children's
book covers

children's book covers

Great book jacket and cover design

ALAN POWERS

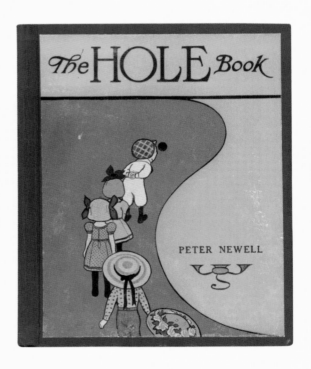

MITCHELL BEAZLEY

children's book covers

ALAN POWERS

Copyright © Octopus Publishing Group Ltd 2003

First published in Great Britain in 2003 by Mitchell Beazley,
an imprint of Octopus Publishing Group Ltd,
2–4 Heron Quays, London E14 4JP

Commissioning Editor **Mark Fletcher**
Managing Editor **Hannah Barnes-Murphy**
Executive Art Editor **Auberon Hedgecoe**
Project Editor **Emily Asquith**
Copy Editor **Penny Warren**
Design **Jeremy Pearce @ 2wo Design**
Picture Research **Emma O'Neill**
Production **Sarah Rogers**
Proof Reader **Claire Musters**
Indexer **Sue Farr**

A CIP catalogue record for this book is
available from the British Library

ISBN 1 84000 693 5

To order this book as a gift or incentive contact
Mitchell Beazley on 020 7531 8481

Set in Clarendon and The Sans
Produced by Toppan Printing Co., (HK) Ltd
Printed and bound in China

Square brackets around dates and names in picture captions indicate that although this information is not given on the book itself it is known to be correct.

(Title Page) *The Hole Book* Peter Newell (author and illustrator), New York, Harper Bros, 1908.
225 x 185mm (8⅘ x 7¼in)
Tom Potts accidentally fires a shot, which goes through a series of holes in the book, causing chaos before it is eventually stopped by a cake. Peter Newell (1862–1924) devised several books in which the physical form of the book is an integral part of the story (see also p. 13).

→ *We Are All in The Dumps with Jack and Guy* Traditional rhyme, Maurice Sendak (illustrator), New York, Michael di Capua Books, HarperCollins, 1993.
210 x 280mm (8¼ x 11in)
An unusual cover by one of the great 20th-century picture-book artists, which carries title information on the back instead of the front. The huge mouth invites the reader inside.

Contents

Introduction

Collectors of children's books pay sums for rare items that would astonish people from outside this arcane world. Books with original jackets may be the most valuable of all, especially if the jackets come from a period when such things were normally thrown away. When books are used by children at home, the jackets are at risk of wear and tear, while the reference collections of great libraries normally discard them as a matter of routine, although public lending libraries are more likely to retain them. As objects in themselves, the jackets that command the highest prices, such as the glassine wrappers placed over the familiar coloured paper binding cases of Beatrix Potter's books, can be surprisingly uninteresting, their value reflecting scarcity and association with a famous book title rather than intrinsic cultural interest. If the book belongs to the period before 1914, the actual cover of the book, whether limp or hard, was usually the focus of design attention, rather than the jacket, although the latter, where it survives, will at least have served to protect what was underneath.

The cultural importance of book covers is still surprisingly neglected by bibliographers. Covers are an integral part of the history of every book and the loose book jacket, in particular, enables us to envisage what the original purchaser would have carried home from the shop, conveying in turn some impression about how the publisher wanted the buyer to view the book. In later periods, book covers may include information about other books, including excerpts from reviews, and sometimes also information about the author.

The neglect of book covers results from a contest between word and image in publishing and reading. The tendency for children to read pictures rather than text has meant that, as can still be the case in academic publishing, a cover that is too attractive is thought to demean an important message. Children do not make such an automatic separation of form and content, however, and may form an emotional attachment to a book as they would to a toy. The cover can play a varied role in this conjunction. With a picture book, it may be a sample of the delights to follow, a kind of window on to an inner world, but not necessarily the richest of them. For a children's novel, it may be the only part that is printed in colour and thus more emotionally engaging. The cover certainly plays a part in the process of physical

← *The Violet Fairy Book* Andrew Lang (author), H. J. Ford (illustrator), London, Longmans, Green & Co., 1901.
187 x 130mm (7⅓ x 5in)
A sumptuous binding from the end of the period of nearly a century when the permanent cover of the book was normally the subject of fine decoration. The gold on this copy, which comes from the Osborne Collection of Early Children's Books in Toronto, has been especially well preserved.

↓ *The Infant's Grammar or a Pic-nic Party of the Parts of Speech* London, John Harris, 1824. 180 x 105mm (7 x 4in)
This copy of one of the most delightful Regency children's books is inscribed 1828. The content is instructional, but the mood is festive as the different parts of speech gather in theatrical costume around the table.

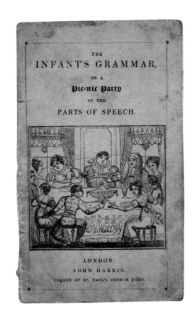

engagement with a book, for while, almost by definition, one cannot look at the cover while reading, it establishes the book as a physical object to be picked up, put down, and perhaps kept over time.

Harold Jones's *Lavender's Blue*, 1954, (see p. 59) was one of my personal favourites as a child, and I think the hieratic organization of the cover, with its figures in different compartments like architectural niches, played a part in this. Brian Wildsmith's supposedly more "child-oriented" watercolours for the *Oxford Book of Poetry for Children*, edited by Edward Blishen in 1963, failed to convert me to a different style. I also remember staring long at the cover by Barnett Freedman for *The Complete Nonsense of Edward Lear*, 1947, (see p. 32) probably because of the way the drawings by Lear, collaged into a background of texture and decorative lettering, had to be looked at carefully, and also because of the *trompe l'oeil* curl and jagged edge on the pretend leaf of paper carrying the title. The Lear cover is one that is still used by Faber & Faber, while *Lavender's Blue* is soon to be republished by Oxford University Press in a facsimile of the original edition. Even so, I feel confident in asserting that no publisher today would allow either of these designs to appear if they were new. They would be seen as too complicated, and as lacking in immediate visual impact of colour and design.

The examples presented in this book are selected in order to illustrate a wide range of periods and styles, and by no means all of them can be claimed as the highest representatives of artistic excellence. Some, such as the covers of A. A. Milne's books, have been selected to represent famous events in publishing history, even though they are clothed with a surprising lack of visual flair. In other cases, books that were never famous at all can reveal wonderful covers, and these have also been included. I apologize in advance to readers who do not find their personal favourites represented, but hope that perhaps memories have been evoked.

Although children's publishing is apparently in a flourishing state at the beginning of the 21st century, the quality of design and production, including that of book jackets, is often put to shame by the products of much earlier periods, when more skill and ingenuity were required to produce clear strong colours, hand-lettering, or pleasantly textured paper. I hope that some of the examples in this book will inspire publishers worldwide to back more dark horses and take more risks, not only in their choice of authors and texts, but also in finding stimulating and original ways of dressing them for their readers.

He filled their listening ears with wondrous things

1

Chapbooks to gift books

In the period from the middle of the 18th century to the First World War there was an extraordinarily wide variety of treatments of the design of children's book covers, with an inventiveness that has not been exceeded in later times. Books varied in size and price, from the humble to the magnificent. They made use of the latest technology in printing and the manufacture of bindings, by means of which new tastes and fashions were made possible. Such books arose out of an increasingly complex but still relatively small world of publishers, booksellers, and printers, at a time when these roles were only gradually becoming separated from one another, and in which the creative hands that produced so many genuinely delightful objects remain largely anonymous. At the end of this period, American children's book publishing began to emerge with an identity of its own, which was to play an important role in developments thereafter.

← *Episodes of Insect Life* "Acheta Domestica" [Miss E. L. Budgen] (author), anonymous binding design engraved by "Staples", London, Reeve, Benham and Reeve, 1849. 208 x 136mm (8¼ x 5⅜in) Here is a fine example of a playful Victorian blocked cloth binding for a natural history text, a popular genre of publishing of the time.

Chapbooks to gift books

Before the 1820s, books were normally issued by publishers in temporary covers, with the expectation that these would be replaced by the purchaser with a more permanent binding in leather, the most resilient material available at the time. The cover might then receive information about the author and title, and perhaps additional decoration, in gold leaf. From the 16th century onwards, a subsidiary genre of publishing, the chapbook, was produced for sale for a few pennies by travelling pedlars (chapmen). The chapbook consisted of a single printed leaf folded into 12 or 16 pages with a title page that usually doubled as a cover, or could be repeated on stronger material. Following the conventions of grander books, the cover was formally organized with centred lines of type to give details of the book title and the printer/publisher. In many cases, there was a small woodcut illustration in between, framed by a decorative border. This style, seen in the publication by John Harris on the opposite page, was perpetuated with variations well into the 19th century. Not all chapbooks were meant for children, but many contained folk tales of giants and magic which children liked and from which they might learn to read. Thus the pictorial book cover began life in association with children, and has remained a constant of children's book publishing which the mainstream book trade later began to imitate.

If any date in the development of children's book publishing is significant, it is 1744, the year when John Newbery (1713–67) produced, for sixpence, *A Little Pretty Pocket Book*, which he described as "neatly bound and gilt". Although Newbery's shop in St Paul's Churchyard, then the chief centre for printing and publishing in Britain, was the first to specialize in books for children, he was essentially only a skilled promoter, and credit for originality should rather be given to Newbery's associate, Benjamin Collins of Salisbury. He claimed to be the inventor of the "battledore", a stiff card with an alphabet and simple reading text. Collins probably began to use colourful and decorative "Dutch" paper (see p. 15) for covering children's books.

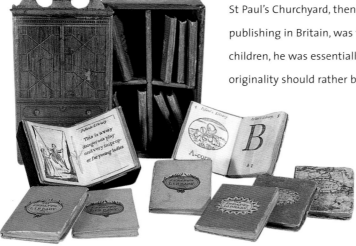

← *The History of Little Goody Two-Shoes*
Thomas Carnan (author), London, T. Carnan, 1783. 102 x 63mm (4 x 2½in)
Thomas Carnan issued attractive books for children with woodcut covers, framed in a border. A similar example is shown on p. 14. In a parody of a scholarly book, the title page of John Newbery's first edition of 1765 advised the reader to "See the Original Manuscript in the Vatican at Rome, and the Cuts by Michael Angelo."

← *Marshall's Easy Lessons for Children*
London, E. Marshall, 1824.
111 x 94mm (4⅓ x 3¾in)
The deep yellow paper cover is speckled with orange, probably applied by flicking a brush over a larger sheet and cutting out pieces from it for binding each book. The label is a hand-coloured engraving. This copy, which carries an inscription of 1827, was published at a late point in the Marshall business. It is of similar format to the books contained in the "Juvenile Library" boxes.

← *Infant's Library*
John Marshall, London, c.1800
This attractive method of packaging books for children was popular between 1800 and the 1820s. Each individual book has a decorative paper cover with an engraved label pasted on to it.

Newbery has won his place in history, however, as the most effective self-promoter, and his success was buoyed up by a general increase in consumerism during his lifetime. In the 18th century parents became more willing to give children things that would please as well as instruct them, and Newbery sometimes played on this, offering books and toys for sale together as a bargain package. In one advertisement he also offered a "free" book; the buyer only had to pay a penny for the binding that enclosed it. Newbery was a creative publisher too, associated with the author Oliver Goldsmith, the alleged author of the perennially popular

moral tale *Goody Two Shoes*, which was published by Newbery in 1765.

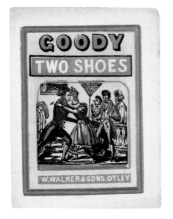

When Newbery died, his business was carried on by members of his family, including his stepson Thomas Carnan, who began to issue books in stiff boards printed with emblematic woodcuts as an alternative to "Dutch" paper and to other more conventional bindings. In 1801, the then manager of a rival Newbery business, John Harris (1756–1846), took over this firm and developed a distinctive style of production, often including attractive hand-colouring, which was then rife in the London print trade. Other publishers in the early 19th century, such as John Marshall (fl. 1783–1828), were prolific and produced titles that were bound as demand arose, in papers that reflected changing styles and taste, such as the fine speckled coloured papers of the Regency period, on which hand-coloured labels were pasted, with the book title in a decorative cartouche.

At this time, publishers competed in inventing new and delightful ways of presenting books. One of the most attractive manifestations of the close affinity between books and toys was the fashion for "Juvenile Libraries", published by Marshall and others. A wooden box with a sliding front, on which a decorative print was pasted to suggest an actual library bookcase, had two shelves of miniature books, half the size of a normal chapbook. These were usually bound in bright paper covers, which, protected by the box, often managed to retain their brightness.

The introduction of cloth binding between 1820 and 1830, originally using curtain material, had an immediate effect on the book trade. Hardback books could be produced in greater numbers than when bound in leather, and the bindings could be decorated as elaborately as anyone wanted with a few strokes of the "arming press". Children's books had pointed the way towards a decorative treatment of the book cover, usually concentrating on the front board and spine, and adult books became in turn increasingly elaborate. Titles were blocked in gold, coloured ink, blind blocking in low relief, embossing, or a combination of all these. In the 1860s, there was a fashion for including printed engravings or photographs pasted on to a book's front board. In the midst of all this richness, the relationship between the binding and the book inside was often almost lost. Even if the book had illustrations, the binding, although the best part, was not necessarily the work of the same hand. The late Victorian and Edwardian pictorial bindings for fiction, as displayed on the covers of the historical adventure stories of G. A. Henty (1832–1902) were a direct continuation of these earlier styles, and were usually the work of anonymous designers in the book trade.

Children's books continued to be produced in paper covers through this period as well, and began to benefit from the development of colour printing using multiple wood blocks, for which a patent was taken out in 1835. Sir Henry Cole (1808–82) added children's books to other areas in which he hoped to reform standards of design and, with the publisher Joseph Cundall, initiated the "Home Treasury" series, with elaborately patterned colour printed covers on paper (see p. 16). Cole helped to reinvigorate children's book publishing, which was adversely affected by evangelical influences in the 1830s and '40s. However, *Struwwelpeter*, arriving from Germany in 1848 (see p. 36), influenced the shape and size of future picture books as well as giving a less reverent tone.

(see p. 16)

(see p. 36)

← **Three Little Pigs**
New York, Raphael Tuck & Sons Co., (Father Tuck's Nurseryland Series) *c.*1890. An example of the chromolithograph covers, mostly printed in Germany, which were popular in Britain and America in the 1890s. These provoked a movement towards more genuinely artistic children's book illustration.

↓ **"An Edwardian Bookshelf"** Photo from "Plain and Fancy", an exhibition of book covers and bindings, from the Osborne Collection of Early Children's Books, Toronto Public Library, 2001. These typical fiction bindings from the 1890s are crowded with colour and detail. The strong colours of the binding cloths were a good background for gold blocking and seem to suggest the military uniforms of this period of British imperialism.

→ **Peter Pan in Kensington Gardens**
J. M. Barrie (author), Arthur Rackham (illustrator), London, Hodder & Stoughton, 1907.
257 x 190mm (10 x 7¹/₂in)
This was one of the most famous of the Edwardian "gift books" with Rackham's memorable colour plates. It has been questioned whether the strange and whimsical text is really a children's book at all. The binding, however, is relatively simple, with hand-drawn lettering showing an Art Nouveau influence.

→ **The Wonderful Wizard of Oz** L. Frank Baum (author), W. W. Denslow (illustrator), Chicago, G. M. Hill, 1900.
245 x 172mm (9²/₃ x 6⁴/₅in)
The first edition of one of the new century's classics has a boldly conceived two-colour blocking on a cloth binding, produced in a range of colours, including a light green. On the back board, the three other companions on the Yellow Brick Road are depicted in medallions, while Toto appears on the spine. The book was issued in a pale green dust wrapper printed in emerald green, a colour of some significance in the story.

→ **The Slant Book** Peter Newell (author and illustrator), New York, Harper & Bros, 1910. 225 x 185mm (8⁴/₅ x 7¹/₄in)
Peter Newell specialized in original book formats in the early 20th century (see The Hole Book on the title page). When the spine is held vertically, the downward slope shows the characters in pursuit of a runaway perambulator. The book was first issued in a blue-and-white dust wrapper with the same running figures, but also with the object of their pursuit, a child in a runaway pram, disappearing off the front board and round the spine.

George Routledge (1812–88) began the series of "Aunt Mavor's Picture Books" in 1852 with the story of *The Old Cornish Woman* who travelled up to London for the Great Exhibition of 1851, largely organized by Cole, with a blue paper cover printed with the standard series design showing "Aunt Mavor" surrounded by children.

The "toy books" that Routledge and his former partner Frederick Warne (1825–1901) developed during the 1850s and '60s were a notable feature of publishing in the second half of the 19th century. Each was a standard

length, and larger in format than most earlier books, although consisting only of a single gathering of pages. These were sewn through the cover which was composed of two leaves of printed paper stuck back to back, or, for books sold at a higher price, with linen sandwiched between them for added strength. From an early period, toy books specialized in brightly coloured covers, most of them printed by Edmund Evans (1826–1905) who preferred to continue using wood blocks rather than the more recent and potentially cheaper process of lithography. During the 1860s, toy books went through a fashion of "fairground" lettering, with bold shaded capitals against plain coloured backgrounds.

Identifiable illustrators began to emerge from the anonymity of the mid century and, when Evans "discovered" Walter Crane (see p. 18), toy books took on a new self-consciousness as works of art. Chromolithography was used alongside woodblock printing in the 1880s, and many publishers commissioned work from the Bavarian firm of Ernest Nister. Arthur Rackham's illustrations for the *Ingoldsby Legends* in 1898 marked a significant moment, when process-colour printing, which allowed a photographic reproduction of a coloured original, was presented as part of a new formula for a "gift book", a luxury item. Unlike toy books, these had pictures mounted on grey card, separated from the text in a group at the end of the book. In Britain Rackham was the chief illustrator of gift books and Howard Pyle occupied that role in the USA. The books usually had a dust wrapper, with a plate from the book pasted on (see p. 33), but the bindings were relatively simple in treatment.

From beginnings to the Regency

Examples on these pages show the emergence of a distinctive style of binding and presentation for children's books. They belong to a society described by F. J. Harvey Darton in his classic history of the subject as "a purely middle-class and purely English society, and mainly urban in temper – unusually so in that agricultural century. Its folk were timid about making mistakes or doing unsuitable things, yet confident and happy about their own judgments… They are little books about little things." Harvey Darton goes on to say of the publisher John Newbery that "binding was one of his most gracious gifts to the nursery library." At a time when publishers usually issued unbound books for sale, this was one of many areas in which Newbery understood children's books could be different.

The age of Newbery's successors, John Marshall and John Harris, is described by historians of children's books as "the Age of Levity". Lasting roughly from 1805 to 1823, illustration played a greater role than it would for many years afterwards. The engraved plates in Harris and Marshall's books were usually hand-coloured, following the custom in the print trade of the time, whether for political caricatures, fashion plates, or juvenile productions, including the toy theatre cut-out sheets first produced around 1811. The delicate transparent washes, skilfully applied without too much detail is seen in three of the cut-out labels here, which incorporate title lettering within an appropriate scene or object. The idea of showing the back of the cart for Hodgson's *History of Whittington and his Cat*, as if disappearing into the book, is a clever realization of the capacity of a cover image to excite some physical feeling about entering the book.

A label on the front board of a book comes closer to the modern idea of a book cover (adult books of this time still carried information only on the spine). It enabled the use of various coloured papers which added so much to the jollity of these small books, but which could not have successfully been printed on directly. In the case of *The History of Little Fanny*, the book is contained in a slipcase with rather grown-up looking Italian style ornament, giving little indication of the delights inside.

→ ***The Good Girl's Soliloquy*** New York, Samuel Wood & Sons, 1820. 130 x 105mm (5 x 4⅛in)
A simple chapbook-style production by an American printer, this shows the longstanding convention of a border composed of moveable type units, which frames a title, stock illustration block, a decorative rule, and the standard publication details, which would also appear on the title page. This is the companion volume to *The Good Boy's Soliloquy*, published by Darton in London as a satire on pious books about self-improvement. The American publisher who commissioned this book failed to notice the satire, however, and this text is "straight".

↑ ***Prints of Natural History with Description*** (volume 1), London, John Marshall, 1802. 98 x 65mm (3⅘ x 2⅗in)
The mottled orange paper has a carefully cut-out hand-coloured engraving showing a collection of rather unnatural-looking creatures. The binding is probably from the 1820s, using printed sheets of an earlier date.

← ***Poetical Flower Garden with Moral Reflections for the Amusement of Children*** J. Bell (engraver), London, T. Carnan, 1778. 118 x 76mm (4⅔ x 3in)
Thomas Carnan (c.1735–88) was the publisher John Newbery's stepson and continued the business. These engravings, as well as two similar ones on the back of the book, have no particular relevance to the subject and are "stock blocks".

→ *The Picture Gallery for all Good Boys and Girls Shewing Them The Cries of London* London, John Wallis, 1802. 175 x 110m (7 x 4⅓in)
An engraved and hand-coloured label, cut in a circle, is pasted on to blue sugar paper. The showman with his horn is exhibiting a live squirrel in what appears to be a revolving cage with a row of bells along the top. It is not surprising that the poet William Blake despaired of a "civilized" nation which could condone such cruelty to animals for entertainment and profit.

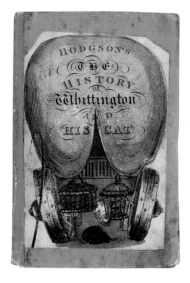

↑ ***The History of Whittington and his Cat*** London, Hodgson & Co., 1822. 139 x 91mm (5½ x 3½in)
The engraved lettering is in a style expected for the title page of a much grander production. The colouring shows the illustrator's ability to work swiftly at this time-consuming task, but the cover benefits from the broad application of different areas of colour.

↑ ***The Wren, or the Fairy of the Greenhouse*** London, John Marshall, 1805. 172 x 112mm (6⅘ x 4½in)
The mottled red binding paper carries oval labels front and back. Books in this style were found in Marshall's "Juvenile Libraries" (see p. 11).

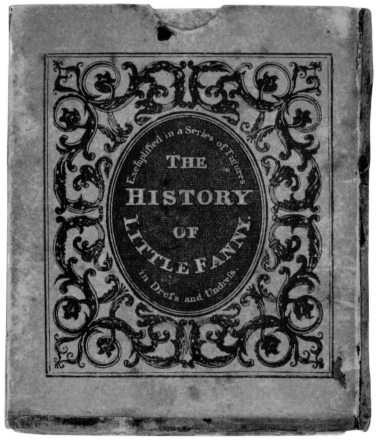

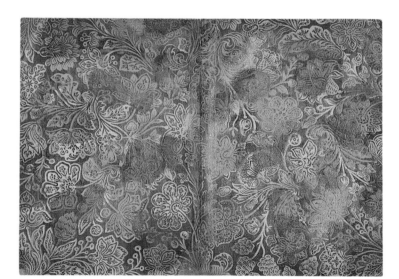

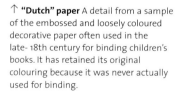

↑ ***The History of Little Fanny, Exemplified in a Series of Figures in Dress and Undress*** (10th edition), London, S. and J. Fuller, 1830. 132 x 100mm (5⅕ x 4in)
The book, which has ribbon ties, comes in a slipcase which repeats the design of a paper binding similar in style to ladies' "annuals" of the period. The real joy is inside, where there is a set of ready cut dresses for a paper doll. The first edition of this popular item was issued in a plain typographic wallet in 1808.

↑ **"Dutch" paper** A detail from a sample of the embossed and loosely coloured decorative paper often used in the late-18th century for binding children's books. It has retained its original colouring because it was never actually used for binding.

Mid-Victorian instruction and entertainment

From the 1830s onward, there was a growing seriousness and attention to factual information in children's books, as offered by the American author S. G. Goodrich (1793–1860), writing in the character of "Peter Parley". Intended as an alternative to fairy tales such as *Jack the Giant Killer*, in the chapbook tradition, Goodrich's books were as popular in Britain as in America. Sir Henry Cole's "Home Treasury" series, begun in 1843, with newly illustrated versions of nursery classics, was a direct attack on "Peter Parleyism", aiming to raise the visual standard while retaining aspects of national culture in Britain that Cole considered important for children's imagination. Cole's cover for *The Mother's Primer*, while displaying the newly developed skill in colour printing, is still a recreation of a historical style of abstract decoration aimed more at adults than children.

It is typical of the general taste of the time, however, when paper covers on boards, often richly coloured and patterned, were often the most interesting aspect of the many "improving" texts that were supplied to an expanding market. The development of machine-made binding cases made hardback children's books much cheaper during this period, and charming blocking designs in the form of ornamental frames wreathed the book titles on the front board. At the same time, the chapbook tradition of limp paper covers continued on both sides of the Atlantic, with retellings of folk tales and, in the absence of effective copyright laws, of stories by more recent authors.

↑ *The Mother's Primer* "Mrs Felix Summerley" [Dame Marian Fairman Cole] (author), London, Longman, Brown, Green, and Longmans, 1844 (facsimile, Osborne and Lilian H. Smith Collection, Toronto, 1970). 167 x 125mm (6½ x 5in) Henry Cole claimed that he based the binding for this and the remainder of his "'Home Treasury" series on a design by the Renaissance artist Hans Holbein.

← *Pretty Poetry for Little Children* Augusta and Mrs Segournay, and Mrs Baker (authors), London, Dean and Munday. 140 x 110mm (5½ x 4¼in) The playful children, classical emblems, and obliging swans were a stock engraving. The cover is an onlay on board in the style of a Regency almanac. This copy is inscribed with the date 1842.

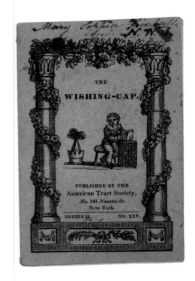

→ *The Wishing Cap* Mrs M. M. Sherwood (author), New York, The American Tract Society, n.d. 98 x 65mm (3⅘ x 2½in). An elegant architectural frame encloses a vignette illustrating a moral tale.

→ The Little Man and The Little Maid
Providence, Winsor & Perrin, 1849,
stereotyped and printed by G. C. Rand &
Co., Boston. 190 x 185mm (7½ x 7¼in)
The backward-sloping capitals in the
title are a distinctive American style of
lettering and are applied to a text and
pictures of Engish origin. The border uses
typefounder's standard repeating units,
framing a caricature illustration.

↓ The Nursery Playmate London,
Sampson, Low, Son & Marston, 1864.
300 x 229mm (11⅘ x 9in). Wood
engraving, printed paper on board.
The style of "rustic" framing for covers
and title pages was introduced from
Germany in the 1840s. It supports a
medley of pictures which indicate
the contents.

↑ Jack the Giant Killer London, J. March,
n.d. 172 x 109mm (6⅘ x 4¼in)
This traditional English folktale first
appeared on the London stage in 1810.
The book consists of a single sheet of
paper, folded twice, with a garish cover
to catch the infant eye.

← Dealings with the Fairies George
MacDonald (author), Arthur Hughes
(illustrator), London, Alexander Strahan,
1867. 140 x 107mm (5½ x 4¼in)
George MacDonald made a lasting
contribution to fantasy literature with
books such as *The Princess and the
Goblin*. He was friendly with several Pre-
Raphaelite artists in Victorian London,
and Arthur Hughes (1832–1915), a
distinguished painter, contributed
evocative illustrations to his many titles.
This is a publisher's series binding rather
than a special one for this book.

Walter Crane & Randolph Caldecott

Despite the moralism of the mid-Victorian period, a lively tradition of picture-book making for children was carried through from an earlier period. It found an appropriate format in the attractively large-sized and colourful "toy books" which were produced from the 1850s onwards. The printer Edmund Evans played an important role in introducing artists to publishers, his first major discovery being Walter Crane (1845–1915) who worked for the London publisher George Routledge from 1865 onwards. The combination of artistic quality with a low price was a winning formula. Crane, who was trained in wood engraving, designed successive standard covers for "Walter Crane's Toy Books", which were printed in a different colourway for each title. These display his early enthusiasm for Japanese decoration, which was then just beginning to penetrate Europe. Crane also produced some covers for individual titles, including a finely dressed pig for *This Little Pig Went to Market* (1871). He recalled the scepticism that greeted his musical volume with paper-covered boards, *The Baby's Opera* (1877), as "a five-shilling book not decently bound in cloth and without any gold on it", but nevertheless this title was just as successful as its predecessors.

Crane left Routledge in 1877 when the firm refused to pay him royalties for this book, which carried on selling successfully year after year. He was replaced by the illustrator Randolph Caldecott (1846–86) who agreed to a profit-sharing arrangement with Evans when his first two books, *John Gilpin* and *The House that Jack Built*, were published in 1878 in editions of 100,000 and immediately sold out. Each of Caldecott's covers was individually designed for the book, and integrated the lettering in a more relaxed way than Crane's. The covers also display his lively sense of humour and skill in drawing action scenes.

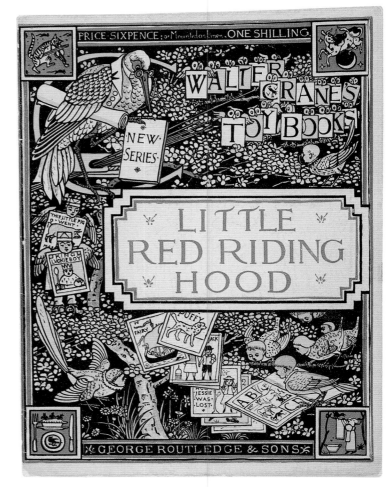

← *Slateandpencilvania* Walter Crane (author and illustrator), London, Marcus Ward & Co., 1885.
224 x 224mm (8⅘ x 8⅘in)
This story, which is based on learning to write, was originally composed by Crane for his own family. The cover, more a design than an illustration, shows the continuing Japanese influence on Crane (see right).

↑ *Little Red Riding Hood* Walter Crane, (author and illustrator), London, George Routledge & Sons, *c*. 1873.
248 x 185mm (9¾ x 7¼in)
This standard series cover for "Walter Crane's Toy Books" series shows the illustrator's Japanese influence in its flat style of drawing and asymmetrical design. He used a crane as a rebus for his own name, being specially skilled at drawing animals. Covers for Crane's "shilling" series in 1874 were even more authentically Japanese in style.

→ **A Frog He Would a-Wooing Go**
Randolph Caldecott (author and illustrator), London, George Routledge & Sons, 1883. 204 x 237mm (8 x 9⅓in)
Engravers working for printer Edmund Evans were able to produce light tonal effects in colour printing that suited the delicacy of Caldecott's originals.

↓ **The Great Panjandrum Himself**
Samuel Foote (author), Randolph Caldecott (illustrator), London, George Routledge & Sons, 1885.
204 x 237mm (8 x 9⅓in)
The text is an 18th-century nonsense "rhyme" (it does not rhyme) which remained in circulation through the 19th century. Caldecott's schoolmaster, in the title role, has begun to write the words on the blackboard, so that the cover works like the credits sequence of a film, launching you in without delay.

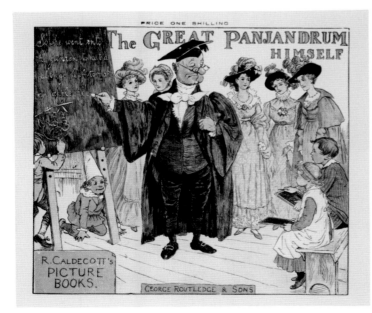

↑ **Sing a Song for Sixpence** Randolph Caldecott (illustrator), London, George Routledge & Sons, 1880.
231 x 206mm (9 x 8in)
The arrangment of the branch of blossom may reflect the Japanese taste, but the drawing style is typical of Caldecott's naturalism.

↑ **The Three Jovial Huntsmen** Randolph Caldecott (illustrator), London, George Routledge & Sons, 1880.
231 x 206mm (9 x 8in)
Nostalgia was in full swing in Caldecott's time, as the Victorians took stock of their achievements, often starting to view earlier periods with greater favour. The title lettering participates in the fun.

Turn-of-the-century classics

During the 1890s it became possible to reproduce an artist's original drawing mechanically for printing, without an engraver needing to copy it by hand, as had always been the case up until then. The fine line quality of the blocking of Andrew Lang's *Violet Fairy Book* (1901, see p. 6) demonstrates the quality that could be achieved with good design and craftsmanship. The two nursery rhyme books on this page, from the previous year, both used this new technology. Mrs Gaskin's *ABC: An Alphabet* represents the Arts and Crafts style in its homely simplicity, while "The Banbury Cross Series", with a similar subject, is in the more continental spirit of Art Nouveau. The selection of binding materials follows a similar stylistic division between restraint shown in the *ABC* and a more expressive form, as seen in the soft leather and ribbon ties of the *Nursery Rhymes*.

Aspects of both these styles continued through into the early 20th century. The naivety of *Stories of Mother Goose Village* can be contrasted with the slightly decadent quality of *Peacock Pie* by Charles Robinson's brother (both on p. 22). Even as late as 1929, Willy Pogány's lettering for *Mother Goose Rhymes* shows an Art Nouveau influence.

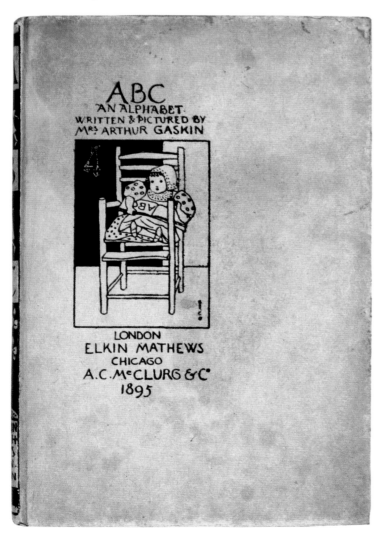

↑ **Nursery Rhymes, The Banbury Cross Series** "Prepared for children by Grace Rhys", London, J. M. Dent & Co., 1895.
149 x 93mm (5⅘ x 3⅔in)
Art Nouveau flame shapes rise up behind a precariously seated child, on a cover that speaks to an adult's understanding of childhood through the "new art" movement of the continent.

← **ABC An Alphabet** "Written and pictured by Mrs Arthur Gaskin", London, Elkin Mathews, 1895.
195 x 135mm (7⅔ x 5¼in)
Bound in an imitation vellum paper, this modest binding speaks of the avant-garde of the 1890s in Britain, even though the imagery is nostalgic.

→ **Mother Goose Rhymes** Willy Pogány (illustrator), London, George G. Harrap, [1929]. 190 x 80mm (7½ x 3in)
Willy Pogány (1882–1955) was born in Hungary and worked in London between 1906 and 1915, as one of the artists well known for gift books. This is a late example of his illustration which continued the Edwardian style.

↓ **Rag, Tag, and Bobtail** Edith Farmiloe (author and illustrator), Winifred Parnell (verses), London, Grant Richards, 1899. 234 x 310mm (9¼ x 12¼in)
This book of illustrated verses is quarter-bound in striped paper, overprinted with a design of artless simplicity by the wife of the vicar of St Anne's, Soho, in London.

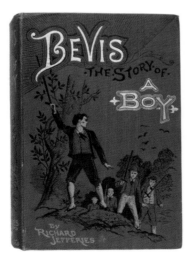

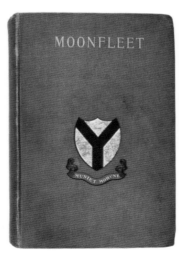

↑ **Bevis, the Story of a Boy** Richard Jefferies (author), London, Sampson, Low, Marston & Co., 1893. 190 x 125mm (7½ x 5in).
Richard Jefferies was an influential writer on country themes who emphasized both the reality and spiritual qualities of nature.

↑ **Moonfleet** J. Meade Falkner (author), London, Edward Arnold, 1898.
200 x 130mm (7⅘ x 5in).
The binding shows the coat of arms of the fictional Mohun family *On a field argent, a cross-pall sable*, which plays a role in the story. Otherwise, this is a typical plain binding of red cloth for late-Victorian serious fiction.

← *The Adventures of Two Dutch Dolls*
Bertha Upton (author), Florence K. Upton (illustrator), London, Longmans, Green & Co., 1895. 222 x 285mm (8¾ x 11⅓in)
This is the first in the series of books by Florence K. Upton (1873–1922) and her mother (1849–1912). The books achieved instant success, with the different-sized dolls, based on the cheap wooden toys made in the Tyrol, and the Golliwogg, a character invented by them who soon became a reality in the toy shops, as well as inspiring the "Golliwogg's Cake Walk" in Claude Debussy's *Children's Corner Suite for Piano* (1906–8).

No sooner had the longstanding business of wood engraving from artist's drawings for illustrations or cover designs been undermined by the new mechanical "process-engraving" in the 1890s, than there was a sense of loss and nostalgia for a method that had produced so many delightful works in earlier periods. Self-conscious playing with primitivism was a feature of children's publishing extending back through the whole Victorian period, for even Henry Cole's "Home Treasury" books were typeset in an 18th-century style, but it worked towards a peak in the 1890s with the deliberately crude evocations of early printing by Andrew Tuer of the Leadenhall Press whose productions were really intended for adults. The same is true of William Nicholson's *An Alphabet*, which recaptures the feel of a chapbook, although it is very much larger in size. It was priced as an art book for adults, which did nothing to curb its popularity. The only competition for such books would have come from the chromolithographed books printed in Germany, but these offended British patriotic sentiment and were variable in artistic quality.

The enthusiasm for archaic styles left its mark in ways we may now take for granted, such as the covers of Beatrix Potter's books from 1902 onwards (see pp. 26–7), which marked a departure from previous fashion with their rough paper finish. It was part of the desire at the time to protect the innocence of childhood from the harsh realities of the modern world. This was exemplified in the extraordinary success of J. M. Barrie's *Peter Pan*, and reflected in the cover for *Anne's Terrible Good Nature*, showing well-behaved children in an idealized setting. After 1895, picture books were partly dominated by the "gift book" format (see p. 13), although Leslie Brooke and the Uptons offered more lively alternatives in which the pictures ran alongside the text.

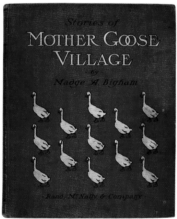

↑ *Stories of Mother Goose Village*
Madge A. Bigham (author), Chicago, Rand, McNally & Co., 1903.
233 x 179mm (9⅛ x 7in)
The repetition of a simple motif was a favourite device of the Arts and Crafts movement, as in this gaggle of geese on an American book cover which might make a good children's wallpaper. The lettering, with the overlapping "O's" in Goose, is equally typical of the period.

↑ *Peacock Pie* Walter de La Mare (author), W. Heath Robinson (illustrator), London, Constable, 1916 .
220 x 175mm (8⅝ x 6⅞in)
William Heath Robinson (1872–1944) was the younger brother of Charles Robinson (see p. 34), and his success as a children's illustrator was achieved with the whimsical, picture-led story of *Uncle Lubin* (1902). This collection of rhymes for children by de la Mare (1873–1956) was first issued in 1913 without illustrations. Of the many illustrated editions published, the poet was most pleased with that by Claud Lovat Fraser, published in 1924 three years after the artist's death.

→ The Story of the Treasure Seekers
"E. Nesbit with pictures by Gordon Browne & Lewis Baumer", Gordon Browne (cover), London, T. Fisher Unwin, 1907. 200 x 125m (7⅘ x 5in)
The cover, blocked in gold on red cloth, reproduces one of Gordon Browne's line drawings from the first of the famous children's novels by Enid Nesbit (1858–1924), concerning the Bastable family.

↓ Anne's Terrible Good Nature and Other Stories E. V. Lucas (author), A. H. Buckland (illustrator), F. D. Bedford (cover), London, Chatto & Windus, 1908.
194 x 132mm (7¾ x 5⅕in)
A fine colour-blocked design by an artist whose training as an architect shows in his confident handling of the park sculpture. Lucas (1868–1958) wrote and edited a variety of children's books.

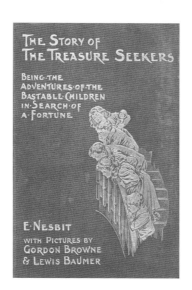

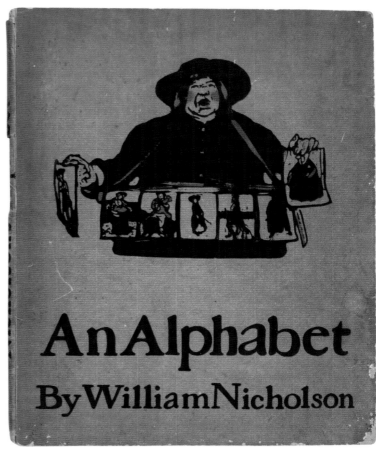

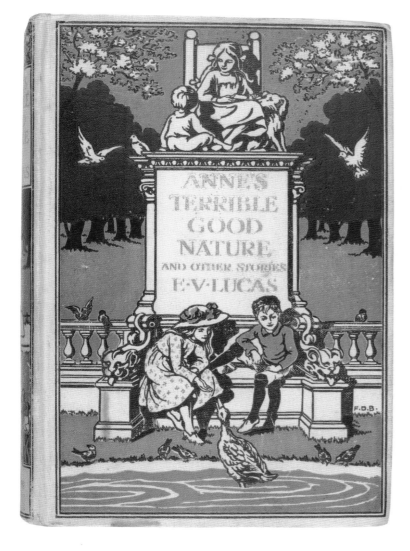

↑ **An Alphabet** William Nicholson (author and illustrator), London, William Heinemann, 1898.
317 x 255mm (12½ x 10in)
This large, magnificent book was the work of a rising graphic artist and painter (1872–1949), best known at this point for his poster art. The flatness of the poster, inspired in turn by France and Japan, is the basis of his effects in *An Alphabet*, where he appears in self-portrait on the first page: "A was an Artist". The back cover carries the windmill colophon designed by Nicholson for Heinemann, which continued in use for many years.

← **Johnny Crow's Garden** "Drawn by L. Leslie Brooke", London, Frederick Warne, 1903. 210 x 165mm (8¼ x 6½in)
The binding style of this popular traditional rhyme book is similar to Warne's *Beatrix Potter* books, with deep blocked lettering on paper-covered boards, and a cut-out colour plate laid on a sunken centre panel.

In the wild wood
Kenneth Grahame

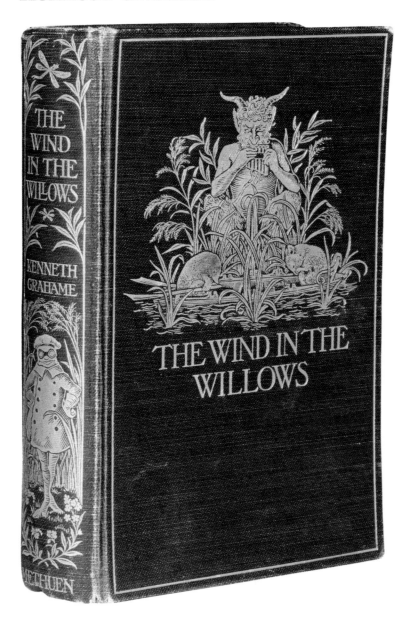

Kenneth Grahame (1859–1932) was Secretary to the Bank of England by day, but he still managed to become established as an author for adults. His early books, such as *Dream Days*, published in 1898, were about children rather than for them. In common with other famous children's books, *The Wind in the Willows* began in the form of bedtime stories which Grahame told to his son and only child, Alastair. They were developed into a book on the urging of an American friend, the magazine editor Constance Smedley.

Although it was difficult to find a publisher at first, the book's strange mixture of humour, action, and character, combined with observations of nature and attempts to speculate more deeply on natural forces, made it popular. It was first published in 1908 and its position was strengthened throughout the 20th century by the many political and social interpretations brought to it, including those emphasized in a popular dramatization by Alan Bennett for the National Theatre in London in the 1980s. Television companies have also dramatized the stories and created apocryphal ones too, using puppets and stop-frame animation to good effect.

The best-known illustrated edition of *The Wind in the Willows* was by Ernest Shepard, who had already established himself with *Winnie the Pooh*. It gave the familiar forms to Mr Toad and the other animal protagonists, with a brilliant realization of the background details and natural settings. The book was also the last title to be illustrated by Arthur Rackham, in an edition brought out by the Limited Editions Club of New York in 1940, the year after his death.

↓ *The Wind in the Willows* Kenneth Grahame (author), E. H. Shepard (illustrator), London, Methuen, 1981. 205 x 139mm (8 x 5½in)
Shepard's illustrations were first printed in 1931, but the long-lived artist (1879–1976) was persuaded to make new watercolour jacket designs, as seen here in this later reprint, and to colour in his original line-work, which was not always to the benefit of the original.

↓ *The Wind in the Willows* Kenneth Grahame (author), Sheila Lane and Marion Kemp (adaption), Helen Fisher (illustrator), Harmondsworth, Penguin Education, 1971. 209 x 149mm (8⅓ x 5⅘in)
The slightly psychedelic ripples on the water would beguile boring hours in class for users of this school edition.

↑ *The Wind in the Willows* Kenneth Grahame (author), London, Methuen, 1908. 195 x 129mm (7⅔ x 5in)
The first edition has a fine gold blocking (also repeated in black on a brown paper wrapper), with a design by W. Graham Robertson. The front board shows "The Piper at the Gates of Dawn", while Mr Toad appears on the spine in his motoring costume.

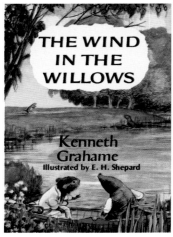

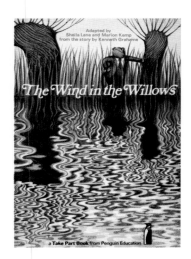

→ **Kenneth Grahame's The Wind in the Willows, A Pop-up Book** Babette Cole (illustrator), London, Methuen, 1983. 274 x 198mm (10⁴/₅ x 7⁴/₅in)
When Kenneth Grahame's copyrights expired in 1982, there were many adaptations of his most famous title. With this pop-up book, the original publisher joined in the fray.

↓ **Sweet Home** "Illustrated in Colour Photography by Paul Henning", London, Methuen, 1946. 213 x 140mm (8²/₅ x 5¹/₂in)
In 1946 the printing of colour photographs was still a novelty, and this story, a single chapter extracted from *The Wind in the Willows*, would have added another title to the publisher's list at a time of paper rationing.

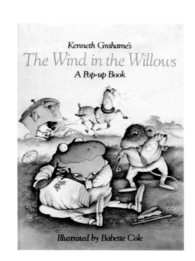

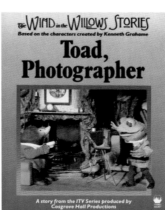

↑ **Wild Wood, The Alternative View of The Wind in the Willows** Jan Needle (author), Andrew Kulman (cover illustration), London, Scholastic Publications, 1993.
215 x 134mm (8¹/₂ x 5¹/₃in)
This is a reissue of a 1981 novel that turns the weasels, who were portrayed as evil in the original, into the heroes. The cover is typical of retrospective graphic design and illustration in the early 1990s.

← **Toad, Photographer** Brian Trueman (author), Cosgrove Hall Productions (illustrations), London, Methuen Children's Books Ltd, 1986.
190 x 150mm (7¹/₂ x 6in)
The characters created by Kenneth Grahame allow for spin-offs into other episodes. This book is based on a children's TV series, using stop-frame animation, made in 1983 by a subisidary of the independent Central and Thames Television Companies.

Peter Rabbit and friends
Beatrix Potter

Beatrix Potter (1866–1943) worked off the frustrations of a lonely, if privileged, childhood in her study of small mammals. Natural history and fantasy merged in stories such as *Peter Rabbit*, composed to entertain young cousins and the children of friends. Privately published in 1901, the book's potential was spotted by Frederick Warne, who issued the trade edition in 1902. After this date, Potter's productivity increased as did her friendship with Norman Warne, which grew to an engagement in 1910, but was sadly curtailed by Warne's early death.

Potter's series of small-format illustrated stories continued to 1913 and her watercolours with ink line tested the printing capabilities of the time. The binding style usually involved pasting one of these as a cut-out into a blind-stamped panel on the front board which was covered in coloured paper. This produced a slightly archaic chapbook feeling in sympathy with the contents. Transparent "glassine" wrappers with the book title were provided to protect the books, and the rarity of their survival gives them a value way beyond any intrinsic interest they possess.

The trade edition of *Peter Rabbit* in 1902 set the style, although later books diverged in various ways before Beatrix Potter's set of titles was standardized in later reprints. W. A. Herring, the production director for Warne, kept a close eye on standards well into the 1950s.

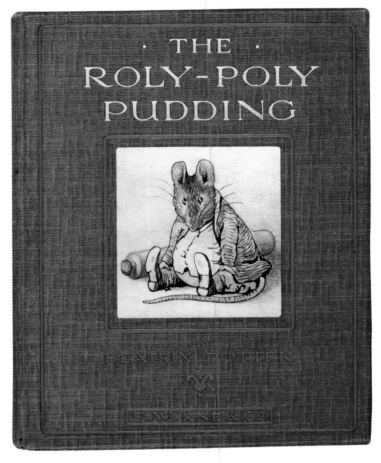

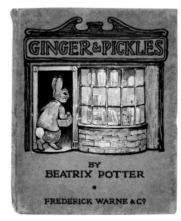

↑ ***The Roly-Poly Pudding*** Beatrix Potter, (author and illustrator), London, Frederick Warne, 1908. 205 x 160mm (8 x 6⅜in) The colour of the crimson binding cloth was copied in later editions where paper was substituted and the book retitled as *The Tale of Samuel Whiskers*. The "Intelligent Pink-eyed Representative of a Persecuted (but Irrepressible) Race" continued to stare out, however.

← ***The Tale of Peter Rabbit*** Beatrix Potter, (author and illustrator), London, Frederick Warne, 1902. 143 x 110mm (5⅗ x 4⅓in) Although the private edition of *Peter Rabbit* was of only 250 copies, this first trade edition is, if anything, rarer. So familiar is this format that we may overlook the skilled integration of contents and book production style.

← ***[The Tale of] Ginger & Pickles*** Beatrix Potter (author and illustrator), London, Frederick Warne, 1909. 183 x 140mm (7⅕ x 5½in) Potter's fable of the perils of consumer credit originally incorporated the title as a fascia board for the eponymous grocery and general store.

THE ROLY~POLY PUDDING

BY BEATRIX POTTER

London · FREDERICK WARNE & Cº LTD · & New York

→ **The Pie and the Patty-Pan** Beatrix Potter (author and illustrator), London, Frederick Warne, 1905. 180 x 140mm (7 x 5½in) The neo-classical cartouche and exaggerated script-style lettering seems appropriate to the contest over gentility which is parodied in the story.

↓ **The Story of a Fierce Bad Rabbit** Beatrix Potter (author and illustrator), London, Frederick Warne, 1906. 95 x 115mm (3¾ x 4½in) Warne's published two of Potter's books as panoramas in wallets, and she prepared a third, "The Story of the Sly Old Cat", before this format was abandoned. The wallets are charming small objects, but the panoramas were fragile for small children and the booksellers hated them because the tabs broke off the upper flap so easily.

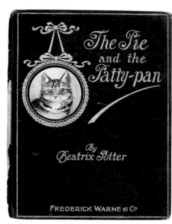

The Pie and the Patty-pan

By Beatrix Potter

FREDERICK WARNE & Cº

The Story of A Fierce Bad Rabbit

Beatrix Potter

THE TALE OF LITTLE PIG ROBINSON

BEATRIX POTTER

↑ **The Roly-Poly Pudding** Beatrix Potter, (author and illustrator), London, Frederick Warne, 1908. 205 x 160mm (8 x 6¼in) Samuel Whiskers, the anti-hero of Potter's tale of catnapping, appeared in two different forms on covers during the first year of publication (see opposite). This quarter-cloth cover reproduces an illustration from the text and features supporting line drawings.

← **The Tale of Little Pig Robinson** Beatrix Potter (author and illustrator), Philadelphia, David McKay Co., 1930. 215 x 165mm (8½ x 6½in) After a long period of absorption in marriage and country matters in the Lake District, Potter was approached by her American publisher for a new work. The result was a longer text in eight short chapters. It was originally in this larger format but was later incorporated by Warne into the standard series. The illustration on the wrapper shows the happy end of the story in which our hero escapes being made into bacon.

Timeless fables
Aesop & La Fontaine

Aesop may have no more secure a historical existence than Homer, but his fables, describing animals, most notably the fox, the wolf, and the lion, as personifications of different human types, are recorded in several Greek manuscripts and were among the first books printed in England. The edition of 1485 by William Caxton was profusely illustrated with nearly 200 wood cuts, but this did not imply that the book was particularly intended for children.

Sir Roger L'Estrange's translation of 1692 gave the *Fables* a Tory political spin, corrected by Samual Croxall in 1722, in an edition evidently intended for children. When John Newbery published *Fables in Verse by Abraham Aesop Esq.* in 1757, Aesop definitively joined the small repertory of texts considered as children's reading. After that, a number of fine illustrators interpreted the fables, including Thomas Bewick, John Tenniel, Randolph Caldecott, and Walter Crane. The opportunity to portray animals is an invitation to the illustrator. Beatrix Potter's *Johnny Town Mouse* is a retelling of an Aesop fable, and is dedicated "to Aesop in the shades".

Jean de la Fontaine (1621–95) was, like his contemporary the folk-story collector Charles Perrault, a member of the new class of French government official who helped to achieve administrative efficiency under Louis XIV. La Fontaine composed his fables in the style of Aesop, borrowing stories from a wide variety of stories and casting them into verse, each with its moral.

→ *Aesop's Fables in Words of One Syllable* Mary Godolphin (text), Harrison Weir (illustrator), H. L. Shindler (cover), London, George Routledge & Sons, n.d.
250 x 160mm (9⁴/₅ x 6¹/₅in)
The lurid process colour images, possibly dating from the 1920s, are pasted on to the boards of what appears to be a much older edition, presumably in an attempt to clear old stock.

↓ *Aesop's Fables* "Retold and presented by Joan Kiddell-Monroe", Oxford, Basil Blackwell, 1972.
247 x 190mm (9³/₄ x 7¹/₂in)
Joan Kiddell-Monroe (see p. 47) was notable for the design quality of her illustrated books. Her "Wonk" series for Ladybird Books was popular in the 1950s.

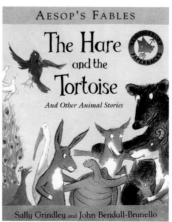

↑ *Three Aesop Fox Fables* Paul Galdone (illustrator), Kingswood, Surrey, World's Work Ltd, 1972.
290 x 173mm (11¹/₂ x 6⁴/₅in)
The well-known American illustrator, Paul Galdone (see also pp.86–7) chose the story of the Fox and the Grapes for the cover of this edition of Aesop's Fables.

← *The Hare and the Tortoise* Sally Grindlay (author), John Bendall-Brunello (illustrator), London, Bloomsbury, [1993].
300 x 240mm (11⁴/₅ x 9¹/₂in)
A jolly group of animals introduce a modern retelling of Aesop's perennially popular stories. The edition pictured here is a 2000 reprint.

Masters of fable and fear

Grimm & Hans Andersen

Jacob and Wilhelm Grimm were born in the 1780s near Frankfurt and began collecting and writing down folktales in 1806 at a time of rising German national feeling. Their first volume, *Kinder- und Hausmärchen*, appeared in 1812, with successors enlarging the canon in the following years. The brothers tapped into a deep vein of authentic oral culture, and their stories have counterparts in other cultures. Only with the first English translation, *German Popular Stories* (1823) illustrated by the popular artist George Cruickshank (1792–1878), did the Grimms understand how illustrations could enhance the text. A later translator and adapter, Wanda Gág, captured their quality when she wrote, "The fairy world of these stories, though properly weird and strange, has a convincing, three-dimensional character. There is magic, wonder, sorcery, but no vague airy-fairyness about it. The German witches are not wispy wraiths flying in the air – they usually live in neat cottages and wear starched bonnets and spotless aprons."

Hans Christian Andersen (1805–75) first published his tales as a little chapbook in 1835, combining fantasy and folklore. If the Grimms' tales are frequently gory, then Andersen's often involve different and more psychological forms of cruelty whose depths may not be grasped by children. He was an enthusiastic visitor to Britain, and his work was translated in 1846. In addition to the artists whose work is shown here, Andersen was illustrated by Mabel Lucie Atwell in 1913 and Arthur Rackham in 1932. The M. R. James translations were illustrated by Robin Jacques in 1953. More recently, Michael Foreman treated them with an adult sensibility in 1976, but there is no accepted current classic version.

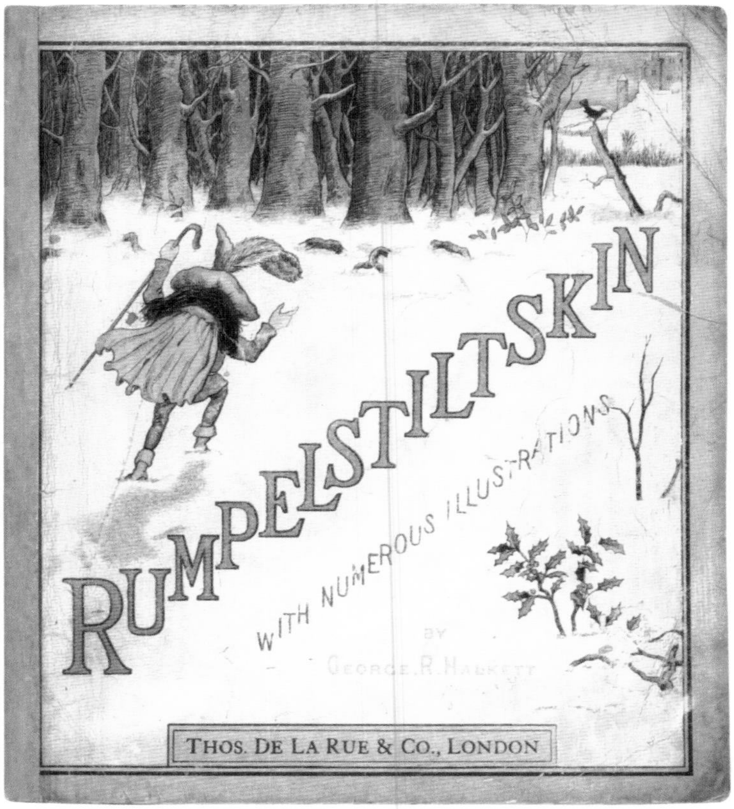

↑ ***Rumpelstiltskin*** **"The Brothers Grimm, a new translation, illustrated by George R. Halkett", London, Thos. de la Rue & Co., 1882. 231 x 201mm (9 x 8in)**
The cover design uses an unusual diagonal lettering layout to fit the illustration. The title was published by a company noted primarily as a printing house for banknotes.

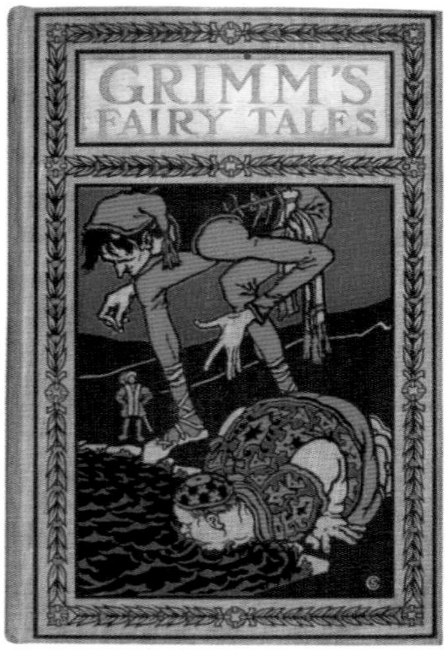

↑ ***Grimm's Fairy Tales*** **adapted by N. J. Davidson, H. M. Brock and Lancelot Speed (illustrators), London, Seeley & Co., *c.*1900. 199 x 130mm ($7\frac{4}{5}$ x 5in)**
A turn-of-the-century gift-book style version of Grimm, with a bold blocked illustration on the cover. The cover is monogrammed "SC" or "CS", but this artist has not been identified.

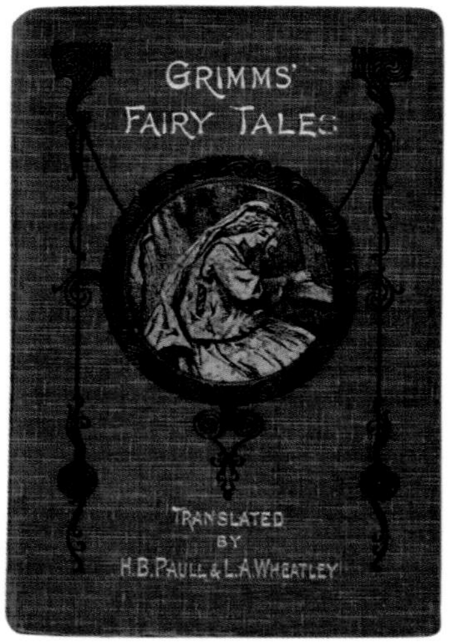

↑ ***Grimms' Fairy Tales and Household Stories*** **H. B. Paul and L. A. Wheatley (translators), New York, Frederick Warne *c.*1890. 202 x 136mm ($7\frac{4}{5}$ x $5\frac{1}{3}$in)**
The central medallion, which has an appropriately circular design, is laid on to the binding case.

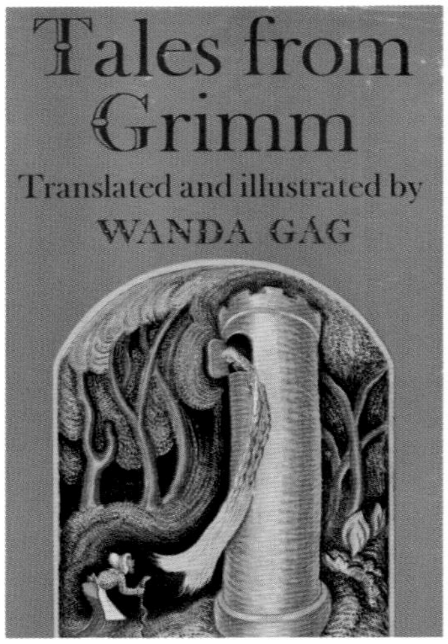

↑ ***Tales from Grimm*** **Wanda Gág (translator and illustrator), London, Faber & Faber, 1937. 212 x 147mm ($8\frac{1}{2}$ x $5\frac{4}{5}$in)**
Wanda Gág (1893–1946), a native German-speaker from Minnesota, translated the stories she had loved as a child and illustrated them with line drawings. The historian Bettina Hürlimann describes her work as "the ideal presentation of the stories for young children."

→ **The Ugly Duckling** "After Hans Christian Andersen", T. van Hoijtema (illustrator), London, David Nutt, 1894. 290 x 240mm (11½ x 9½in)
Theo van Hoijtema (1863–1917) was strongly influenced by Japanese and Indonesian art. He printed his own lithographic illustrations for a number of different Andersen stories including this.

→ **Andersen's Fairy Tales: The Mother's Love** London, Frederick Warne, n.d. 205 x 147mm (8 x 5⅘in)
Although the book is undated, the cover, designed for a series of single publications of Andersen's stories, is typical of the rather Germanic taste of the 1870s.

↓ **Andersen's Fairy Tales** Frederick Richardson (illustrator), Philadelphia, The John C. Winston Company, 1926. 220 x 155mm (8⅔ x 6in)
Frederick Richardson (1862–1937) designed this gift book which has a lavish cover illustration of *The Snow Queen*.

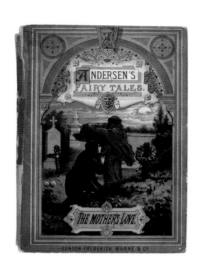

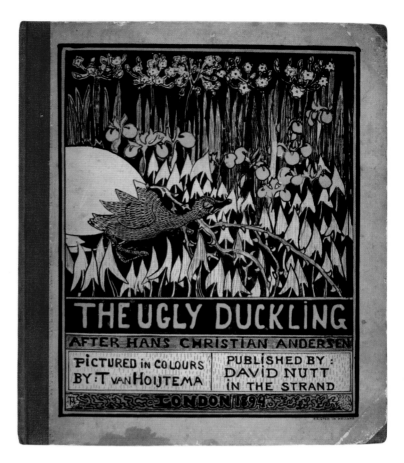

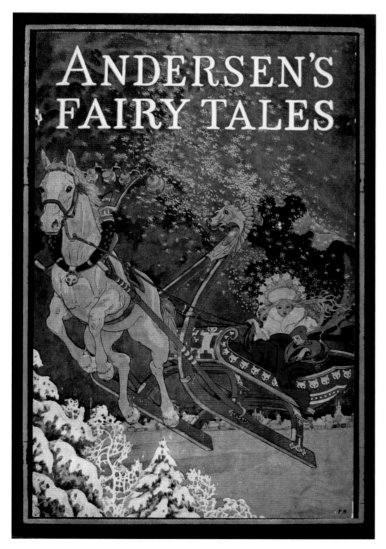

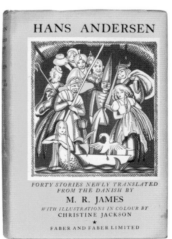

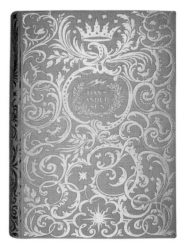

↑ **Hans Andersen Forty Stories** M. R. James (translator), Christine Jackson (illustrator), London, Faber & Faber, 1930. 215 x 142mm (8½ x 5⅗in)
Faber & Faber, founded in 1923, maintained high standards of book design. The translator was the author of famous ghost stories, while the illustrator is less well known.

↑ **Fairy Tales and Legends** Hans Andersen (author), Rex Whistler (illustrator), London, R. Cobden-Sanderson, 1935. 215 x 140mm (8½ x 5½in)
Rex Whistler (1905–44) made scraper-board illustrations for Hans Andersen. This gold blocking on cream buckram, in a Rococo style typical of Whistler's work, was the binding for a special signed edition of 200 copies. It was also used for the jacket and cloth case of the standard edition and reprints until the 1980s.

English eccentrics
Edward Lear & Lewis Carroll

Edward Lear (1812–88) earned a living as a landscape painter and ornothological artist. While staying with the Earl of Derby to make drawings of his menagerie, Lear entertained the children of the house with illustrations to nonsense rhymes. This led him to start writing and illustrating his own texts. From these almost accidental beginnings, Lear became far better known to posterity for his nonsense, which was first published in an obscure edition in 1846, but became widely popularized in Routledge's edition of 1861. His own illustrations are unsurpassable, although he never designed a standard cover.

With the publication of *Alice's Adventures in Wonderland* in 1865, the shy Oxford academic Charles Lutwidge Dodgson (1832–98) assumed his second persona as Lewis Carroll. He changed children's literature with the freedom of his invention that seems to touch on some deeper structure of language and logic underlying everyday life. John Tenniel (1820–1914) illustrated the first edition, which was largely scrapped because the artist complained of the printing quality of the pictures. *Through the Looking Glass* (1871) followed the success of the first book, and *The Hunting of the Snark*, with illustrations by Henry Holiday, was published in 1876. The classic status of the Tenniel illustrations has not deterred many other artists from revisiting Carroll's texts after they came out of copyright in 1907, including Norman Ault (1907) and Mabel Lucie Atwell (1910).

↓ *Laughable Lyrics: A Fresh Book of Nonsense Poems, Songs, Botany, Music etc.* Edward Lear (author) London, Robert John Bush, 1877.
208 x 166mm (8⅕ x 6½in)
This was Lear's last new book of nonsense and contains poems that express sadness through humour. The cover depicts the "two old bachelors" who go in quest of sage and onion stuffing.

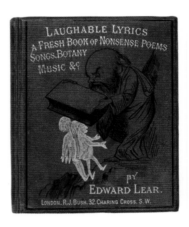

↓ *Nonsense Songs & Stories* (9th edition, revised), Edward Lear (author), London, Frederick Warne, 1894.
220 x 174mm (8⅔ x 6⅘in)
This collection, with its tame and conventional cover redrawn from Lear's originals, included some new material. This edition was published six years after the author's death.

← *The Complete Nonsense of Edward Lear* Holbrook Jackson (editor), Barnett Freedman (cover illustration), London, Faber & Faber, 1947.
230 x 165mm (9 x 6½in)
This handsomely designed edition has remained the standard one, and still sells in its jacket by Barnett Freedman (1901–58), an artist who worked a great deal for Faber. The jacket, which has a collage of Lear's illustrations, was also printed on the binding cloth, as seen here.

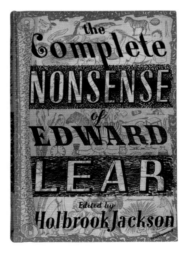

← *The Owl and the Pussycat* Edward Lear (author), Louise Voce (illustrator), London, Walker Books, 1991.
266 x 231mm (10½ x 9in)
A fresh approach to a familiar theme, with lettering and characterization that seem in sympathy with Lear's text.

↑ *A Book of Nonsense* "Derry Down Derry" Edward Lear (author), London, Thomas McLean, 1846, 2 vols.
149 x 216mm (5⅘ x 8½in)
This was the first printed version of Lear's nonsense and is incredibly rare. It was published ten years after the original composition of the limericks contained within. The cover shows the imagined author presenting his book to children, as described in the rhyme printed below it.

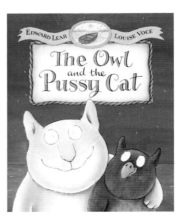

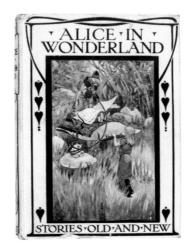

← *Alice in Wonderland, Stories Old and New* Lewis Carroll and Frank Adams (authors), London and Glasgow, Blackie & Son Ltd, *c.*1910. 183 x 126mm (7⅕ x 5in) This is a cheap gift book edition of *Alice*, decorated in the style of Blackie's Art Nouveau designer Talwyn Morris, with a colour plate stuck on.

↓ *Alice's Adventures in Wonderland* Lewis Carroll (author), Tony Ross (editor and illustrator), London, Andersen Press (Random House), 1993. 250 x 190mm (9⅘ x 7½in) Modern reworkings of *Alice* can be sentimental, but Tony Ross captures the nightmare quality of the story while retaining enough of the comic-book style to offset it.

↑ *Alice's Adventures in Wonderland* Lewis Carroll (author), Arthur Rackham (illustrator), London, William Heinemann, 1907. 204 x 148mm (8 x 5⅘in) In the year that Alice came out of copyright, the artist Arthur Rackham (1867–1939) illustrated a gift book edition with a sumptuous blocked binding. The dust wrapper, without lettering but repeating the process block from the frontispiece, is a rare survival.

→ *The Hunting of the Snark* Lewis Carroll (author), Henry Holiday (illustrator), London, Macmillan, 1876. 186 x 126mm (7⅕ x 8½in) This was the first edition of Carroll's "Agony in Eight Fits". Henry Holiday, a well-known stained-glass artist, drew nine illustrations as well as the cover, which was printed on to cloth and shows the Bellman who commands the crew of the strange vessel.

LEWIS CARROLL

ALICE'S ADVENTURES IN WONDERLAND

ABRIDGED & ILLUSTRATED BY TONY ROSS

Interpreting "A Child's Garden of Verses"

← *A Child's Garden of Verses* R. L. Stevenson (author), Charles Robinson (illustrator), London, John Lane, The Bodley Head, 1896.
194 x 125mm (7²/₃ x 5in)
Charles Robinson established his reputation with *A Child's Garden of Verses*. He understood the new technique of process reproduction from line drawings well enough to get the best results from it. The gold blocked cloth case has an elaborate spine, a more restrained front board, and a humorous additional design on the back.

→ *A Child's Garden of Verses* R. L. Stevenson (author), Millicent Sowerby (illustrator), London, Chatto & Windus, 1907. 234 x 170mm (9¹/₅ x 6²/₃in)
This is a gift-book treatment of Stevenson's poems, with colour plates and black-and-white headpieces by Millicent Sowerby (1878–1967), a popular postcard artist. The paper dust jacket is shown. Underneath, the book is bound in imitation vellum with gold blocking.

↓ *A Child's Garden of Verses* R. L. Stevenson (author), H. Willebeek Le Mair (illustrator), Philadelphia, David McKay Co., 1926. 231 x 288mm (9 x 11⅓in)
The Dutch artist Henriette Willebeek Le Mair (1889–1966) was popular in Britain and America, with elegant and well-printed work that was influenced by the French illustrator Boutet de Monvel.

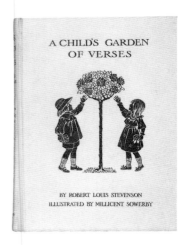

Robert Louis Stevenson (1850–94) felt the experience of childhood deeply. He wrote essays on the subject, contributing to the late 19th-century revolution in attitudes to the relationship between childhood and creativity, and happiness in later life. *Treasure Island* (1883) and *Kidnapped* (1886) have established his reputation as a writer of adventure stories most firmly.

A Child's Garden of Verses, published in 1885, shows a different aspect of Stevenson, as he projected himself into childhood through the power of imagination. It was stimulated by the publication of *A Birthday Book for Children*, illustrated by Kate Greenaway with poems by Mrs Sale Barker, on which Stevenson thought he could improve. Helped by his stepson, Stevenson typeset and printed many of the poems in an edition of two copies with the title *Penny Whistles*. The first commercial edition had no illustrations to assist it, but in 1896 the edition published by John Lane of The Bodley Head (the publishers of the illustrated quarterly *The Yellow Book*), launched the career of illustrator Charles Robinson (1870–1937) with fashionable Art Nouveau line drawings. The whole book was presented in a matching binding. The verses were still deservedly popular when Stevenson came out of copyright in 1924, and their vivid visual imagery has attracted many illustrators, including Tasha Tudor in 1947 and Martin and Alice Provensen in 1951; some in period style and some updated.

↓ *From a Railway Carriage* R. L.
Stevenson (author), Llewellyn Thomas
(illustrator), London, Orion Children's
Books, 1993. 180 x 275mm (7 x 10⁴/₅in)
Stevenson's poem from *A Child's Garden
of Verses* is given a full picture-book
treatment by an illustrator who began
his career in the 1980s.

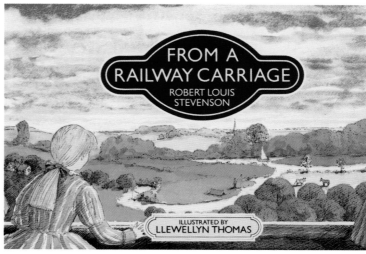

↑ *A Child's Garden of Verses*
R. L. Stevenson (author), Eve Garnett
(illustrator), Harmondsworth, Puffin
Books (Penguin Books), 1948.
177 x 110mm (7 x 4¹/₃in)
Trained as an artist, Eve Garnett became
even better-known as the author of *The
Family from One End Street* (1937) and its
sequels. In the cover of this Puffin
edition, some of Stevenson's
sentimentality comes through.

→ *A Child's Garden of Verses*
R. L. Stevenson (author), Brian Wildsmith
(illustrator), Oxford, Oxford University
Press, 1966. 313 x 223mm (12¹/₃ x 8⁴/₅in)
Brian Wildsmith (b. 1930) followed the
success of his *ABC* with a similarly loose
and colourful interpretation of Stevenson's
poems, sending sentimentality flying.

Struwwelpeter through the ages

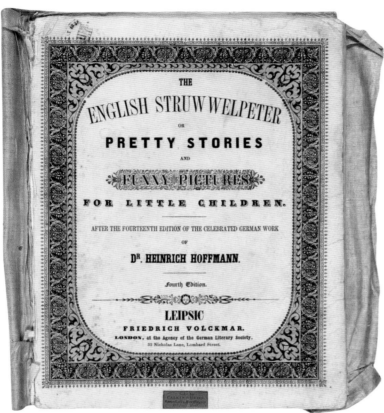

← *The English Struwwelpeter* (4th edition) Dr Heinrich Hoffmann (author), Leipzig, Friedrich Volckmar; London, at the Agency of the German Literary Society, 1848. 245 x 190mm (9²⁄₃ x 7¹⁄₂in) This first translation came from the same press as the original. The pink paper label is pasted on thin board and linen, which forms a wrapper sewn to the spine.

→ *The English Struwwelpeter* (38th edition), Dr Heinrich Hoffmann (author), London, Griffith, Farran, Okeden & Welsh, *c*.1868. 266 x 203mm (10¹⁄₂ x 8in) After 1868, the original drawing of "Shock-Headed Peter", with even longer nails and more unruly hair, was modified into this familiar form, and the base became a plinth to hold the title information.

↓ *The English Struwwelpeter* Dr Heinrich Hoffmann (author), London, Forum Books Ltd, 1990. 253 x 206mm (10 x 8in) The image is the same as in the 19th century, and is one of the most enduring classic cover designs.

As later editions of his classic book helpfully relate, Dr Heinrich Hoffmann (1809–94), a specialist in mental illness, went out into Leipzig one day in the autumn of 1844 to look for a picture book to amuse his three-year-old son. He found only high-minded and elegantly designed books which did not appeal to him, so he came home and composed and illustrated verses for a Christmas present. The result, published in 1845 as *Lustige Geschichten und drollige Bilder*, or *Merry Stories and Funny Pictures*, but prefaced by the same, single image of "Shock-Headed Peter", who later became the title of the book, has fascinated succeeding generations with its grotesque parody of admonitory verses for the young. They are described by the children's book historian Bettina Hürlimann as "a kind of symbolic hyper-reality".

Struwwelpeter was one of the first picture books to appear in the relatively large quarto size, reproducing the original manuscript. The early editions were hand coloured, and often assumed to be printed by lithography, although they may in fact have been woodcuts. These followed each other in quick succession, with the addition of extra verses. When the text was translated into English in 1848, the printing still took place in Leipzig. Editions were published in London by George Routledge from 1858.

Some classic children's books are impossible to parody, but since *Struwwelpeter* is already within such a well-understood genre of tales of punishment and retribution, it has lent itself to numerous variations, in words and pictures. In 2002 it was the basis for a highly successful stage production which toured many cities, augmenting the grotesqueness, but no less popular for that.

← **Slovenly Peter** (23rd edition of the original, with additional material), Philadelphia, The John C. Winston Co., *c.*1870. 254 x 199mm (10 x 7⅘in)
This characterful blocked binding from an American publisher takes the general style of Hoffman's drawings.

↓ **Struwwelpeter** "Specially illustrated by Janet and Anne Grahame Johnstone", London, John Gifford Ltd, 1950. 248 x 186mm (9¾ x 7⅓in)
A post-war reworking of the illustrations to Hoffman's texts loses the primitive savagery of the original.

↑ **Inquisitive Peter and Other Funny Tales** "Daddy John" (author), illustrator unknown, London and Belfast, Marcus Ward & Co., *c.*1880. 259 x 225mm (10⅕x 8⅘in)
This paper-covered toy book with a bright cover, imitates the genre of *Struwwelpeter*.

→ **Max and Moritz, A Story in Seven Tricks** Wilhelm Busch (author and illustrator), cover artist unknown, London, George Routledge & Sons Ltd, 1865. 250 x 190mm (9⅘ x 7½in)
Presented in a form of comic strip, this tale of pranks which lead to a grisly end was especially popular in America. The copy shown here comes from George Routledge's *Struwwelpeter* series.

→ **Schicklgrüber** Robert Colling-Pyper and Margaret Stavridi (authors), Walter Sauer (introduction and translation), Andernach, Kari Verlag, 2000. 278 x 220mm (11 x 8⅔in)
This parody of *Struwwelpeter* was originally created in the Second World War by an English artist and author based in India. It was "mainly addressed to the British and American soldiers stationed in India and served as propaganda against the German and Axis enemies." Verses include Adolf playing with Joe (Stalin) the dog, Roumania playing with Nazi fire and getting burned, Fidgetty Finland, and so on.

THE FOOTBALL'S REVOLT

by

Lewitt-Him

COUNTRY LIFE BOOK

2

Precious children: the '20s and '30s

The period between the wars produced many books that are still read and remembered today. During the 1920s, many features of modern life were becoming well established, with suburbs expanding around cities to accommodate new families in houses and gardens whose styles and colour schemes were matched in the way that books were presented in coloured dust jackets. If suburban architecture was conservative and nostalgic, many children's books in the 1920s tended to be the same way. Similarly, the gradual reawakening of writing and illustration during the 1930s had some features in common with modern architectural styles. The original impulse came largely from continental Europe where there was an attempt to see the social problems of the modern world more clearly, in order to give opportunities to everyone. Children could enjoy the risks that adult publishers took on their behalf.

→ *The Football's Revolt* Lewitt-Him [Jan Lewitt and George Him] (authors and illustrators), London, Country Life Ltd, 1939. 285 x 235mm (11¼ x 9¼in)
Two Polish graphic artists (see p. 68) arrived in London just before the Second World War and produced this story about two footballs that object to being kicked and stay suspended in the air over the pitch. The comic fireman is trying unsuccessfully to catch them. This large picture book, with colour plates, was one of several that brought new vitality to children's publishing.

Precious children: the '20s and '30s

The First World War marked the moment of transition when the book jacket, rather than the decorated binding, became the focus of attention in presenting the book for sale. The change was gradual but irreversible, because the reasons were primarily economic. Blocking book cloth in several colours was too expensive, and it also looked out of date. Paper jackets were already quite common before 1914, although, like the brown paper wrapper for *The Wind in the Willows*, they were usually a repeat of the design on the binding case itself. The wrappers had a dual function: they served to protect the proper book cover while it was in a shop or warehouse, and at the same time gave the prospective purchaser an immediate indication of what they were buying, not only in terms of decoration, but in the flavour of the book's contents.

The book jacket had existed for a long time as an idea, but its potential was undeveloped. After 1920 its moment arrived, and publishers became more aware that additional sales could be made through the immediate outward appearance of the book, something that may be obvious to us today but was only reluctantly accepted within the conservative book trade. The pioneer American bookseller and critic, Bertha Mahony Miller, looked back in the 1950s to record the pioneering work, thirty-five years earlier, of an exceptional retailer, Frederic J. Melcher, who stirred up interest in the ways that children's books could be displayed in shops, including furniture shops as well as book shops, where their jackets were seen as part of a scheme of decoration and a way of life.

Book jackets had to overcome a dubious reputation acquired in their early days, largely based on the perception that they were badly designed and printed. This criticism applied mainly to those printed using the process colour technique. Various examples can be seen illustrating "School stories through the ages" (pp. 54–5), beginning with the earliest, from 1909, which takes a colour plate from the book itself and pastes it on to a striped paper, overprinted with title details – the Arthur Rackham cover for *Alice in Wonderland* on p. 33 uses the

→ **Kidnapped** R. L. Stevenson (author), N. C. Wyeth (illustrator), New York, Charles Scribner's Sons, 1913. 255 x 190mm (10 x 7½in)
Newell Convers Wyeth (1882–1945) was a well-known American artist and a pupil of Howard Pyle at the Brandywine School of Illustration. The second of Wyeth's illustrated editions of Stevenson's classic tale of 18th-century Scotland has a lively jacket illustration in full colour on this dust wrapper, repeated as an onlay on the binding underneath.

→ **Rip Van Winkle** Washington Irving (author), N. C. Wyeth (illustrator), Philadelphia, David McKay Co., 1921. 255 x 190mm (10 x 7½in)
This first edition of the American classic, first published in a miscellany in 1819, has a full-colour dust wrapper, indicating the shift to this form of presentation after the First World War.

→ **Flower Fairies of the Summer** Cicely Mary Barker (author and illustrator), London and Glasgow, Blackie & Son Ltd, 1925. 142 x 110mm (5⅝ x 4⅜in)
Although apparently whimsical, the *Flower Fairies* books by Barker (1895–1973) show genuine observation both of children and of flowers. The cover format looks back to the 1912 style of central Europe with its chequerboard panels in the corners of the frame design.

→ **The Squirrel, the Hare and the Little
Grey Rabbit** Alison Uttley (author),
Margaret Tempest (illustrator), London,
William Heinemann, 1929.
175 x 140mm (7 x 5½in)
This is the first in a series which
contained at least twenty-six titles
illustrated by Tempest (1892–1982), who
also contributed to the books' design. It
was also the first book written by Alison
Uttley (1884–1976), who was a prolific
children's author. The central panel with
the illustration is slightly raised.

→ **Number 4 Joy Street, A Medley of
Prose and Verse for Boys and Girls**
Coloured wrapper designed by Alec
Buckels, Oxford, Basil Blackwell, 1927.
249 x 185mm (9⅘ x 7¼in)
Alec Buckels produced a busy but well-
ordered design in flat colours for the
cover of Basil Blackwell's annual
miscellany, which rose above the general
standard of "reward books" with literary
contributions from Eleanor Farjeon,
Hilaire Belloc, and Edith Sitwell.

→ **Tippenny-Tuppenny's Happy Book**
Author and illustrator unknown, London,
Humphrey Milford, Oxford University
Press, 1938. 85 x 65mm (3⅓ x 2½in)
This is one of a steady stream of books
from Oxford University Press in the
period of "Herbert Strang", the
pseudonym of the publisher's editors.
The bright covers redeem the rather
routine content.

same technique more elegantly on a plain white paper.
A pasted picture was a cheaper solution than
commissioning an extra, large colour print to make a
whole jacket, but it has an improvised feeling to it. As
colour printing became more affordable in the 1920s, it
was the cheap books that tended to have full colour
covers, but the technique was still unreliable and, unless
great care was taken in the printing, the colour of the
original would become muddy. In the world of adult
publishing, pictorial jackets were looked down on as a
gimmick which lured uneducated readers into purchasing books by the use of over-dramatized
imagery. There were further grounds for criticism because this kind of printing could only be

done on smooth-coated paper, which chipped and
damaged easily. In addition, this type of paper would be
more likely to slip off the book and was less pleasant to
handle than a traditional binding or a jacket printed on
heavier and rougher paper. It is not surprising that some
of the book jackets that we enjoy today as period pieces,
if not as great art, were thrown away or simply fell apart.

During the 19th century, book bindings acquired a life
of their own, not commonly related to the style of the
book. If a binding carried an illustration, it might be the

work of a different artist to the main illustrator of the book, as with the Seeley & Co. edition of
Grimm's Fairy Tales (see p. 30). Publishers kept longer back lists of publications in their catalogue
than they do today and when an edition was printed it was economical to commission a fairly
long run, although the binding was often carried out only in small batches to meet demand.
The unbound sheets were retained in a warehouse and
new bindings could be applied to them to create a more
up-to-date look, as with the Routledge's *Aesop's Fables in
Words of One Syllable* (see p. 29). Such deception added to
the equivocal reputation of the illustrated cover.

In the 1920s and '30s, many of the children's books still
to be found in great numbers in secondhand bookshops,
were "got up" in coloured jackets or blocked bindings by
publishers, but were of low quality inside. They were
known as "reward" books, as their principal destination

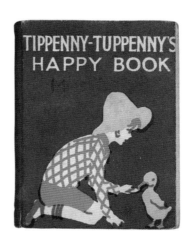

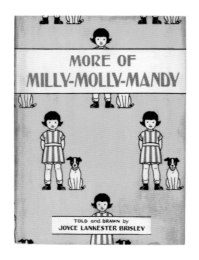

was to serve as prizes. They were often given away by schools at the end of term, or used as prizes by church Sunday schools. Reward books were low-grade imitations of the Edwardian "gift books", but instead of a rich bank of colour plates, the hapless recipients were lucky to get a single colour frontispiece, which might be cut into a medallion and pasted on to the front board, amidst formalized decoration by a different hand. The Blackie edition of *Alice in Wonderland* on p. 33 is an example of the gift-book genre. The paper for these "reward" titles was artificially "bulked" with air to make it thicker without providing the strength or solidity that this ought to imply. As the librarian and historian Marcus Crouch wrote, "it was... virtually impossible for any story of literary or sociological value to be produced in this machine." Book critics were delighted when thousands of "rewards" went up in flames when the centre of English publishing, then located in the Paternoster Square area north of St Paul's Cathedral, was hit during the London Blitz of the Second World War. Afterwards the book trade was able to turn over a new leaf.

Opposition to book jackets was more deep-rooted than a simple objection to shoddy design or printing, however. The Arts and Crafts movement had generated a feeling on both sides of the Atlantic that a book ought to be an object of integrity. This implied that a unified design idea followed through all the elements, from the size of the page and its layout to the choice of paper, type, illustration, and binding. Integrity demanded that, as far as possible, each part of the book should honestly display the methods by which it was produced. As a result, photomechanical techniques of reproduction were only approved if they were of the highest quality and served a purpose that

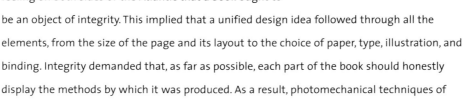

no other form of printing could replace. A good designer would choose a method, such as wood engraving, which was more direct in its method, unless it was absolutely necessary to reproduce a photograph. Even if photo-etched line blocks were used, it was considered preferable to design these to print in flat colours or pure line rather than using the dot screen. All book jackets were suspect

← *More of Milly-Molly-Mandy* Joyce Lankester Brisley (author and illustrator), London, George G. Harrap, 1928.
192 x 130mm (7½ x 5in)
The second book in a popular English series uses a repeat pattern like a wallpaper for its jacket. The way that the lettering overlays the images is charming, as too is the useful picture map of the village on the endpapers.

← *Nursery Rhymes* "With pictures by Claud Lovat Fraser", London, T. C. & E. C. Jack Ltd, 1919.
272 x 200mm (10¾ x 7⅘in)
Claud Lovat Fraser (1890–1921) was a highly influential artist who revived an 18th-century chapbook style, and gave it widespread popularity before the First World War with broadsheets of verse and illustration published by a small company, The Flying Fame, of which he was a partner. *Nursery Rhymes* was first published by The Poetry Bookshop in 1916. The critic Marcus Crouch called it "the most forward-looking of English picture-books since Nicholson's *Alphabet* in 1898," adding that "like Nicholson's book it had at least half an eye on the adult bookman."

← *Mr Tootleoo and Co.* Bernard Darwin (author), Elinor Darwin (illustrator), London, Faber & Faber, 1935.
190 x 242mm (7½ x 9½in)
The previous two titles in this popular fantastical series of rhymed tales about a shipwrecked sailor and various fabulous creatures were published by the Nonesuch Press, one of the notable upholders of the fine printing revival of the 1920s. The attractive drawings by the author's wife are printed to resemble *pochoir*, or stencil colouring, and make a fine showing on this first "trade" title in the series.

→ **The Twins & Tabiffa** Constance
Heward (author), Susan Beatrice Pearce
(illustrator), London, George G. Harrap,
1923. 160 x 110mm (6⅓ x 4⅓in)
The script lettering, presumably by the
illustrator, is a pleasing feature of this
cover pasted as an onlay on the front
board. Showing the back view of figures
is a common device for suggesting a
forward motion into the book on the
part of the reader.

→ **Ameliaranne and the Green Umbrella**
Constance Heward (author), Susan
Beatrice Pearce (illustrator), London,
George G. Harrap, 1920.
160 x 113mm (6⅓ x 4⅓in)
The first in a long series, which
unusually always had the same
illustrator, although the authorship
changed over time to include, rather
unexpectedly, Eleanor Farjeon, one of the
most distinguished children's writers of
the period. As for *The Twins and Tabiffa*,
Pearce uses a back view of the central
figues in a symmetrical design.

because they were not physically part of the book, but those printed by process colour were the worst in terms of integrity because the artist had less control over the result than could be offered by other processes.

Alternative printing techniques required more skill on the part of the artist or designer, but the results restored a sense of integrity to the jacket or printed binding because it was a well-considered piece of print production in its own right. If the artist wanted to use flat colour, which could be obtained from printing off line blocks, someone needed to draw each colour as a separate original, known as a "colour separation" and plan the sequence of printing to get the best results. Claud Lovat Fraser, whose early work before the First World War was part of the chapbook revival associated with William Nicholson, was one of the first artists to study this technique and demonstrate how successful it could be in recapturing some of the singing quality of colour found in Regency hand-colouring.

The technique was not too difficult to learn, and the covers for *Number 4 Joy Street* and *Tippeny-Tuppeny's Happy Book* (see p. 41) are examples showing how this technique could produce sparkling results at different levels of complexity. The poster-like simplification of the latter is typical of the 1920s and associated Art Deco movement that loved bright and contrasted colours. On these pages, the cover of *More of Milly-Molly-Mandy* is a simple application of flat colour, while *Mr Tootleoo and Co.* is a hybrid: it includes areas of mechanical tone but is still printed in specially mixed individual colours for maximum brightness. The jacket for John Masefield's *The Box of Delights* (see p. 45) shows how a white background can help to set off a simple choice of colours supported by black outline drawing.

These covers were unusual in their time, but represented a growing awareness in publishing that a good book should be treated as an integral whole, with a consistent style carried throughout. Edy Legrand's work was widely noticed in Britain and America (see p. 48). A young illustrator, Douglas Percy Bliss, wrote in the *Artwork* magazine in 1929, "Before I encountered the books of Edy Legrand the brightest and jolliest picture books that I had seen were those by Crawhall and his followers, Nicholson and Lovat Fraser. The discovery of Legrand's delightful *Macao et Cosmage* was a shock of delighted surprise."

Once book jackets were established in the field, they gave opportunities for a wide variety of design styles. One purpose was to establish the identity of books published in series. Some of the series published during the inter-war period are still produced today, for example the *Just William* or the *Chalet School* books. Both these series had colour jackets, although the books themselves were illustrated in black and white. Beginning in the middle of the 1930s, Harold Jones produced a more artistically distinguished series treatment for the books of M. E. Atkinson (see p. 58), in which the way the lettering is incorporated into the design suggests that he had been studying book covers of the 1860s or 1870s and reworking them in a sophisticated way. These marked the beginning of his long career as a children's book illustrator which extended into the 1970s.

Hugh Lofting drew his own illustrations and jackets for his *Dr Dolittle* books. These have a frame – each title has a different design and colour – with the frontispiece image reproduced within. Similarly, Arthur Ransome (see pp. 56–7) took over the illustration and jackets of his books from the other artists who had illustrated the early editions. Each of his books has a jacket with images from that title reduced and arranged as a collage, with a second colour unique to the book, making a pleasing set of different colours when the series is lined up together. Other distinguished authors who chose to make their own jacket designs, suitable for line block reproduction, included J. R. R. Tolkein for *The Hobbit* published by George Allen & Unwin in 1937, and T.S. Eliot for *Old Possum's Book of Practical Cats*, published by Faber & Faber in 1939. (Both titles are reproduced in *Front Cover*, a companion volume to this.)

Adult book jackets from publishers such as Faber & Faber, Jonathan Cape, The Bodley Head, and Chatto & Windus made use of the talents of some of the best graphic artists of the period. Rex Whistler made

← *Just William's Luck* Richmal Crompton (author), Thomas Henry (illustrator), London, George Newnes, 1948.
190 x 130mm (7¹⁄₂ x 5in)
Thomas Henry illustrated and provided distinctive red-backed jackets for the first thirty-eight titles in the *William* series, up to 1965, latterly in collaboration with Peter Archer. This mid-period jacket depicts the hero with his dog Jumble, in a habitual plight, desperate with desire for something but short of ready cash.

← *Doctor Dolittle's Circus* Hugh Lofting (author and illustrator), London, Jonathan Cape, 1925.
204 x 145mm (8 x 5¹⁄₄in)
Hugh Lofting (1886–1947) began his series about a doctor who talks to animals in 1922, with his own illustrations and cover designs. The covers are particularly delightful in a slightly naïve way, with a pleasing use of colour. As the critic Edward Blishen wrote in 1968, "It is possible to guess at the styles of drawing that influenced him – a curious range from early Victorian grotesquerie to art nouveau" and the general character of his illustrations ties the books very firmly to the 1920s. Blishen felt "a special supercharge of high spirits and invention" in this book and thought it possibly Lofting's best.

← *The Head-Girl of the Chalet School* Elinor M. Brent Dyer (author), Nina K. Brisley (illustrations and cover), London and Edinburgh, W. & R. Chambers, 1928.
190 x 125mm (7¹⁄₂ x 5in)
Up to 1941, the *Chalet School* books were all illustrated by Nina Brisley, the sister of the creator of *Milly-Molly-Mandy*. This process-colour jacket captures the quality of a watercolour design on its chalky white "calendered" paper.

→ *The Camels are Coming* "W. E. Johns" [William Earle] (author), London, John Hamilton, 1935.
190 x 125mm (7½ x 5in)
This is a reissue of the first Biggles title, and is named after the Sopwith Camel, an early fighting plane. The cover has jolly Art Deco lettering and an effective use of the three planes coming out of the sky. The series was taken over by Oxford University Press in 1935 and developed a standard series cover, with illustrations by Howard Leigh and Alfred Sindall.

→ *The Box of Delights* John Masefield (author), Judith Masefield (illustrator), London, William Heinemann, 1935.
195 x 130mm (7¾ x 5in)
Masefield wrote two books about a boy called Kay Harker, *The Midnight Folk* (1927) and *The Box of Delights*, the latter seen here in the first edition with a cover designed by the author's daughter. The images suggest the occasional comedy in a story that is probably better known for wonder, mystery, and even a slightly Kafkaesque terror. This cover design was retained for later hardbacks, but modified in design and printed in alternative colours.

illustrations and jackets for Walter de la Mare's stories, *The Lord Fish* for Faber & Faber in 1933, and the publishers were proud enough of their commission to bind in extra prints of the front of the jacket and its spine at the front and back of the book. In contrast with the the low standard of reward books, with their tired reworkings of old material, these publishers not only commissioned good jackets but took part in the general raising of book production standards during the 1920s. Basil Blackwell, the owner of the leading bookshop in Oxford, published a small but distinguished children's list, headed by anthologies from the annual magazine *Joy Street*, which ran from 1923 to 1926. On these pages, writings by several important authors including Eleanor Farjeon first appeared. The jackets for the *Joy Street* books by Alec Buckels (see p. 41) were designed on a much more sophisticated level than those of other children's annuals which flooded the market, although the designs by Alfred Bestall for the *Rupert* annuals, produced from 1936 onwards, have their loyal devotees (see p. 53). At Faber & Faber, a firm started in 1923, the director in charge of production was Richard de la Mare, the son of the author of *Peacock Pie*. Faber published William Nicholson's superb picture books *Clever Bill* (1926) and *The Pirate Twins* (1929, see p. 49), and during the 1930s issued English editions of several of the best picture books to come out of America.

On the other side of the Atlantic, a new enthusiasm and professionalism had been developing since the early years of the century, in contrast to which British book publishing, despite increasing volumes of book production, looked confused and amateurish. Beatrix Potter had reached the conclusion that English children's authors "used to write down to children, now they write twaddling dull stories or odious slangy stuff." Authors, illustrators, publishers, retailers, and librarians formed a linked network in America, serviced by new organizations and publications such as the *Horn Book*, a bi-monthly magazine from Bertha Mahony Miller's children's bookshop in Boston, which was first published in 1924. The children's sections of public libraries were often the most important part of the chain and so were librarians such as Anne Carroll Moore of the New York Public Library. Moore, who wrote reviews in the *New York Herald Tribune*, was a friend of Beatrix Potter, who valued her serious understanding of children's literature. The opinions of Miller, Moore, and

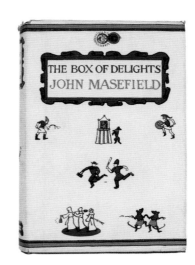

others, predominantly professional women in what was in other respects still a man's world, were valued by publishers who were stimulated to experiment with new authors, covers, designs, and stories. A small sample of the results is shown on pp. 60–1 and, for books after 1940, on pp. 82–3, but there are many more that could be selected. The beginning of the twin annual prizes in the USA, the Newbery Medal (awarded from 1922 onwards for the best children's American literature) and the Caldecott Medal (presented from 1938 for the most distinguished picture book), did much to stimulate public interest in the field of children's books.

The new American confidence in the production of picture books owed much to the combination of open-minded editors and newly arrived émigré authors and illustrators from central Europe. If they had passed through Paris on their journey, they would have become familiar with the *Père Castor* (*Father Beaver*) series, produced by lithography in a fresh style (see p. 49), to which the Russian artist Feodor Rojankovsky (1891–1970) who came to the United States in 1941, contributed many titles under the Gallicized name "Rojan". *Père Castor* books were influenced in turn by the picture books produced by artists in Russia following the 1917 revolution which were drawn in a brisk and lively style and printed directly from the artist's drawings on to lithographic printing plates. Although this printing medium had been available

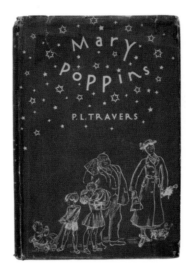

for many years, its potential for conveying loose and rapid drawing, combined with strong colour, had been strangely unexplored. American publishers sought out printers who could get good results from the process, and artists who knew how to work in the medium and make their own colour separations. When successful, lithography could save the publisher a great deal of money while offering customers cheap books that were actually original artist's prints, for example Rojankovsky's book about Daniel Boone, produced in Paris for the American market in 1931. After books like this had shown

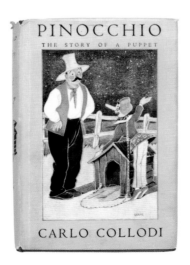

← *Emil und die Detektive* Erich Kästner (author), Walter Trier (illustrator), Berlin, Williams & Co. Verlag, 1933.
200 x 160mm (7⅘ x 6⅓in)
This is a German edition from the year in which this classic of 1929 by a left-wing writer was banned by the Nazis. The cartoon-like cover is bold in its use of so much blank space, with a high viewpoint. Walter Trier (1890–1951) later came to London and illustrated *Blitz Kids* by Elinor Mordaunt (1941) among others.

← *Mary Poppins* P. L. Travers (author), Mary Shepard (illustrator), London, Gerald Howe, 1934.
190 x 130mm (7 x 5in)
This book was already famous in America (although not on the same scale as in Britain), when Walt Disney made it into a film in 1966. The simple original jacket, printed in a single working of pale purple on yellow paper, is by the daughter of the better-known illustrator, E. H. Shepard.

← *Pinocchio, the Story of a Puppet* Carlo Collodi (author), M. A. Murray (translator), Kurt Wiese (illustrator), London and Edinburgh, Thomas Nelson, 1938.
208 x 140mm (8⅕ x 5½in)
Collodi's classic morality tale was first published in English in 1892. This edition, illustrated by a well-known German-American artist, predates Walt Disney's film by two years.

→ **Adventures of the Little Wooden Horse**
Ursula Moray Williams (author), Joyce
Lankester Brisley (illustrator), London,
George G. Harrap, 1938.
225 x 165mm (9 x 6½in)
Ursula Moray Williams (b. 1911) was herself
an illustrator, as seen in her *Jean-Pierre*
books, but the illustrator for the jacket of
this book, which became a well-established
classic, was the author-illustrator of the
Milly-Molly-Mandy books. (see p. 42)

→ **Sharp Ears, The Baby Whale** John Y.
Beaty (author), Helene Carter (illustrator),
Oxford, Basil Blackwell, 1939.
213 x 213mm (8⅜ x 8⅜in)
This was originally an American book,
printed by lithography, and republished
in Britain, as were several of the best
American picture books of the 1930s. The
cover shows how a skilled artist, in this
case the same who illustrated the
American edition of *Swallows and
Amazons* (see p. 56), could work with a
limited selection of colours and combine
them to create a strong sense of design.

→ **In His Little Black Waistcoat** "Story and
decorations by Joan Kiddell-Monro",
London, Longman, 1939.
380 x 275mm (15 x 11in)
Joan Kiddell-Munroe (b. 1908), was
inspired by the arrival of a baby giant
panda at London Zoo to write and
illustrate her first book, which is on the
same scale as the *Babar* books. As the
critic Frank Eyre wrote, it was "remarkable
for its fearless use of white space, at a
time when most conventional picture
books appeared to be designed upon the
principle of giving the public as many
colours as possible."

the way, the impulse to design more boldly was carried over into other print media. With the new generation of picture books, the jacket usually became an integral part of the whole production, although, as in the case of Wanda Gág's *Millions of Cats* or Viriginia Lee Burton's *Choo Choo: The Story of a Little Engine Who Ran Away* (see pp. 49 and 61), it was the only part of the book that made use of other colours in addition to black and white.

Lithographic presses, usually intended for printing posters, had no difficulty coping with large page sizes, and a fashion for very large picture books began with Jean de Brunhoff's *Babar* books (see p. 50). Edward Ardizzone's *Little Tim and the Brave Sea Captain*, published in 1936 (p. 76), whose size was based on the sketchbook in which it was originally drawn, was commissioned by the New York branch of Oxford University Press rather than by the London office. Even with the more technically advanced printers in America, its production was a perilous adventure, although it paid off.

In Britain, Kathleen Hale's first *Orlando* book (see p. 51) was published in 1938, from plates drawn by artists at the printers, W. S. Cowell. After that, Kathleen Hale had to learn to draw her own plates to save costs, and regularly worked for four months on each title. All these books are quarter-bound, with prints pasted on to the front and back boards, although they also had jackets of magnificent size with the same designs. Hale worked on the *Orlando* plates herself, without any additional financial reward, because she wanted to put so much detail into the drawings.

The cover for Joan Kiddell-Monroe's *In His Little Black Waistcoat* (right), which was also very large, was based on simplification and, as the critic Marcus Crouch remarked, "a subtle balancing of black and white masses". With books such as these, and the beginning in 1940 of the lithographed Puffin Picture Books, which were based on Noel Carrington's experience of producing *Orlando* for the publishers Country Life Books, as well as his admiration for Russian books and *Père Castor*, British children's book publishing took a step forward and began to catch up with America's lead.

The rebirth of the picture book

The concept of the *livre d'artiste* developed in France in the late 19th century. It was distinguished from the luxury illustrated book by the primacy given to illustration over text, and the implied avant-garde character of the work. Because of Modernism's interest in folk art, children's creativity, and other manifestations of the primitive, children's books, or sophisticated reworkings of them, became one aspect of the genre. Once the precedent was set, an in-between genre developed in the 1920s of books that were ostensibly for children, but were largely intended for adult enjoyment. These included Edy Legrand's magnificent *Macao et Cosmage* (1919) which carries a political and moral message amid its sumptuous *pochoir-* (stencil-) coloured plates.

On a more modest scale, the artist David Jones was one of several artists who worked for Harold Munro's Poetry Bookshop in London in the 1920s. Also in London, William Nicholson, who had flirted with children's books at the turn of the century, responded to the birth of a daughter, Elizabeth, by producing two all-time classics – *Clever Bill* (1926) and *The Pirate Twins* (1929) – described by the critic Brian Alderson as "quite simply the finest and most fluent picture books of the century."

In post-revolutionary Russia, many artists turned to designing lithographed children's books which were admired in the West and in turn influenced the *Père Castor* (*Father Beaver*) series published in Paris by Flammarion. These were mostly books about everyday life, nature, and science. With lithographic printing, it was simpler from the production point of view if the artists drew their own lettering, both for the cover and often for the text of the book as well. This helped to give an intimate and informal quality to the work, and thus the lettering became a more integral part of the cover design.

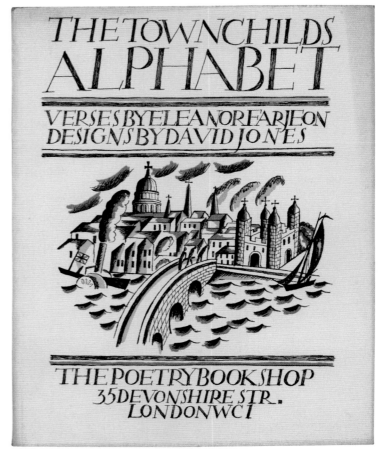

↑ *The Town Child's Alphabet* "Verses by Eleanor Farjeon, designs by David Jones", London, The Poetry Bookshop, 1924.
210 x 170mm (8¼ x 6⅔in)
David Jones (1895–1974) was a distinguished painter and poet who was very concerned with the relationship of text and image. This early work shows the distinctiveness of his line work. There was a companion title, *The Country Child's Alphabet*, with illustrations by Michael Rothenstein.

← *Macao et Cosmage, ou l'Expérience du Bonheur* Edy Legrand (author and illustrator), Paris, Editions la Nouvelle Revue Française, 1919.
330 x 330mm (13 x 13in)
The cover is perhaps the least part of this fine book, although it shows in faded colours the effect of hand stencilling with watercolour. Edy Legrand (1892–1970) relaunched his career with spectacular success with this and other titles in the 1920s.

↓ **The Pirate Twins** William Nicholson (author and illustrator), London, Faber & Faber, 1929. 187 x 250mm (7¹⁄₃ x 9⁴⁄₅in)
Nicholson changed his style from the severe figures of his *Alphabet* when devising this delightful fantasy story, illustrated with a few colours. Note how the smoke from the ship's funnel curls round to make a decorative border.

→ **Ils Font Comme Ci, Elle Fait Comme Ça** "Père Castor" [Paul Facher] (author), Chacane (illustrator), Paris, Flammarion, 1934. 170 x 190mm (6²⁄₃ x 7¹⁄₂in)
The *Père Castor* series began in 1932 and was influential in Britain and America. This is a cut-out book, with perforated card pages, making a game about occupations with words on the back of each figure as clues.

← **Das Zauberboot** Tom Seidmann-Freud (author and illustrator), Berlin, Herbert Stuffer Verlag,1929.
241 x 208mm (9¹⁄₂ x 8¹⁄₃in)
The work of the German woman illustrator Tom Seidmann-Freud (1892–1930) was based on the discoveries of child psychology that children benefit from an active role in looking at pictures. Thus, in the tradition of pop-up books, there are things to pull, lift, or revolve on almost every page.

↑ **Millions of Cats** Wanda Gág (author and illustrator), London, Faber & Faber, 1928. 185 x 250mm (7¹⁄₄ x 9⁴⁄₅in)
This is a classic of simple storytelling in folk style, with strong black-and-white pages and a brightly coloured cover. Wanda Gág (1893–1946) was a writer and illustrator who brought authentic fantasy into the whimsical world of the 1920s.

Big books
Babar & Orlando

Jean de Brunhoff (1899–1937) was, in his way, as significant as Beatrix Potter in changing the shape of children's books. Potter 's miniature titles matched the animals she wrote about and de Brunhoff's large books suited the elephants he first immortalized in 1931. The bold colours printed from lithographic plates, with charming handwritten texts, were replicated in the first English edition issued by Methuen. Brunhoff wrote the stories when ill with tuberculosis, as a way of keeping in touch with his children, and the last of his four original books was published after his tragically early death.

The illustrator Maurice Sendak, a great admirer of Babar, has written, "These books are so traditionally French, filled with what might be considered old-fashioned ideas of manhood, womanhood and manners. But there is always an underlying emphasis on developing a child's (an elephant child's) personal freedom and individuality through self-control."

The charm and success of Babar and other French titles influenced the publisher Noel Carrington in Britain. Kathleen Hale brought him the idea of Orlando the Marmalade Cat, based on stories for her own children. These books, produced before and after the war in a format deliberately similar to Babar's, were printed from colour separations drawn by Kathleen Hale, who took four months on each one. Henrietta the Faithful Hen was a later invention of Hale's, less well known than Orlando but equally inventive.

↑ *Babar's Travels* Jean de Brunhoff (author and illustrator), London, Methuen, 1936.
362 x 267mm (14¼ x 10½in)
"Full of alarming and very amusing twists of fate" says Maurice Sendak of the second *Babar* book, in which Babar and Celeste have many adventures on their honeymoon.

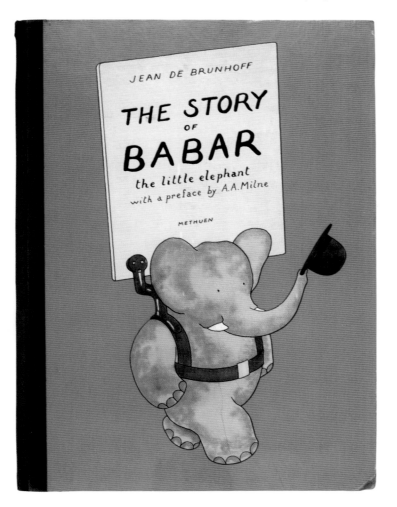

← *The Story of Babar, the Little Elephant* Jean de Brunhoff (author and illustrator), A. A. Milne (preface), London, Methuen, 1934. 362 x 267mm (14¼ x 10½in)
Babar became a firm favourite in Britain and America. This is the first English edition. The handwritten text was printed by the lithographic specialists W. S. Cowell. After the Second World War, the production became more conventional and smaller, but the original large version was reissued in the 1980s.

→ **Henrietta the Faithful Hen** Kathleen Hale (author and illustrator), London, George Allen & Unwin, 1967. 213 x 285mm (8²/₅ x 11¹/₅in)
This is the second edition of a book first published in 1943 by Hale's original editor, Noel Carrington, with his post-war company Transatlantic Arts. Henrietta appeared in a later book with Allen & Unwin in 1973.

→ **Orlando's Home Life** Kathleen Hale (author and illustrator), London, Puffin Picture Books (Penguin Books), 1942. 180 x 220mm (7 x 8²/₃in)
When Noel Carrington started Puffin Picture Books, Kathleen Hale's experience with drawing for lithography was a good reason for extending the *Orlando* series with three additional titles.

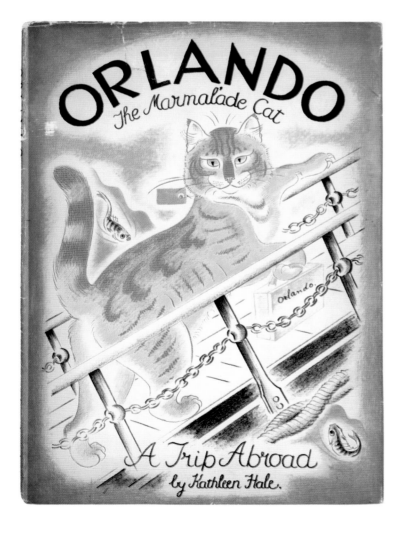

↑ **Orlando (the Marmalade Cat) Keeps a Dog** Kathleen Hale (author and illustrator), London, Country Life Books, 1949. 370 x 270mm (14¹/₂ x 10²/₃in)
Hale's sense of the design of a page comes across in the shaping of the white space in the centre of the cover.

← **Orlando the Marmalade Cat: A Seaside Holiday** Kathleen Hale (author and illustrator), London, Country Life 1952. 370 x 270mm (14¹/₂ x 10²/₃in)
This was the last *Orlando* book in the original large format. The cover shows an old boat converted into a holiday home that was a feature of the river at Aldeburgh in Suffolk for many years.

← **Orlando the Marmalade Cat: A Trip Abroad** Kathleen Hale (author and illustrator), London, Country Life Books, 1939 370 x 270mm (14¹/₁ x 10²/₃in)
This was the second of Kathleen Hale's large size *Orlando* books and the first for which she drew her own lithographic plates. It was issued with a loose wrapper, with the same design on the boards of the book.

English bears
Winnie the Pooh & Rupert

The cultural significance of Winnie the Pooh is not to be summarized in a few sentences. His creator, A. A. Milne (1882–1956), would be forgotten but for the verses and stories inspired by his son, Christopher Robin Milne, who was born in 1920. With Ernest Shepard's illustrations, the set of four books became bestsellers which, while redolent in some ways of the whimsy of the 1920s, have proved among the strongest survivors in the whole genre of children's books. Published in uniform editions by Methuen, more attention was lavished on the bindings, in good buckram with gold-blocked drawings from the books, than on the jackets.

Rupert Bear, drawn by Mary Tourtel (1874–1948), first appeared as a comic strip in the British *Daily Express* in 1920. Soon the daily cartoons were gathered into story books, printed on "featherweight" paper. They are interesting for the evolution of the hero, whose head changes shape and becomes more human. When Tourtel's eyesight began to fail, Rupert was taken over by Alfred Bestall (1892–1986), who was a better inventor of stories and used colour printing for the covers and endpapers of the series of Rupert annuals, which begun in 1936 and remained popular for ever after.

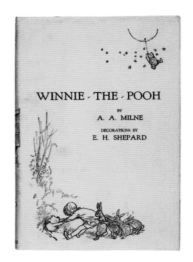

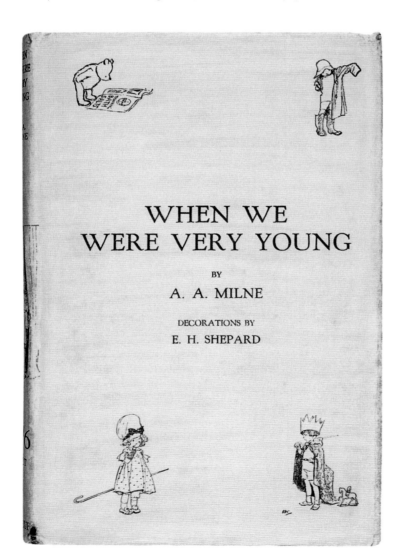

← **Winnie the Pooh** A. A. Milne (author), E. H. Shepard (illustrator), London, Methuen, 1926. 190 x 128mm (7½ x 5in) The most famous bear in literature originally appeared in a rather plain cover, with two illustrations taken from the text, which are carefully positioned on the page in a manner appropriate to the action depicted. The same concern for layout makes for lively reading of the text and undoubtedly contributed to the success of this book and its companions.

↓ **A. A. Milne's titles** This group of spines of A. A. Milne's four books (two of verse and two of stories), shows how they would have appeared to a buyer in a bookshop in the 1920s. Each has a small drawing by Shepard to make it more decorative, but otherwise not much effort has been taken to make the books attractive; in fact the price is one of the most prominent features.

↑ **Winnie ille Pu** A. A. Milne (author), Alexander Lenard (translator), E. H. Shepard (illustrator), London, Methuen, 1960. 190 x 127mm (7½ x 5in) This Latin translation was first published in Sao Paulo in 1958 and was eagerly taken up by school classics teachers in Britain. Pooh as Centurion is a perfect cover image, and he also appears crowned with laurels on the title page.

← **When We Were Very Young** A. A. Milne (author), E. H. Shepard (illustrator), London, Methuen, 1924. 190 x 128mm (7½ x 5in) *When We Were Very Young* sold half a million copies in its first ten years. Shepard (1879–1976) was a frequent illustrator for *Punch* magazine, where Milne worked as a young man, and where some of his poems, later collected in this book, were first published with Shepard's illustrations.

← *Little Bear and the Fairy Child* Mary Tourtel (author and illustrator), Edinburgh and London, Thomas Nelson, 1921. 152 x 155mm (6 x 6in)
This is the format of the first set of *Rupert* newspaper cartoon strips put into book form. The main illustration is taken directly from the book, which is similarly printed in two colours. The binding paper is a smooth imitation vellum.

← *Rupert and the Magic Toy Man* Mary Tourtel (author and illustrator). London, Sampson Low, Martson & Co., *c.*1933. 185 x 122mm (7⅓ x 4⅘in)
The *Rupert* books changed into this distinctive yellow-covered format in 1923, with a text in verse as shown on this cover.

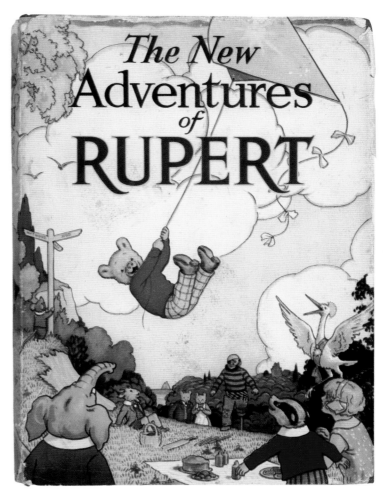

↑ *The New Adventures of Rupert* Alfred Bestall (author and illustrator), London, *Daily Express*, 1936. 253 x 192mm (10 x 7½in)
Alfred Bestall's jackets and covers for *Rupert* annuals fascinated generations of children with their rich detail and carefully reproduced watercolour. This is the first that Bestall designed. The style of drawing landscape features and clouds is a continuation from the work of W. Heath Robinson at the beginning of the century. The later annuals had laminated covers with similar illustrations and illustrated coloured endpapers, the latter being more atmospheric and evocative.

School stories through the ages

Stories set in the British boarding school, or its imitators, were a substantial genre, much of it submerged below the tideline of literary respectability. This scarcely matters where the design of covers is concerned, since the earnestness of the titles and imagery are often unconsciously humorous and even touching in their emotional naivety. While *Tom Brown's Schooldays* by Thomas Hughes established the genre in 1857, *The Fifth Form at St Dominic's* by Talbot Baines Reed (1852–93), launched a greater wave of stories. School stories before the Second World War were usually segregated by gender, and Angela Brazil (1869–1947) became the most popular author of girls' school stories after the publication of *The Fortunes of Philippa* in 1906.

Desmond Coke (1879–1931), himself a schoolmaster, set out to parody the genre in *The Bending of a Twig* (1906) and a series of other titles, although much school-story writing is beyond parody.

The intense enclosed world of the boarding school survived the Second World War but ceased to be a respectable literary theme. Lacking an American equivalent, it remained essentially an English subject. Later, authors on both sides of the Atlantic made the mixed day school a credible focus for discussing the perennial tribulations of growing up.

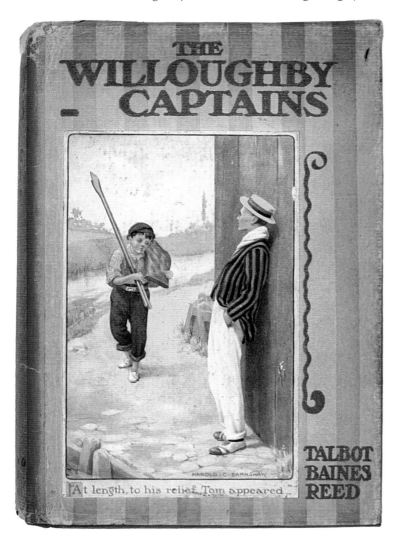

↑ *That Fellow Hagan!* Sydney Horler (author), Frank Gillett (illustrator), London, Cassell, 1927. 197 x 127mm (7¼ x 5in)
Although this kind of cover art was often condemned for being too obvious, it is not without skill.

← *The Willoughby Captains* Talbot Baines Reed (author), Harold Earnshaw (illustrator), London, Hodder & Stoughton, 1909. 190 x 127mm (7½ x 5in)
Here is an early example of a pictorial wrapper, printed on a striped paper with hand lettering overprinted and a process colour plate from the book laid on.

→ *The Chaps of Harton* "Belinda Blinders" [Desmond Coke] (author), London, Chapman and Hall, 1913. 192 x 125mm (7½ x 5in)
The pseuydonym and the style of illustration convey that this is a parody.

→ *School! School!* Sydney Horler and Archibald Webb (authors), London, S. W. Partridge & Co., 1925.
125 x 190mm (5 x 7½in)
The cover follows a formula, as did most of the writing of school stories during the 1920s.

↓ *The Best Bat in the School* Dorita Fairlie Bruce (author), London, Oxford University Press, Humphrey Milford, 1933.
190 x 125mm (7½ x 5in)
The cover is colour printed and pasted on to the binding. It was written by a prolific author of "reward books" and published by Oxford University Press in the days before it had a more discriminating policy towards children's fiction.

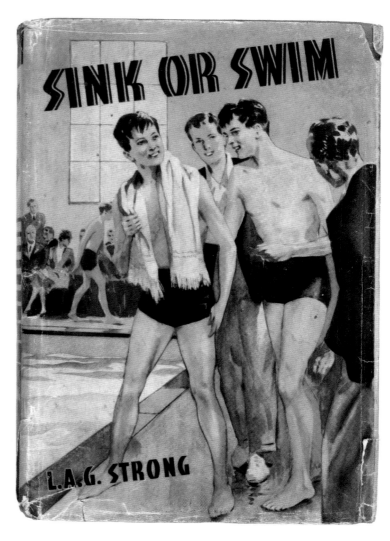

↑ *Sink or Swim* L. A. G. Strong (author), London and Redhill, Lutterworth Press, 1946. 190 x 130mm (7½ x 5in)
Strong was a children's editor for Basil Blackwell, the Oxford bookseller and publisher. This wrapper, designed for two-colour printing, reflects the wartime economy standard of book production and interpets literally the book's title which pursues the theme of a school misfit.

← *Autumn Term* Antonia Forest (author), Margery Gill (jacket design), London, Faber & Faber, 1962.
205 x 135mm (8 x 5⅓in)
This is a reprint of a title first published in 1948. The cover has been updated by a noted illustrator, working with three colours in the colour line-block technique. *The Listener* commented, "A likely and likeable school tale; the dialogue is good and the characters are flesh and blood."

Swallows and Amazons for Ever!
Arthur Ransome

In the summer of 1928, the Altounyan family returned to England from Syria, with their children, to spend a long holiday on Coniston Water in the Lake District. The writer Arthur Ransome (1884–1967) was a family friend and keen sailor who joined in the children's experiences on the lake in two small boats, one of which was called "Swallow". Ransome's fictionalized version of their experiences was written during 1929 and published by Jonathan Cape in 1930 as *Swallows and Amazons*. The adventures feature the Walker children (the Swallows), the Blackett sisters (the Amazons), and other child characters becoming slightly older in a progression of holidays, free from concerns of school and, for the most part, of parental interference. The *New Statesman* wrote, "the child reader will be delighted to find nothing so uninteresting to him as child-psychology, and the things that do interest him are treated on a real and serious plane." The books were immediately successful, and Ransome wrote twelve books in the series, ending with *Great Northern?* in 1947.

Ransome was very particular about the way the books and their covers were illustrated. He was dissatisfied with the romanticism of Steven Spurrier, whose map appears on the covers and endpapers of the first edition of *Swallows and Amazons,* and preferred the work of Helene Carter for the first American edition. After Clifford Webb had illustrated two of the books, Ransome started drawing illustrations himself, beginning with *Peter Duck* in 1932, with help from Taqi [Titty] Altounyan.

Ransome's own pen and ink drawings were amateur in many ways, but they were accurate in respect of technical matters of boats and their fittings, as he required, and went well with the stories. Clifford Webb's jacket for *Swallowdale* introduced the idea of composing drawings from the text in a collage manner, with a second colour filling in the gaps between them. Ransome took over this idea for use with his own illustrations, and the whole set of books was brought into a uniform look which has continued unchanged for the hardback editions.

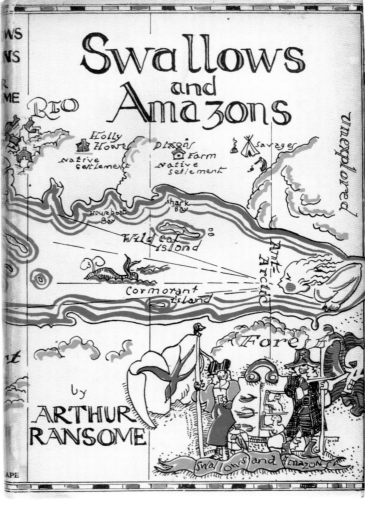

→ **Swallowdale** Arthur Ransome (author), Clifford Webb (illustrator and jacket), London, Jonathan Cape, 1931. 206 x 140mm (8 x 5½in)
Clifford Webb illustrated the second edition of *Swallows and Amazons* as well as its sequel, *Swallowdale*, and Ransome liked those of his illustrations where the faces were not too apparent "throwing the whole energy of the artist into setting the adventure in its romantic landscape that no child can invent but that every child needs as food to its own fancy." This jacket also introduced the "collage" theme which was later adopted for the whole series.

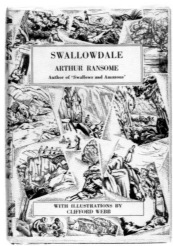

↑ **Swallows and Amazons** Arthur Ransome (author), Steven Spurrier (jacket and maps), London, Jonathan Cape, 1930. 206 x 140mm (8 x 5½in)
This is the first edition, whose jacket adds title lettering to the coloured endpaper maps of the imaginary lake, its islands and shores, drawing on the pirate story themes which the children introduce into their adventures.

← **Swallows and Amazons** Arthur Ransome (author), Helene Carter (jacket, maps, and illustrations), Philadelphia, J. B. Lippincott, 1931. 210 x 145mm (8¼ x 5¾in)
Ransome thought the illustrations of the first American edition beat those of Steven Spurrier "to blazes in picturesqueness and general interest." The three colours and aerial view give it a strong design.

→ *Swallows and Amazons* Arthur Ransome (author), "illustrated by the author with help from Miss Nancy Blackett", London, Jonathan Cape, 1953. 190 x 127mm (7½ x 5in)
Ransome's own illustrations, first made for *Swallows and Amazons* itself in 1938, were used in the book, but he left the original endpapers cover by Stephen Spurrier in place.

↓ *Peter Duck* Arthur Ransome (author and illustrator), London, Jonathan Cape, 1932. 206 x 140mm (8 x 5½in)
Ransome followed up a suggestion for a story offered by the Altounyan children, and wrote part of it when staying with them in Aleppo in the winter of 1932. *Peter Duck* opens on the Norfolk broads in winter, and leads on to tales of pirates on the high seas. This was the first book for which Ransome made his own drawings and created his own collage for the cover.

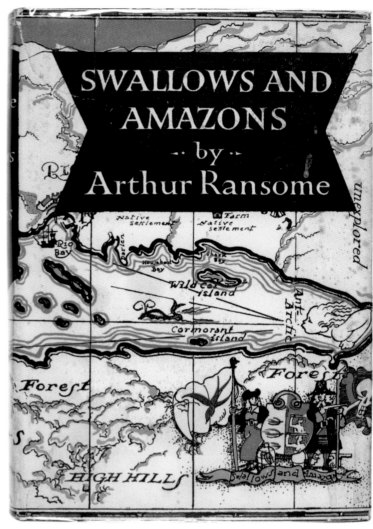

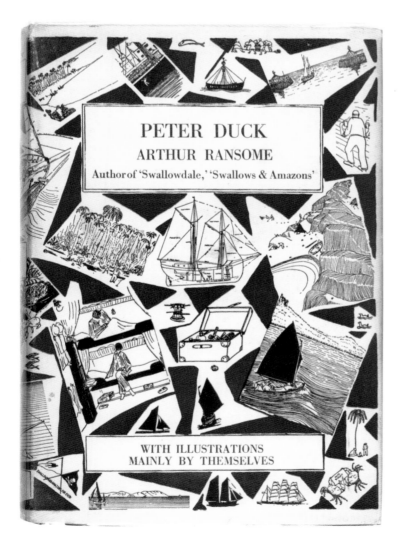

← *The Far-Distant Oxus* Katherine Hull and Pamela Whitlock (authors), Pamela Whitlock (illustrator), Arthur Ransome (introduction), London, Jonathan Cape, 1937. 207 x 140mm (8½ x 5½in)
Hull (1921–77) and Whitlock (1920–82), schoolgirls in their teens, were inspired by Ransome's work to write their own child-based adventure, involving ponies on Exmoor. They submitted their manuscript to Jonathan Cape and the fresh style of storytelling and illustration won Ransome's support. Three titles were published in the series.

"His love for what he sees so well"
Harold Jones

With the publication in 1954 of the nursery rhyme collection *Lavender's Blue*, Harold Jones found a place in the affections of generations of children who could appreciate the combination of innocence and sophistication in his delicate outline drawings and colour washes. His details are always faithful to the text, yet they bring an added element of strangeness.

Born in London in 1904, Jones became established as a children's illustrator in 1936 with the series of adventure stories, similar to those of Arthur Ransome, by the author M. E. Atkinson. In 1937, Faber & Faber published *This Year, Next Year*, conceived by Jones as a picture book with his own verses. Before he had finished writing these, Walter de la Mare saw the illustrations and offered to write poems to fit them, which Jones considered a high compliment, returned by de la Mare in the line that titles this page.

Jones continued to illustrate into the 1980s, and some of his later work is striking in its evocation of dream-like imagery. His attitude to Christianity was simple, enabling him to approach texts such as Blake's *Songs of Innocence* and Kingsley's *The Water Babies* with a fresh eye. He had a clear sense of the "architecture" of a book and the relationship between type and illustration on the page, as well as skill in drawing his own lettering.

↑ ***This Year: Next Year*** Walter de la Mare (author), Harold Jones (illustrator), London, Faber &Faber, 1937.
294 x 255mm (11½ x 10in)
This cover, repeated in identical form on the paper-cover boards, brings together fragments of images from the book, printed throughout in five colours from the artist's hand-drawn colour separations on lithographic stone at the Baynard Press.

← ***Mystery Manor*** M. E. Atkinson (author), Harold Jones (illustrator), London, John Lane, The Bodley Head, 1937. 205 x 135mm (8 x 5¼in)
A series of six titles (1936–39) came out of the collaboration of Atkinson and Jones. Each had a handsome coloured jacket and endpapers.

→ ***Songs of Innocence*** William Blake (author), Harold Jones (illustrator), London, Faber & Faber, 1958.
210 x 158mm (8¼ x 6¼in)
Since Blake was his own first illustrator in 1789, it takes courage to illustrate his work again. Jones's cover shows his training in the discipline of life drawing.

→ *Lavender's Blue, A Book of Nursery Rhymes* Kathleen Lines (compiler), Harold Jones (illustrator), London, Oxford University Press, 1954. 257 x 195mm (10 x 7¾in)
Jones's best-known work has been frequently reprinted, but the early editions have the best quality of soft colour. The printers, Jesse Broad of Old Trafford, worked from separations drawn by Jones on transparent overlays, producing a disciplined range of colours laid like hand-colouring on to a fine black outline. The vignette on the back cover illustrates the book's title verse.

↑ *The Enchanted Night* Harold Jones (author and illustrator), London, Faber & Faber, 1947. 254 x 190mm (10 x 7½in)
For this book, one of a pair produced for his own children, Jones used a robust technique of wood engraving rather than the delicate line for which he is best known. In a typical touch, the collection of emblems on the cover hints at the mystery within.

← *The Water Babies* Charles Kingsley (author), Harold Jones (illustrator), London, Victor Gollancz, 1961. 220 x 157mm (8⅔ x 6in)
Charles Kingsley's allegory of spiritual discovery in a Victorian setting, first published in 1863, perfectly suited Jones's combination of the mystical and the down-to-earth. The cover shows his attention to detail, such as the title lettering made out of bent water reeds while the picture captures the dream-like condition of the underwater world.

Illustration in America in the 1930s

The reasons for a growth in the vigour of American children's publishing have been explored at the beginning of this chapter. The first important changes began to take place around the First World War, but Edwardian styles of illustration lingered on. Wanda Gág's *Millions of Cats* (p. 49) was rejected by many American publishers before it finally came out to great acclaim in 1928, and was one of the first picture books to demonstrate the potential for a new approach.

Gág drew inspiration from her German immigrant background (see p. 30), and many illustrators who created the classics of the 1930s had arrived as immigrants themselves, like Ludwig Bemelmans, from the Austrian Tyrol, Ingri and Edgar Parin d'Aulaire, who were born in Norway and Munich respectively and who came to America together in 1929, and Maud and Miska Petersham, earlier immigrants from Hungary. Kurt Wiese was born in Germany in 1887 and worked in several countries, including Brazil, before coming to America. He mastered the lithographic process successfully, carrying out colour separations for Bemelmans who found the work irksome. Picture books by these and other artists often drew on the colourful folk costumes of their native countries, although the d'Aulaires turned to a patriotic American subject with *Abraham Lincoln* in 1939, which was the third book to win the Caldecott Medal.

These artists were able to adapt to the new fashion for lithographic printing coming from Russia and Paris, and inspired American illustrators such as William Pène du Bois and Virginia Lee Burton to work in the same way. The medium seemed to go well with a new graphic boldness in the way that covers were designed, usually with the artist's own lettering in a style to suit the subject. The first titles of Dr Seuss (see p. 84) also appeared just before the Second World War to great acclaim.

↑ *Hansi* Ludwig Bemelmans (author and illustrator), New York, Viking Press, 1934. 310 x 232mm (12⅕ x 9in)
The boy's cheeks are a good display of the soft grainy texture obtainable with lithographic crayons. The cover is a bold piece of design by the creator of *Madeline* (see p. 86).

→ *The Story of Ferdinand* Munro Leaf (author), Robert Lawson (illustrator), New York, Viking Press, 1936. 211 x 185mm (8⅓ x 7¼in)
The story of a bull that refuses to fight was the most successful work of a prolific author. James Roginski writes, "The universal message of the flower-smelling bull escapes no one."

→ *Giant Otto* William Pène du Bois (author and illustrator), New York, Viking Press, 1936. 158 x 156mm (6⅕ x 6in)
The otterhound Otto uses his giant strength to perform good deeds. This is one of three books written and illustrated by William Pène du Bois at the age of twenty.

← **Mike Mulligan and His Steam Shovel** Virginia Lee Burton (author and illustrator), Boston, Houghton Mifflin, 1939. 220 x 245mm (8⅔ x 9⅕in)
Like *Choo Choo*, this story was based on observation, in this case, Burton wrote, "'Mary Ann', Mike Mulligan's steam shovel, I found digging the cellar of the new Gloucester High School." The jacket, which is different, is illustrated on the jacket of *Children's Book Covers* itself.

← **Abraham Lincoln** Ingri and Edgar Parin d'Aulaire (authors and illustrators), New York, Doubleday & Co., 1939. 319 x 225mm (12½ x 8⅘in)
As war approached, patriotic American subjects became increasingly popular among American children's publishers. "The more we studied Lincoln the closer he came to us, the greater he became, the more necessary for our present life, the closer related to us and our times," said Ingri Parin d'Aulaire in her Caldecott Medal acceptance speech in 1940.

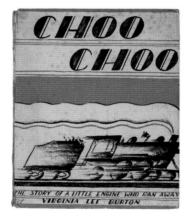

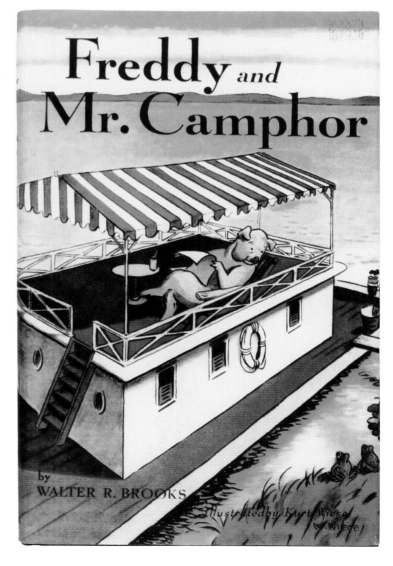

↑ **Choo Choo: The Story of a Little Engine Who Ran Away** Virginia Lee Burton (author and illustrator), London, Faber & Faber, 1937. 289 x 230mm (11⅓ x 9in)
Burton explained, "An engine on the Gloucester branch of the Boston and Maine is the heroine of *Choo Choo*," a story written for her own two young children. With its "Broadway" lettering and wavy speed lines, the cover is in an Art Deco style.

→ **Freddy and Mr Camphor** Walter R. Brooks (author), Kurt Wiese (illustrator), New York, Knopf, 1944 (reprint by The Overlook Press, Woodstock NY, 2000). 203 x 135mm (8 x 5⅜in)
Walter Brooks (1886–1958) began his series of books about "the Renaissance pig" Freddy in 1928. It was described in *The New York Times' Book Review* as "the American version of the great English classics, such as the *Pooh* books or *The Wind in the Willows*." Kurt Wiese provided characterful covers which have been revived for a series of recent reprints.

3

Wartime and reconstruction: the '40s and '50s

There is a special fascination about children's books produced during and after the Second World War. Small formats and cheap paper did not prevent some brave efforts in publishing. Even in neutral Sweden, the first edition of *Pippi Longstocking* (see p. 70) was a small-sized book on poor quality paper. After the war, one can contrast the growing confidence of the United States with a more hesitant approach in Britain, although this is considered a great period for children's writing as well as illustration. Paperbacks began to replace hardbacks, and picture books flourished on both sides of the Atlantic with the career of Edward Ardizzone in Britain who became, perhaps, the best-known children's illustrator, while in the United States, Maurice Sendak began to introduce some cultural complexity into what previously seemed an uncomplicated activity.

← *Diana and her Rhinoceros* Edward Ardizzone (author and illustrator) London, The Bodley Head, 1964. 203 x 260mm (8 x 10¼in) A landscape format suits drawings of a rhinoceros, whether he is seen in a garden, as on the cover, or lying in front of a coal fire receiving Diana's cure for a bad cold. This is one of Ardizzone's most appealing books.

Wartime and reconstruction: the '40s and '50s

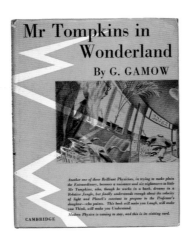

Those who lived through the Second World War attest to the great growth in reading during this time. Whether people were in barracks, shelters, or simply confined to home by danger, blackouts, or shortage of transport, there was little to do except read. Despite paper shortages, new books were produced and sold quickly. For children, the effect was scaled down and publishers relied heavily on reprints of older texts. Although the *Rupert* cartoon series in the *Daily Express* managed to avoid the war altogether, established authors such as Richmal Crompton and Angela Brazil found it a welcome new theme, introducing relatively harmless tales of spies or evacuees.

Not all publishing activity was of a high standard, however. The critic Frank Eyre, writing in 1952, remembered how "a very high proportion of the books that would figure in any list of the best modern children's books were unobtainable during the war years, and far too many inferior books were produced." This situation was all the more apparent since the 1930s had been a time of vigour. On the other hand, as the author Geoffrey Trease observed, the restrictions on paper meant that the artificial "bulking" found in pre-war books ceased, and "children's books underwent a healthy slimming process." In America, where the war did not engage the population until 1941, and then had a less devastating effect than in Britain, the disruption was less apparent.

Captain W. E. Johns had launched Biggles as a pilot in the First World War Royal Flying Corps in 1932 and during the pre-war decade had strongly advocated building up the strength of the RAF. His sequence of stories were believed to have influenced recruitment during the war, and, in 1941, *Biggles defies the Swastika* was set in Nazi-occupied Norway. At the request of the Air Ministry, Johns agreed to write books that would similarly support recruitment to the Women's Royal Air Force and, in books such as *Worrals of the WAAF* (1941), created Joan Worralson and Betty Lovel, based on women pilots who flew non-combat missions.

André Maurois (1885–1967), a well-known French adult author whose life of the poet Shelley was the first title published by Penguin Books in 1935, wrote a children's book, *Patapoufs et Filifers*, published in France in 1930. Two boys, one fat, one thin, enter an underground kingdom and find themselves the guests of the two rival populations, in a Gulliver-like fantasy of exaggerated human foibles. While the "Fattypuffs" (as they were translated in the later English version) exemplify what outsiders consider a typically French love of food and a

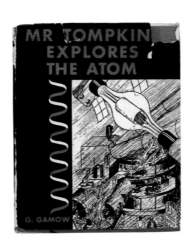

← Mr Tompkins in Wonderland G. Gamow (author), John Hookham (illustrator), Cambridge, Cambridge University Press, 1939. 215 x 170mm (8½ x 6⅔in)
Gamow went to the USA in 1934 and became an American citizen in 1940. He made an important contribution to the understanding of nuclear fission, and was also a successful popularizer of science.

← Mr Tompkins Explores the Atom G. Gamow (author and illustrator), Cambridge, Cambridge University Press, 1945. 215 x 170mm (8½ x 6⅔in)
The jacket states, "The pictures that have resulted from this bold effort may look somewhat crazy, but after all the stories themselves are rather crazy too" – not surprisingly, since it contains a summary of the making of the atomic bomb.

→ **Biggles Defies the Swastika** "Captain W. E. Johns" [William Earle] (author), Howard Leigh and Alfred Sindall (illustrators and cover illustration), London, Oxford University Press, 1941. 190 x 130mm (7½ x 5in)
Biggles acts as a counter-agent for the British in Norway where he is captured by the Germans after their invasions.

→ **Fatapoufs & Thinifers** André Maurois, (author) Rosemary Benét (translator), Jean Bruller (illustrator), New York, Henry Holt, 1940. 285 x 210mm (11⅕ x 8¼in)
A cartoon-style jacket introduces the theme of two worlds in which the humans' charcters match the geography and the manmade environment.

→ **Fattypuffs and Thinifers** André Maurois (author), Norman Denny (translator), Fritz Wegner (illustrator), London, The Bodley Head, 1968. 255 x 190mm (10 x 7½in)
The first English edition of Maurois's classic was in 1941, but it was revived with splendid drawings by Fritz Wegner in a large format.

Mediterranean sense of time, the "Thinifers", who eat meagrely while standing up to save time, cannot tolerate this defiance of their ideology and create a pretext for war. Inevitably, the Thinifers win through their superior equipment and training, but in the post-war condition of coexistence, they are gradually subverted by Fattypuff values. It has been interpreted as a commentary on England and France, but may equally reflect Germany and France. Either way, its first English translation in 1941, a year after the fall of France, seems to indicate a topical commentary offering hope for the future. Much of the humour, captured in Fritz Wegner's illustrations to the 1968 edition, derives from the differences in architecture, furnishings, and transport between the rival groups, reflecting their opposed beliefs.

If many children's books were preoccupied by traditional values of heroism or, less often, stoicism, two scientific fantasies by the Russian-American scientist, G. Gamow (1904–68), published in the years that the war began and ended, were something different. *Mr Tompkins in Wonderland* is dedicated to Lewis Carroll and to the Danish physicist Nils Bohr. On its cover it carries the text, "Modern Physics is coming to stay, and this is its visiting card." Bohr's research contributed to the creation of the atomic bomb, whose contribution to ending the war in 1945 was accepted more willingly at the time than later on. The jacket of *Mr Tompkins Explores the Atom* explains that "Although this book was written some months before the surrender of Japan it contains the clearest, fullest account of the physical principles and the forces involved in the action of the atomic bomb, describing the stages of theory and experiment by the outcome of which (as we now know) the traffic lights of human history may have been changed forever."

Instead of science, children in America, especially boys, developed a taste for science fiction. The interest came not from books but from comics and magazines, which were based in turn on radio serials that the guardians of culture considered a threat, although there was little they could do to prevent them.

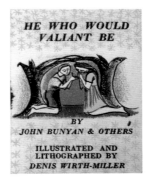

The restrictions of wartime publishing, especially in Britain, had the advantages of reducing books in format and bulk and of concentrating the minds of designers on defying adversity in order to restore fun and fantasy. In contrast to the elephantine scale of the *Babar* books in the 1930s, picture books now were dependent on small off-cuts of paper from other jobs, which were too valuable to throw away and were well-suited to formats that revived the simple production and scale of the chapbook (see p. 10), while adding the advantages of lithographic printing in colour.

Unfortunately only a small number of printers were willing to negotiate with their workforce for artists, who were not members of printing trade unions, to come into the printing works, which was necessary in order to benefit from the cost-saving that artists could bring to the colour printing process. As the designer Enid Marx recalled in later years, "the upper end of the publishing trade became aware ... that they could get more lively illustrations by employing artists to work autolithographically, and still at the same time retain the skills of the trade printers. For litho needs not only the skill of the draftsman but also that of the printer."

Perhaps the times or the fashion deterred artists from simply revisiting the slightly *faux-naive* quality of the chapbook revival begun by Joseph Crawhall in the 1880s and continued in the work of Claud Lovat Fraser before and after the First World War. Artists trained in the '20s and '30s were aware of Cubism and other modern movements which went deeper into modes of representation, and even if they chose not to absorb all aspects of these searching reconstructions of reality, they learned a new sense of designing a picture and organizing its surface. Thus traditional subject matter could be tackled afresh without loss either of artistic integrity or of a popular audience.

Children in whose path this new breed of picture book fell became the recipients of some of the best illustration around. Richard Chopping, who illustrated several books for Noel Carrington's own company Transatlantic Arts as well as for Penguin where Carrington also worked, was

← *He Who Would Valiant Be* (The Challenge Miniature Books, 41) "By John Bunyan & Others", Denis Wirth-Miller (illustrator), London, The Challenge/SPCK, n.d. 75 x 60mm (3 x 2⅜in)
Seldom have religious texts for children been given such an attractive presentation as these chapbook-style titles from the years of wartime scarcity.

← *Heads Bodies & Legs* Denis Wirth-Miller and Richard Chopping (authors and illustrators), Harmondsworth, Puffin, (Penguin), 1946. 177 x 109mm (7 x 4¼in)
The fine outline drawing and clear colours contribute to making this one of the best small books of a vintage era. The cover is notable for its gathering of puffins, the emblem of the children's division of Penguin.

← *My Kingdom for a Cow* A. de Quincy (author), Brian Robb (illustrator), London, Hamish Hamilton, 1948.
180 x 120mm (7 x 4¾in)
This is a hardback with wrappers pasted down over the boards, an economical but effective production method.

→ **Mary Belinda and the Ten Aunts**
Norah Pulling (author), Suzanne Einzig (illustrator), London and New York, Transatlantic Arts, 1946.
160 x 125mm (6⅓ x 5in)
Here is a small hardback stylishly illustrated in accordance with the neo-Victorian theme. It was printed by W. S. Cowell of Ipswich, who were one of the leading firms of printers willing to work with artists on lithography. At this point the German-born author, who came to England in 1939, was using the German version of her first name, but she later changed this to Susan when illustrating Philippa Pearce's classic children's novel, *Tom's Midnight Garden* (see p. 71).

→ **My Toy Cupboard** (Bantam Picture Book No. 33), Claudia Freedman (author and illustrator), London and New York, Transatlantic Arts, c.1945.
135 x 95mm (5⅓ x 3¾in)
Typography and illustration combine seamlessly on the cover of one of Noel Carrington's revived chapbooks.

later chosen by Ian Fleming as the jacket artist for the *James Bond* books. Chopping's *Heads Bodies & Legs* is a printed version of a favourite game in which strips of paper are passed round and each person adds an extra part of a figure without seeing the earlier contributions. The book version has three separate sets of pages which can be turned to make bizarre combinations.

Other prominent illustrators of the time included Chopping's partner, Denis Wirth-Miller, who created small booklets for SPCK, the religious publishing house. Enid Marx (1902–98), who created similar small-scale books during and after the war, was famous for designing seating fabrics for the London Underground and (albeit anonymously) for the government's wartime Utility Furniture scheme. Another artist, Trekkie Ritchie (1902–96), was married to Ian Parsons, one of the directors of the London publishers Chatto & Windus, the publishers of many of Enid Marx's small books. Ritchie created "Midget Books", each 85 x 65mm (3⅓ x 2½in), with twelve pages including the cover, all printed, like chapbooks, on the same paper stock.

Claudia Freedman has been overshadowed by her husband, Barnett Freedman, a contemporary of Enid Marx, Edward Bawden, and Eric Ravilious at the Royal College of Art. Bawden and Ravilious who, even in their twenties were among the best-known book illustrators in Britain, both had families but did not illustrate more than a handful of children's books, while Freedman illustrated none at all, even though he did create a classic cover for Edward Lear in 1947 (see p. 32). *My Toy Cupboard*, by Claudia Freedman, has some of the closely hatched quality found in her husband's work, but in this case the medium is colour-separated line block.

Another eminent publisher of titles in the chapbook style was the Saltire Society of Edinburgh. Dedicated to the preservation of Scottish culture, they issued traditional stories such as *Rashie Coat* (1951), in Scots, illustrated with wood engravings by Joan Hassall who at the time was teaching

at Edinburgh College of Art. Ruari MacLean wrote of these in 1960, "she has done more ambitious work since, but it is doubtful whether she will do anything more beguiling."

My Kingdom for a Cow (1948), is a slightly more substantial book, but the bright cover with its wiry drawing by Brian Robb (1913–79) shares the chapbook style of immediacy and folk-art charm. Robb, a much respected teacher of illustration at the Royal College of Art, later illustrated the series of "Odd and Elsewhere" stories by James Roose-Evans.

The popularity of books about trains and other forms of transport in the 1940s must have some deep underlying sociological explanation connected to the importance of transport in wartime. Or perhaps it reflects the approaching obsolescence of the steam engine in the war period and after. Again, the special and perennial appeal to small boys of large vehicles, whether powered by steam or diesel, must touch on a psychic inclination towards power and domination. It cannot be accidental that most engines in stories are masculine, with the exception of Virginia Lee Burton's *Choo Choo* (see p. 61) and the steam shovel, Mary Ann. It is enough to bring to mind the synaesthesia of the steam locomotive in action – sight, sound, smell, and trembling earth and air – to realize that this was a sensation not easily replicated by later modes of traction.

Like *Choo Choo*, Jan Lewitt and George Him's *Lokomotywa* was published shortly before the outbreak of the war. This was the title of the original Polish edition of 1938, but the same book was issued in translation, as *Locomitive*, by Minerva Publications of London, where the two artists, who worked as a team, emigrated in the year of original publication. This story of men

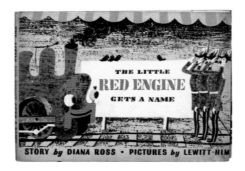

and machines was followed by their illustrations to a counterpart of English origin, *The Little Red Engine Gets a Name* (1942) by Diana Ross, a story in which the engine takes on the attributes of a child in adult society, a creature of habit, pleased to receive recognition for faithful service. The illustrations have a special quality which was successfully reproduced by Leslie Wood when he took over as illustrator of the series in 1945. The same quality is found in books produced by Jack Townend for the same publisher, Faber & Faber. Although his achievement was physically

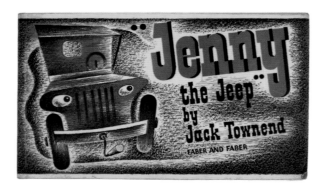

small, it has a special quality. Little is known of Townend's career: his first book was *A Railway ABC* (1941), followed by *Jenny the Jeep* (1944), a story with a wartime theme, *Ben* (1944), about the love between two steam-rollers, and *A Story*

← *Lokomotywa* Juljan Tuwim (author), Jan Lewitt and George Him (illustrators), Warsaw, J Przeworskiego, 1938. 185 x 260mm (7¼ x 10¼in)
Lewitt and Him make their first appearance in a cartoonish style. The same book was published in translation by Faber & Faber in 1939.

← *The Little Red Engine Gets a Name* Diana Ross (author), Jan Lewitt and George Him (illustrators), London, Faber & Faber 1942. 179 x 245mm (7 x 9⅔in)
The full-bleed colour picture spreads in this book mark a new sense of the autonomy of the picture book. Diana Ross's well-pruned text gives the story wheels.

← *Jenny the Jeep* Jack Townend (author and illustrator), London, Faber & Faber 1944. 130 x 220mm (5 x 8⅔in)
Townend worked in lithography with great skill, adopting some of the non-realistic conventions of contemporary art. This thin book has a wrapper over boards with the same design underneath.

→ **Wheels** Oliver Hill (author), Hans Tisdall (illustrator), London, Pleiades Books, 1946. 259 x 205mm (10¹/₅ x 8in)
Oliver Hill (1887–1968) was a well-known architect whose talents were lying idle during the war. Tisdall (1910–97) had already collaborated with Hill as a mural painter, and went on to design a notable series of book jackets for the London publisher Jonathan Cape.

→ **The Book of Railways** Arthur Groom (author), Rod M. Clark (illustrator), London, Benn Brothers, n.d. 275 x 210mm (10⁴/₅ x 8¹/₄in)
Many fine books of this kind introduced children to the glamour of railways with stirring patriotic sentiments.

→ **The Three Railway Engines** (11th edition), The Rev. W. Awdry (author), C. Reginald Dalby (illustrator), Leicester, Edmund Ward, 1951. 109 x 145mm (4¹/₄ x 5³/₄in)
It was unusual to print a children's book in colour throughout at this date. The cover repeats the illustration from page 59, from "The Sad History of Henry". This title, published in 1945, was the first in the series.

BY OLIVER HILL & HANS TISDALL

about Ducks (1945), involving a roller coaster ride and a train journey. Townend also contributed to the Puffin Picture Books series (see pp. 72–3).

Hans Tisdall (1910–97), who illustrated two books with texts by the architect Oliver Hill for Pleiades Books Ltd, emigrated from Germany to Britain at the beginning of the 1930s, by choice rather than from political pressure. He achieved a reputation as a textile designer and mural painter under his original name of Hans Aufseeser, and continued to play a distinctive role during and after the war years as an illustrator, painter, and teacher. *Balbus*, a picture book of building (1944), was the first of his collaborations with Hill, followed by *Wheels* (1946), which, as its cover indicates, is not only about transport but also about the use of wheels in engineering and even, in the final spread, about the legend of St Catherine and her wheel. These books are equivalent to Picture Puffins,

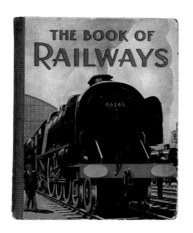

and it is strange that Tisdall's considerable graphic talents were never employed for that better-known series.

The most famous of all the railway books came into being as the result of a Church of England minister, the Rev. Wilbert Vere Awdry (1912–97), telling stories about trains to his children. This association between the clergy and railways was far from unique, and in the Ealing film, *The Titfield Thunderbolt* (1953), the enthusiasm of the village vicar for running a railway is compounded when his bishop shares the footplate for the dramatic final run, in defiance of the forces of modernity represented by a rival bus company and a government inspector. Now known by the name of *Thomas the Tank Engine*, the title of the second book in the series in 1946, these small full-colour books have, as it were, gathered steam over time to become a global brand in the English-speaking world. *The Three Railway Engine*s, the first book, includes Thomas as a character in a moralistic tale which leaves no doubt that the engines are actually small boys.

Documentary books about trains also proliferated at this time, illustrated in a realistic style heightened by perspective and scale to impress child readers with the majesty of the railway network, which was nationalized in 1948 and soon began to lose its distinctive separate liveries and engine types. In those days, there were few boys in Britain who did not consider being an engine driver the pinnacle of career aspiration.

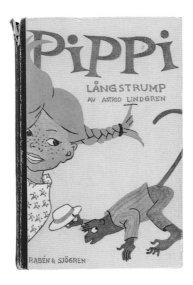

The period between 1945 and 1960 is widely considered to be a special one for children's book publishing and the reasons are not hard to see. The baby boom at the end of the Second World War was combined with a new seriousness in all aspects of child-rearing and education, in a determined effort to put the disruptions of the war as firmly into the past as possible. This was a period of high cultural aspirations, while the pressures of commerce were moderated by the presence of cultural elites who had powerful controls over the publishing and distribution of children's books. In this atmosphere, a cadre of illustrators had grown up who were inspired by the pioneer achievements of the 1930s and were ready to continue the work.

Many of these factors tended to produce books whose dullness has led them to be deservedly forgotten. At the same time, many books were produced whose timeless quality allows them to be classified as classics and, in many cases, to remain more or less continually in print. Of these, only a scattered selection is represented here, among which *Pippi Längstrump* (*Pippi Longstocking*) by Astrid Lindgren, first published in 1945, has a special place as the first book from a Nordic country to gain a firm footing in the international field since those by Hans Christian Andersen. Pippi is a girl who lives an entirely independent life. She is anarchic but considerate of others, in defiance of conventional behaviour, which is represented by the children from the neat house next door. This was a lesson gladly absorbed by a world in the '50s and '60s learning to be free.

Angela Banner's *Ant and Bee* series, begun in 1950, belongs in a long tradition of didactic

stories based on counting, telling the time, and the elements of reading. The clear, flat colour illustrations with black outline, combined with a strange imaginative quality, seem to set them apart from others of their kind, and the effect is helped by the comfortable, small landscape format.

In 1958, Michael Bond published the first of what became a series of nine original books

← *Pippi Längstrump* Astrid Lindgren (author), Ingrid Vang Nyman (illustrator), Stockholm, Rabén & Sjörgren, 1945. 160 x 107mm (6⅓ x 4¼in)
The independent, super-strong heroine with red plaits was based on stories told by Lindgren to her daughter, and reflect the social rejection she had suffered as an unmarried mother. The academic writer on children's books Nicholas Tucker writes, "Here at last was a girl character truly following in the steps of other famous and attractive child rebels from Huckleberry Finn onwards."

← *A Bear Called Paddington* Michael Bond (author), Peggy Fortnum (illustrator), London, Collins, 1958. 206 x 140mm (8 x 5½in)
The illustrator of the series Peggy Fortnum wrote, "After reading the story I draw directly with pen and ink, often producing many versions and sometimes choosing the first. I work from imagination, memory and reference more than from direct studies." The author and illustrator together make the idea of an English-speaking bear at large in London's Portobello Road entirely believable.

← *Ant and Bee: An Alphabetical Story for Tiny Tots* Angela Banner (author), Bryan Ward (illustrator), London, Kaye & Ward Ltd, 1972. 102 x 124mm (4 x 5in)
First published in 1950 and continuing as a series over a number of years, the *Ant and Bee* books brought fantasy into routine learning. This is a reprint of the first title.

about Paddington, a bear from Darkest Peru who arrives at Paddington station in London and is adopted by the Brown family who live near Portobello Road. The hardbacks were beautifully illustrated with the loose line drawings of Peggy Fortnum, and the books' covers, even up to 1970, show a pleasing lack of concern with marketing – unlike the image of Paddington which became increasingly commercialized after he appeared on television.

While *The Cow Who Fell in the Canal* (1957) is not a classic like Paddington or Pippi, it has

been reprinted regularly owing to the witty story and the evocation of a clear-skied Holland in the drawings of Peter Spier, a Dutchman who emigrated to the USA in 1951.

Tom's Midnight Garden and *Tintin* represent opposite poles of children's book publishing in the post-war world. Philippa Pearce's story has the stature of an adult novel and has been the subject of lengthy critical analysis, but it is close enough to a child's eye view to deal effectively with emotional issues about separation on a number of levels. Susan Einzig's cover captures its vivid imaginative quality. By contrast, Hergé's Tintin has almost no emotional life at all; he seems to feel by proxy through those around him, such as his dog Snowy and his companion, Captain Haddock. The strip cartoons are as much beloved by children for their portrayal of action as they used to be disdained by adults.

At a time when sales to public libraries were particularly important for publishers, they were keen to find a successful way to protect books from wear. *Schoolmaster Whackwell's Wonderful Sons* (p. 90) carries a note that its "Gibraltar Library Binding" of glazed printed cloth is "guaranteed for the life of the sheets" and is "washable, damp proof and soil-resistant". Original printings of books from the 1940s and '50s are attractive, if they have survived in good condition, because they belong to a time before laminated bindings and jackets. Although lamination is useful for protecting a book while it is in a shop as well as when it is being used, it makes the colours much harsher and introduces a clinical feeling.

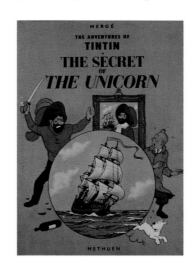

The virtues of scarcity
Puffin Picture Books

In 1939 Noel Carrington (1894–1989), a publisher and advocate of good design, who was dissatisfied with the children's books available, had lunch with Allen Lane, who four years previously had founded Penguin Books. Lane's bold gamble with Penguin revolutionized British publishing, and Carrington explained how Lane might also provide well-printed, colour children's books that were cheaper than their competitors. The secret lay in the technique of autolithography, with colour separations drawn by the artist. Carrington was inspired by lithographed children's books from Soviet Russia and also by the *Père Castor* series from France. As well as others, he used W. S. Cowell, a printer in Ipswich, who had developed a specialism in autolithography through working on Kathleen Hale's early *Orlando* books.

Carrington was commissioned by Lane to start "Puffin Picture Books", at sixpence each the same price as the adult Penguins. The first four books were published at the end of 1940, but the series continued to expand into the 1960s, with Carrington remaining as part-time editor, after he had founded his own imprint, Transatlantic Books. The series was mainly non-fiction, and the author and illustrator were often the same. Titles ranged from serious, almost technical, information about industry and architecture, to illustrated nursery rhymes; and two *Orlando* stories also appeared. The adoption in 1946 by Cowells of a transparent plastic printing plate which artists could draw on made it simpler for them to work in the medium.

← *A Book of Rigmaroles or Jingle Rhymes*
Enid Marx (author and illustrator), Harmondsworth, Puffin Picture Book No. 12 (Penguin Books), [1945]. 180 x 225mm (7 x 8⁴⁄₅in)
A designer of textiles with a strong interest in folk art, Enid Marx illustrated a number of children's books with lithography and wood engravings.

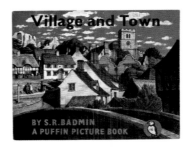

← *Village and Town* S. R. Badmin (author and illustrator), Harmondsworth, Puffin Picture Book No. 16 (Penguin Books), [1942]. 180 x 225mm (7 x 8⁴⁄₅in)
Badmin's detailed observations of buildings and backgrounds are meticulously drawn as separations of soft muted colours to encourage responsible post-war planning and design.

→ *The Magic of Coal* Peggy M. Hart (author and illustrator), Harmondsworth, Puffin Picture Book No. 49 (Penguin Books), [1945]. 180 x 225mm (7 x 8⁴⁄₅in)
Coal was vital for Britain's wartime economy, and the hardship suffered by miners in the 1930s had captured public sympathy, leading to nationalization of the industry.

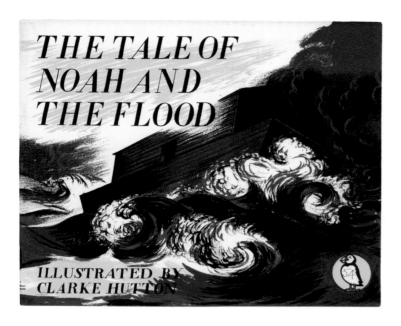

← **The Tale of Noah and the Flood**
W. E. Williams (author), Clarke Hutton (illustrator), Harmondsworth, Puffin Picture Book No. 54 (Penguin Books), [1946]. 180 x 225mm (7 x 8⅘in)
The dramatic cover shows Hutton's skill in drawing his own colour separations for lithographic printing, a subject that he taught at the Central School in London from 1930 to 1968.

← **The Clothes We Wear** Jack Townend (author and illustrator), Harmondsworth, Puffin Picture Book No. 64 (Penguin Books), [1947]. 180 x 225mm (7 x 8⅘in)
The skill in lettering and graphic design, typical of Townend's story books, is evident in the cover of his Puffin book. Part of Puffin's policy was to make children interested in the processes of industrial production and their historical origins.

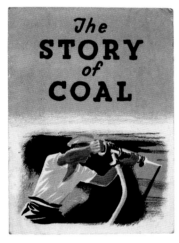

↑ **The Story of Coal** Clifford Rowe (author and illustrator), London, Transatlantic Arts/London and New York, Bantam Picture Book No. 34, c.1946.
135 x 95mm (5⅓ x 3¾in)
This alternative book on coal, also commissioned by Noel Carrington, was the work of a well-known left-wing artist.

→ **Printing** Harold Curwen (author), Jack Brough (illustrator), Harmondsworth, Puffin Picture Book No. 70 (Penguin Books), 1948. 180 x 225mm (7 x 8⅘in)
Harold Curwen had recently retired from the Curwen Press, a leading firm in the printing revival of the 1920s (and the printers of this book). The cover shows aspects of some of the printing techniques available at the time.

Mervyn Peake/Early Puffins

Mervyn Peake (1911–68) achieved his greatest fame after his death when his series of novels about the fantasy castle-city of Gormenghast became cult books and, in 2000, a television series. He studied painting but joined the distinguished line of author-illustrators with his first book, *Captain Slaughterboard Drops Anchor* (1945). With his sensitive line work, Peake was also a compelling illustrator for a number of Victorian classics that were reissued in the 1940s.

Soon after the start of Puffin Picture Books, Allen Lane, the founder of Penguin, summoned Eleanor Graham, a well-known authority on children's books, to invite her to start a companion paperback series. The series Puffin Story Books, which later became simply Puffin Books, was launched in 1941. Graham wanted to avoid too many reprints of classics, although she picked a few with care. She mixed in with these a number of new or recent titles, creating a new standard for children's paperback publishing in the same way Penguin Books had done before for adults. The covers were printed on card and were mostly in full colour, with commissioned illustrations that were reproduced with a soft dot-screen. By the time of Graham's retirement in 1961, 150 Puffin Story Books had been published, at an average rate of well over one per week.

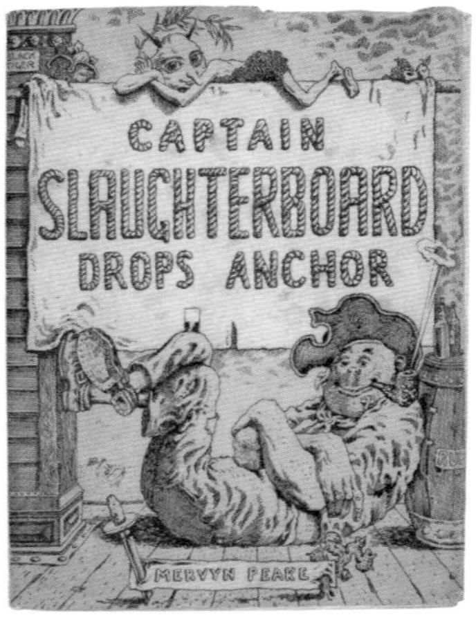

↑ ***Captain Slaughterboard Drops Anchor*** Mervyn Peake (author and illustrator), London, Eyre & Spottiswoode, 1945.
250 x 189mm (9 4/5 x 7 1/2in)
The first edition of this handsome nonsense tale was published in black and white in 1939, but only a handful of copies escaped a bombing raid. The cover of the second edition, with its two colours and fine rope lettering, shows Peake's skill as a designer.

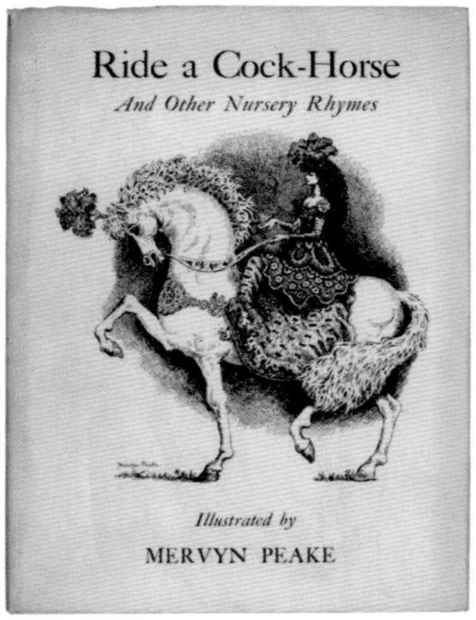

↑ ***Ride a Cock-Horse and Other Nursery Rhymes*** Mervyn Peake (illustrator), London, Chatto & Windus, 1940.
250 x 186mm (9 4/5 x 7 1/3in)
The intricate textures of mane, tail, fabric, and feathers are evidence of Peake's extraordinary imaginative transformation of the everyday, which is also evident in his writing. This book is a rare example from its period of stencil colouring applied by hand.

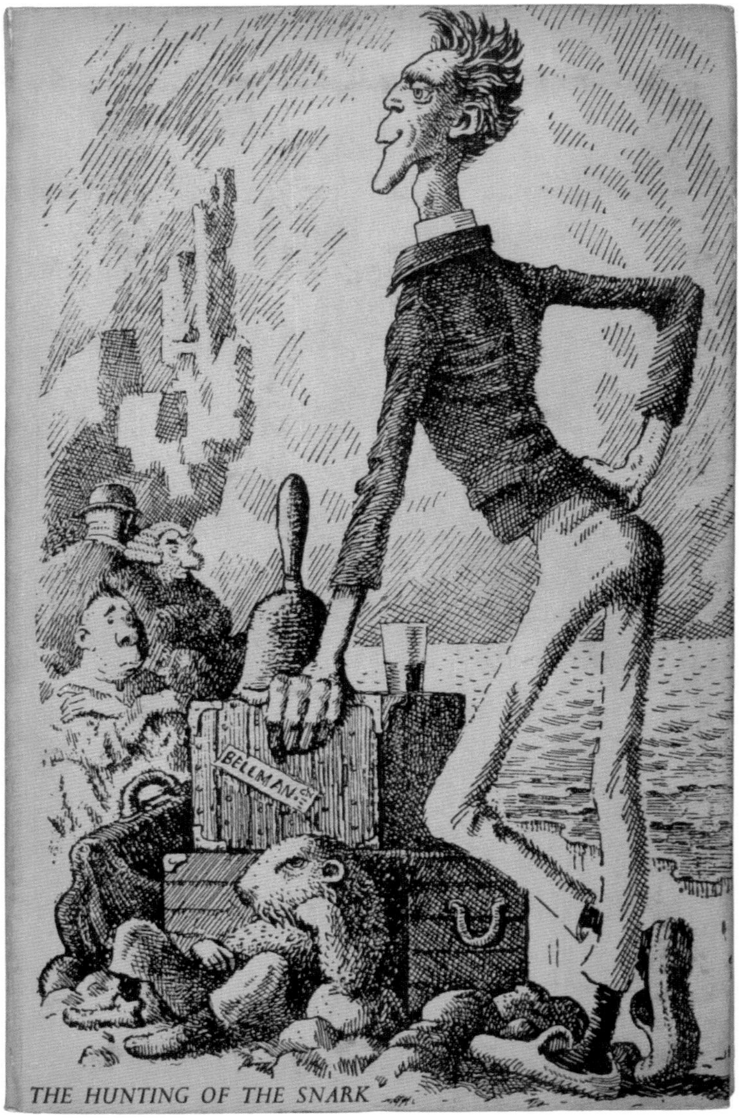

↑ ***The Hunting of the Snark: An Agony in Eight Fits*** Lewis Carroll (author), Mervyn Peake (illustrator), London, Chatto & Windus, 1941. 187 x 116mm (7 1/3 x 4 1/2in)
This superb reinterpretation of Carroll's ballad was printed with illustrated boards. Peake also illustrated Carroll's two *Alice* books in 1954.

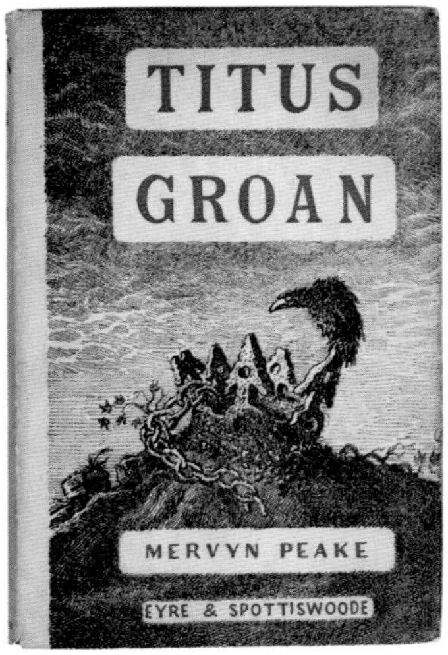

← ***Titus Groan*** Mervyn Peake (author and cover illustrator), London, Eyre & Spottiswoode/New York Reynal & Hitchcock, 1946.
220 x 145mm (8 2/3 x 5 3/4in)
The first of a trilogy of novels on which Peake's fame has continued to grow. *Titus Groan* may not be a children's book, but it uses many of the devices of fairy tale and fantasy.

→ **Worzel Gummidge: The Scarecrow of Scatterbrook** Barbara Euphan Todd (author), Elizabeth Alldridge (illustrator), Harmondsworth, Puffin Story Books PS1 (Penguin Books), 1981.
180 x 110mm (7 x 4⅜in)
This cover is a reproduction of the Puffin edition of 1941. First published in 1936, *Worzel Gummidge* achieved fame on the BBC's *Children's Hour* radio programme and was a worthy title for the launch of the Puffin series, which looked at this point very similar to its grown-up Penguin counterpart.

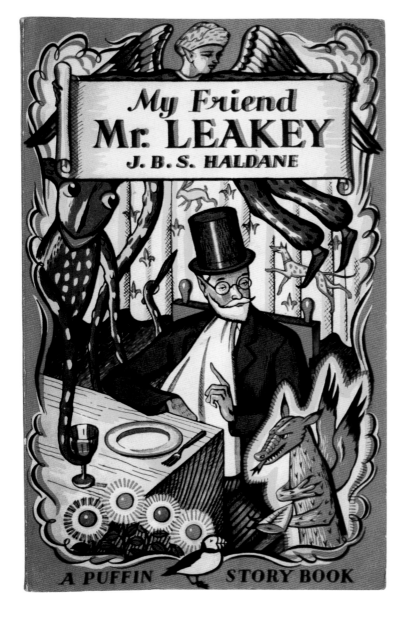

↑ *Treasure Island* R. L. Stevenson (author), "cover by 'Lake'", Harmondsworth, Puffin Story Books PS36 (Penguin Books), 1946.
180 x 110mm (7 x 4⅜in)
The "seafaring man with one leg" appears dramatically on the front cover of this early Puffin paperback, while the back cover (left) helpfully reprints Stevenson's map of the island itself.

← *My Friend Mr. Leakey* J. B. S. Haldane (author), L[eonard] H. Rosoman (illustrator), John Harwood (cover), Harmondsworth, Puffin Story Books PS16 (Penguin Books), 1944. 180 x 110mm (7 x 4⅜in)
The only fictional work by a distinguished scientist was published in 1937 with illustrations by the young Leonard Rosoman, later a well-known painter. The Puffin edition affirms the educational aspirations of the series, for Mr Leakey expounds scientific knowledge through his fantastical activities.

A born illustrator
Edward Ardizzone

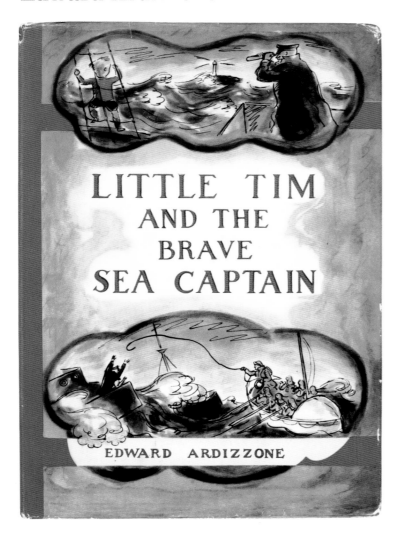

Edward Ardizzone (1900–79) made his mark as a children's illustrator with the first version of *Little Tim and the Brave Sea Captain*. It was commissioned by Grace Hogarth, the New York editor for Oxford University Press, and printed from colour separations in a large format made popular by the *Babar* books, but in this case resulting from the large sketchbook in which Ardizzone first drew the story for his son, Philip. It was a turning point, since he had abandoned a business career in order to become a full-time artist, but until this point had difficulty in supporting his family. Several of Ardizzone's stories are tales in this spirit of idealistic hard work which is rewarded.

Ardizzone used the title "The Born Illustrator" for the publication of a talk he gave in 1958 discussing what illustration was really about. It involved, he said, a close relationship between the drawings and the text, and a strong visual memory supported by continuous observation of actual life. While Ardizzone wrote a number of original stories, he worked equally well with the texts of other authors, including such well-established figures as Eleanor Farjeon and Walter de la Mare. He was prolific, and his work, often using speech balloons, is instantly recognizable. His covers engage immediately with the story, and are often clever works of graphic design with a Victorian flavour, combining separate episodes within a single composition, incorporating well-drawn lettering within the loose line work of the drawings themselves. Ardizzone used colour in a way that was sensitive yet supported the strength of his line drawings. In many cases the cover offered the only colour printing in a book which was illustrated in black and white.

Ardizzone wrote, "The author-artist does not primarily create his books for children, but rather to amuse that childish part of himself... Little children love all books. They have no taste, and rightly so, and of course will read and look at anything with pleasure. All the more reason, therefore, that we should give them the best."

↑ *Little Tim and the Brave Sea Captain*
Edward Ardizzone (author and illustrator),
New York, Oxford University Press, 1936.
330 x 233mm (13 x 9¼in)
The cover depicts episodes from the story of a boy who goes to sea, first told by Ardizzone to his own children. In later books, his drawing and lettering skills became more sure, and his colour range broader, without any loss of vitality.

→ *Desbarollda The Waltzing Mouse* Noel Langley (author), Edward Ardizzone (illustrator), London, Lindsay Drummond, 1947. 194 x 138mm (7⅔ x 5½in)
Ardizzone enjoyed exaggerating faces with a relish for the grotesque, often contrasting the struggles of his protagonists to survive in a hostile world.

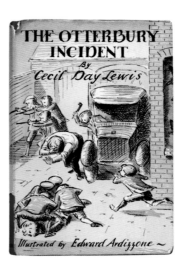

← *The Otterbury Incident* Cecil Day Lewis (author), Edward Ardizzone (illustrator), London, Putnam & Co., 1948.
210 x 140mm (8¼ x 5½in)
Written by a future British poet laureate, probably now best remembered as the father of film star Daniel Day Lewis, this is a modern life story of out-of-school exploits by a group of boys. It was based on the plotline of a French film, *Nous les Gosses*. Ardizzone's cover anticipates the dramatic conclusion.

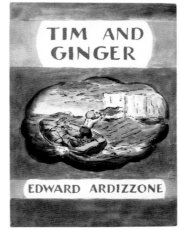

← **Tim and Ginger** Edward Ardizzone (author and illustrator), Oxford, Oxford University Press, 1965.
260 x 195mm (10¼ x 7⅔in)
For his later series of nine *Tim* books, Ardizzone worked with transparent overlays to translate his wash drawings to the press, adding the black key drawing at the end of the process. The colour-washed bands and background of the cover simplify the 1936 version.

← **J. M. Barrie's Peter Pan** Eleanor Graham (author), Edward Ardizzone (illustrator), Leicester, Brockhampton Press, 1962. 165 x 235mm (6½ x 9¼in)
Eleanor Graham of Puffin Books wrote a version of the famous story that is considered to be one of the best, and Ardizzone illustrated it. The book appeared with variant cover designs on both sides of the Atlantic.

↓ **The Little Steamroller** Graham Greene (author), Edward Ardizzone (illustrator), London, The Bodley Head, 1974.
185 x 245mm (7¼ x 9⅔in)
This was one of four children's stories by Graham Greene which he wrote between 1950 and 1953 with illustrations by Dorothy Craigie. The publishers of Greene's adult books, The Bodley Head, commissioned Ardizzone to illustrate them for a reissue in the 1970s.

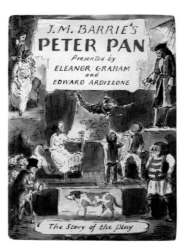

↑ **Stig of the Dump** Clive King (author), Edward Ardizzone (illustrator), Harmondsworth, Puffin Books, 1963.
182 x 110mm (7⅕ x 4⅓in)
Unusually for Puffin, this was not a reprint but a first publication of a book. The story, which has become a classic, describes a boy's discovery of a caveman living in the local rubbish dump.

← **Nurse Matilda Goes to Town** Christianna Brand (author), Edward Ardizzone (illustrator), Leicester, Brockhampton Press, 1967.
160 x 108mm (6⅕ x 4¼in)
The two books in this series, written by Ardizzone's cousin, were beautifully produced in a small format by a minor British publisher. This is a story of unruly children and their mysterious nurse.

"Wholesome reading for your children"
Enid Blyton

Born in 1897 in south London, Enid Blyton had published some thirty titles by the outbreak of the Second World War, but this was nothing compared to the rate of about thirty per year that she sustained from the war years until around 1960. Slowing down only a little before her death in November 1968, she was still writing between six and ten thousand words a day. The quantity was not only a measure of her productivity, but also of the receptiveness of her child readership, for whom her books have continued to offer a way into reading like no others. Her books still sell millions of copies annually.

Blyton's storytelling was based on the improvisation she used when she worked as a nursery governess as a young woman. She understood the difficulties of childhood having been deeply hurt by the collapse of her parents' marriage when she was thirteen. Later she was to find happiness when she married Hugh Pollock, her editor at George Newnes in 1924, but she separated from him and married again.

Blyton occupies an equivocal place in the history of children's books. It is her very qualities of fast-moving action, her shallow characterization, and her repetitive vocabulary which most appeal to a six- or seven-year-old and which have been most condemned by critics and upholders of cultural standards. With hindsight, much of the criticism seems exaggerated, and it serves to overlook other positive aspects of Blyton's work. These are listed by the critics Peter Hollindale and Zena Sutherland, "Her prose is clear and precise, her sense of narrative sequence immensely skilful and compelling, her wit and psychological shrewdness far greater than she is given credit for… and her graphic observation of the natural world is gravely underrated."

Blyton's galloping career swept up many illustrators in its wake. Among the more distinguished of these were Stuart Tresilian, who illustrated the *Adventure* series, and Eileen Soper, who gave form to the *Famous Five*, the series of books with which, Enid Blyton is probably most associated. As the books have gone through successive paperback editions, the line illustrations and the covers have been updated, but the rather poor quality paper has remained a consistent feature.

↑ *Five on a Treasure Island* Enid Blyton (author), Eileen Soper (illustrator), London, Hodder & Stoughton, 1942. 190 x 130mm (7½ x 5in) The cover of the first of the series, which eventually numbered twenty-one, illustrates the wrecked ship that lands on Kirrin Island. "'There she is,' said Julian, in excitement. 'Poor old wreck! I guess she's a bit more battered now.'"

↑ *Five on a Secret Trail* Enid Blyton (author), Eileen Soper (illustrator), London, Hodder & Stoughton, 1956. 190 x 130mm (7½ x 5in) The typical Enid Blyton signature had arrived for this, the fifteenth of the books which were published with annual regularity.

↑ *Five are Together Again* Enid Blyton (author), Eileen Soper (illustration), London, Hodder & Stoughton, 1963. 190 x 130mm (7½ x 5in) Eileen Soper's covers gave unity to the original series, with unpretentious use of full colour. This is the final title.

↑ *Five Go Off in a Caravan* Enid Blyton (author), London, Hodder & Stoughton, 1978. 179 x 113mm (7 x 4½in) Even by the late 1970s, Blyton's most famous children's stories were not too anachronistic to be brought up to date as a TV series, complete with a jaunty signature tune song. This title was originally published in 1946.

↑ **The Magic Faraway Tree** Enid Blyton (author), Dorothy A. Wheeler (illustrator), London, George Newnes, 1943.
209 x 142mm (8¼ x 5½in)
Newnes, who were primarily magazine publishers, had issued Blyton's first book, *The Enid Blyton Book of Fairies*, in 1924. In this story and its successors, which have shades of Norse mythology, a group of children discover a magic tree,which reaches up to the sky and has the varied population of a modern high-rise apartment block.

→ **The Castle of Adventure** Enid Blyton (author), Stuart Tresilian (illustrator), London, Macmillan, 1946.
203 x 140mm (8 x 5½in)
The clothes show the summer holiday adventure story format, with boys and girls together, which Arthur Ransome pioneered. Kiki the parrot provides comic relief to these stories.

← **The Secret Seven** Enid Blyton (author), George Brook (illustrator), Leicester, Brockhampton Press, 1949.
196 x 137mm (7¾ x 5⅓in)
In contrast to the rural holiday themes of the *Famous Five*, who are all at boarding school, (including Timmy the dog), the *Secret Seven* series of fifteen books, beginning with this one, depicts similar adventures in the life of day-school children during term time.

↓ **Hurrah for Little Noddy** Enid Blyton (author), Harmsen van Beek (illustrator), London, Sampson Low, 1950.
190 x 140mm (7½ x 5½in)
The *Noddy* books, illustrated by "Beek", were early examples of plastic lamination which would have been thought suitable for these books for younger children.

Other worlds beneath and beyond
The Borrowers & C. S. Lewis

Apart from being an actress and playwright, Mary Norton (1903–92) was the author of two famous children's book series, *Bedknob and Broomstick* (1947), made famous by a Disney film, and *The Borrowers* (1952), filmed in 1997. Both books share a serious attitude to issues of magic and imagination which are usually treated as pure fantasy. In *The Borrowers* books, which were all originally illustrated by Mary Stanley (b. 1909), readers were introduced to a completely plausible parallel universe on a small scale: the Borrowers are very small humans and behave as such. As the children's book historian Bettina Hürlimann wrote, "a world where safety pins become giant tools, where cotton reels become stools, and chess-men classical statues, has a glamour of its own, regardless of any profounder readings which can be made of this nether-nether land." The Borrower Clock family – Pod, his wife Homily, and their daughter Arietty, around whom each of the five books revolve, begin to lose control of this world owing to Arietty's desire to widen her horizons. It has been noted, by those seeking profounder meanings, how accurately Mary Norton reflected issues about class mobility through education and improved opportunities in the post-war years.

In the *Narnia* books of C. S. Lewis (1898–1963), the sense of escape is from the everyday world to another that focuses on moralism and myth intertwined together in an underlying purpose of religious teaching. A few lapses apart, Lewis was good enough at storytelling and characterization to escape the overloading such a description implies, although recent critics, notably the writer Philip Pullman, have attacked his covert intentions. *The Lion the Witch and the Wardrobe* was begun in 1939 and finished ten years later, partly as a result of Lewis's being worsted in a debate with a non-believing philosopher, Elizabeth Anscombe. The other books followed in rapid succession, all illustrated by Pauline Baynes (b. 1922). She responded to Lewis's request to "pretty up" the children, and showed a sensitive response both to the the books' imaginative and realist aspects.

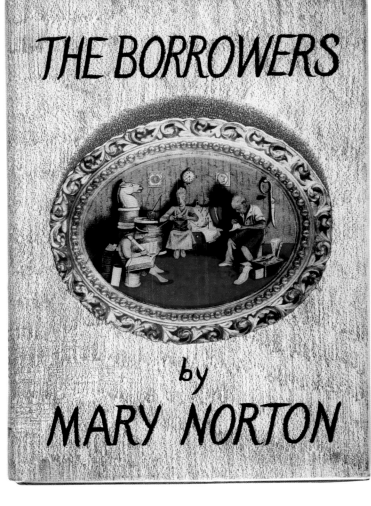

→ **The Borrowers** Mary Norton (author), Beth and Joe Krush (illustrators), New York, Harcourt Inc., 1998.
200 x 135mm (7⅛ x 5⅓in)
The cover of the American edition, first issued in 1953, attributes more Victorian period charm and comedy to the book than is justified, although some of the line drawings in the text are imaginative.

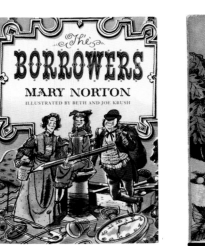

↑ **The Borrowers** Mary Norton (author), Mary Stanley (illustrator), London, J. M. Dent, 1952. 205 x 145mm (8 x 5¾in)
The cover reproduces the frontispiece. The colour illustration, surrounded by a black-and-white photograph of a frame, shows the Borrowers' adaptation of objects from the full-size world. Arietty is learning to read and write, the first in her family to do so. The illustrated endpapers of the original hardback are particularly well illustrated.

← **The Borrowers Afield** Mary Norton (author), Diana Stanley (illustrator), Harmondsworth, Puffin Books, 1960.
181 x 111mm (7 x 4⅜in)
In the second book, originally published in hardback in 1955, the Borrowers learn to live out of doors and become accustomed to nature after their entirely housebound earlier life.

→ The Lion, the Witch and the Wardrobe
C. S. Lewis (author), Pauline Baynes
(illustrator), Harmondsworth, Puffin
Books, 1959. 181 x 111mm (7 x 4⅖in)
The full-colour cover of the Puffin edition
gave Pauline Baynes an opportunity for
delicate miniaturist painting, which
continues on to the back cover to depict
a distant landscape.

↓ The Lion, the Witch and the Wardrobe
C. S. Lewis (author), Pauline Baynes
(illustrator), London, Geoffrey Bles, 1950.
203 x 140mm (8 x 5½in)
The wrapper for the first edition has a
decorative cartouche of fauns and trees,
enclosing the lion, Aslan, flying with
Susan and Lucy on his back. The subdued
colours are typical of British taste during
the austerity of the post-war years.

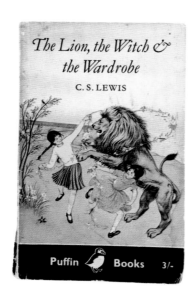

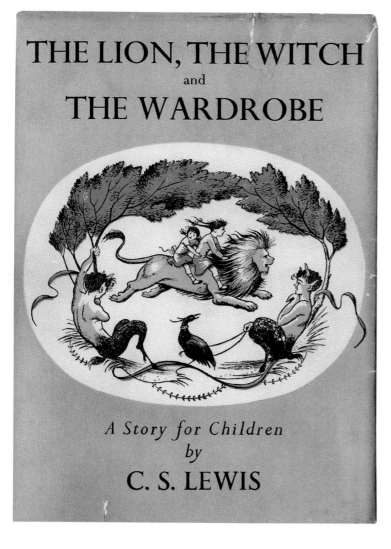

↑ The Magician's Nephew C. S. Lewis
(author), Pauline Baynes (illustrator),
London, The Bodley Head, 1955.
203 x 140mm (8 x 5½in)
Having written the central five books in
the series, which are loosely linked in
sequence, Lewis extended the set by
writing the beginning of the saga, *The
Magician's Nephew*, in a style which is
reminiscent of E. Nesbit.

← The Last Battle C. S. Lewis (author),
Pauline Baynes (illustrator),
Harmondsworth, Puffin Books, 1964.
181 x 111mm (7 x 4⅖in)
There is a specially fine cover by Pauline
Baynes for the last of Lewis's books,
which rounds off the story. Although it
was acknowledged not to be as good as
the earlier ones, it was awarded the
Carnegie Medal in recognition of Lewis's
total achievement.

In the land of the free
American classics of the '40s and '50s

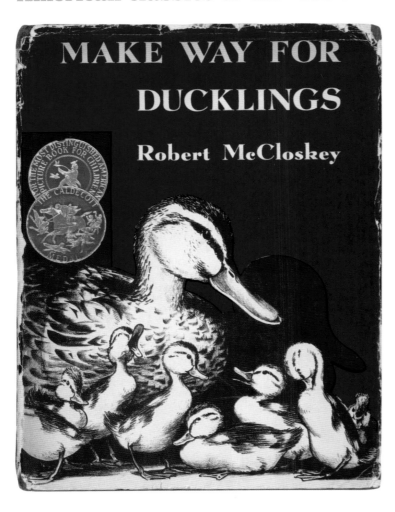

The strength of the American revival in children's book publishing that began in the 1930s continued through the succeeding decades. In the mid 1950s, looking back at the acceptance speeches by the recipients of the Newbery Award, Elizabeth Nesbitt wrote, "It is extraordinarily heartening to reread these, to perceive how clearly so many writers for children recognise the separateness and importance of the child's world." The Newbery and Caldecott awards were undoubtedly a good way of boosting sales, as the medallions applied to the jacket of *Make Way for Ducklings* indicate. This book continued the fashion for hand-drawn lithographs started by Virginia Lee Burton, and for reasons of economy McCloskey drew on stone in one colour only, in a style that achieves the best qualities from the medium.

H. A. Rey's *Zozo*, better-known by his original title of *Curious George*, was a deliberate, and highly successful, attempt to adapt the rapid action of the newly-popular comic books to a more permanent format. Rey in fact made a number of cartoon films about George's antics. The illustrator Clement Hurd, who provided the pictures for Margaret Wise Brown's most enduring titles, studied painting in France under Fernand Léger – to whom he may have owed his use of bold saturated colour. Wise Brown was a highly prolific author who worked with many illustrators, including Garth Williams, who also illustrated the two children's books by E. B. White, a contributor to the *New Yorker*, that have secured his reputation.

↑ *Make Way for Ducklings* Robert McCloskey (author and illustrator), New York, Viking Press, 1959. 310 x 235mm (12¼ x 9¼in) First published in this format in 1941, this simple story is set in a Boston neighbourhood, where the sight of a family of mallards holding up the traffic gave McCloskey the idea.

→ *Zozo* H. A. Rey (author and illustrator), London, Chatto & Windus, 1942. 256 x 215mm (10 x 8½in) The monkey likes investigating the world around him, usually ending in chaos. The original American title, *Curious George*, was considered to be a risk to the dignity of the British king.

→ *Little Fur Family* Margaret Wise Brown (author), Garth Williams (illustrator), New York, Harper & Brothers, 1946. 95 x 75mm (3¾ x 3in) (size of box) An opening in the box, in the bear's tummy, reveals the real fur in which the book is bound. The originals were subject to moth attacks in the warehouse.

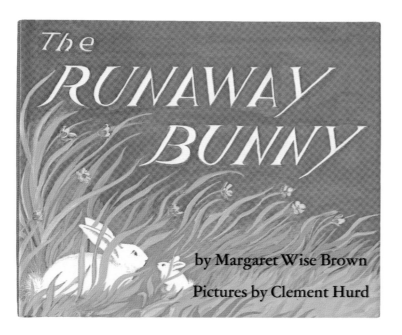

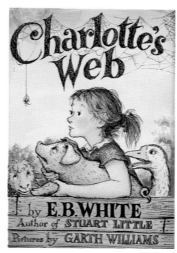

← **Charlotte's Web** E. B. White (author), Garth Williams (illustrator), New York, Harper & Row, 1952.
202 x 133mm (8 x 5¼in)
The cover could introduce any farmyard story, but this one is, in the words of writers Michael and Margaret Rustin, "one of the very best children's stories to be published since the war."

↓ **Stuart Little** E. B. White (author), Garth Williams (illustrator), New York, Harper & Brothers, 1945. 205 x 140mm (8 x 5½in)
The cover shows the intrepid mouse hero surviving a world that exaggerates the ordinary differences in scale and assumptions between children and adults.

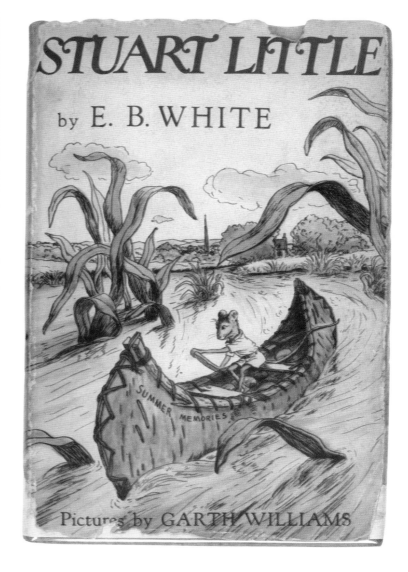

↑ **The Runaway Bunny** Margaret Wise Brown (author), Clement Hurd (illustrator), London, Collins, 1992.
177 x 210mm (7 x 8¼in)
Whatever form the little rabbit tries to take to run away, its mother finds a way to follow. This is a subtle tale about the ties of family and love, originally published in 1942.

↑ **Goodnight Moon** Margaret Wise Brown (author), Clement Hurd (illustrator), New York, Harper & Row, 1947 (1982 edn). 176 x 207mm (7 x 8in)
This popular night-time picture book travels round the objects in a child's room, including a reference to *The Runaway Bunny*, illustrated in complete colour spreads.

Sweet medicine for reluctant readers
Dr Seuss & Richard Scarry

Theodor Seuss Geisel (1904–91) intended to become a professor of English Literature but as he wrote, "he could not break himself of an old habit of putting on paper the unusual pictures conjured up in his dreams." He worked as a newspaper cartoonist and in advertising before launching his career in children's books with two pre-war titles under his famous pseudonym. The elderly Beatrix Potter was sent a copy of *And to Think that I Saw it on Mulberry Street*, and admired its qualities. Like her, Seuss had a talent for combining pictures and text, and for entering a child's mind. This was most famously displayed in *The Cat in the Hat*, the first of Seuss's books expressly intended for beginners. The series continues to deserve its success through the linking of cartoon-style drawings with texts that convey humour and irony in the simplest choice of words.

Richard Scarry (1919–94) started illustrating in 1946. Although he began to write his own texts in 1951, based on an assemblage of individual episodes rather than a story line, his great success came in 1963 with *Richard Scarry's Best Word Book Ever*, which used the anthropomorphic animals for which he is best known. Elaine Moss wrote in *Signal* that Scarry was "totally unpretentious, bubbling with humour, alive with activity, peppered with words of wisdom and corny jokes... Scarry books are a marvellous combination of entertainment, always on a child's level." In 1969, Scarry moved to live in Switzerland, and his later work, which reflects a global view, often teaches children about different parts of the world.

↑ *The 500 Hats of Bartholomew Cubbins*
"Dr Seuss" (author and illustrator),
London, Oxford University Press, 1940.
305 x 232mm (12 x 9in)
Bartholomew Cubbins meets the king, but whenever he tries to doff his hat in respect, there is another hat underneath. The title was originally published in New York by Vanguard Press in 1938.

← *And to Think That I Saw it on Mulberry Street* "Dr Seuss" (author and illustrator), London, Country Life, 1939.
268 x 212mm (10½ x 8½in)
The original American edition was published by Vanguard Press, New York, in 1937. This is a New York story, about the things a child imagines seeing on the way back from school.

→ **Horton Hatches the Egg** "Dr Seuss"
(author and illustrator), New York,
Random House, 1940.
260 x 209mm (8⅕ x 10¼in)
The cover is self-evidently ridiculous.
Having seen it, you have to read the book
to discover how this situation arose.

↓ **The Cat in the Hat** "Dr Seuss" (author
and illustrator), New York, Random
House, 1957. 235 x 170mm (9¼ x 6⅔in)
The most famous of Dr Seuss's books
was issued in laminated boards, so that
no dust wrapper would be needed.
The back cover carries testimonials
from educationalists.

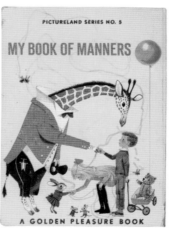

↑ **The Great Big Car and Truck Book**
Richard Scarry (author and illustrator),
New York, Simon & Schuster, 1951.
325 x 244cm (12¾ x 9⅔in)
This was Scarry's first picture book. Its
delight in modes of transport is typical
of much that was to follow, although it
does not yet have animal characters.

← **My Book of Manners** Richard Scarry
(author and illustrator), New York,
Golden Press, 1962.
267 x 204in (10½ x 8in)
Without black outlines, the Scarry
drawing style is not instantly
recognizable, although the humour is
characteristic of the author.

"In an old house in Paris"
Francophile books

The contribution made by France to international 20th-century children's books includes titles by French authors and illustrators that have been adopted in English-speaking countries, and books by English and American authors who have used France (usually Paris) as a setting. This tendency was particularly strong in the 1940s and '50s when France was recovering from wartime occupation and seemed irresistibly attractive from the point of view of the countries that had helped to liberate it. Bettina Hürlimann linked the success of *Le Petit Prince* (1943) by Antoine de Saint-Exupéry (1900–44) to the pathos of occupied France, as well as to the author-illustrator's death while flying for the Free French in Morocco.

French-speaking Ludwig Bemmelmans (1892–1962), creator of the *Madeline* books, was just one example of talent brought to the USA by political uncertainty in Europe, while Kay Thompson used France as a setting for her *Eloise* novels. The precocious six-year-old was based on the young Liza Minelli, brilliantly characterized in Hilary Knight's drawings.

The *Anatole* books, nine in total between 1956 and 1973, were the creation of two Americans, the author Eve Titus (b. 1922) and the Hungarian-born illustrator Paul Galdone (1914–86). Anatole, a mouse who, like a pre-war intellectual, considers his role as a citizen to be a sufficient *raison d'être*, is drawn into the cash-nexus of business, but strictly in the anonymous role of cheese-taster in a factory. *The Red Balloon* meanwhile drew on nostalgia for Paris, with a story about a small boy's dream, represented by a magic balloon, and those who threaten to steal it.

↑ *Madeline* Ludwig Bemelmans (author and illustrator), London, Verschoyle, 1938. 305 x 235 cm (12 x 9in)
Madeline, the plucky orphan girl, has climbed to stardom since her appearance in 1939. Bemelmans saw himself primarily as a painter, saying "I wanted to paint purely what gave me pleasure and one day I found the audience for that kind of painting… I addressed myself to children."

→ *Madeline's Rescue* Ludwig Bemelmans (author and illustrator), New York, Viking Press/London, Verschoyle, 1953. 305 x 235 cm (12 x 9in)
Awarded the Caldecott Medal for the "most distinguished picture book" in 1953, this was the second title in the series.

← *The Little Prince* Antoine de Saint-Exupéry (author), New York, Reynal & Hitchcock, 1943. 225 x 185mm (8⁴/₅ x 7¹/₄in)
Although issued in New York, this edition is in French. The whimsical story, more directed to adults than to children, was an immediate success.

→ *Eloise in Paris* Kay Thompson (author), Hilary Knight (illustrator), New York, Simon & Schuster, 1957.
Following the success of *Eloise* (1955), Kay Thompson (1902–98) sent her heroine to Paris. We discover, inter alia, that Eloise's pet turtle, Skiperdee (thoughtfully accommodated by Sabena Airlines) acquires a favourite French word " 'zut' which is oh hecko."

↓ *Anatole* Eve Titus (author), Paul Galdone (illustrator), London, The Bodley Head, 1957. 255 x 185mm (10 x 7¼in)
First published by McGraw Hill in New York in 1956, Anatole was an international success, helped by the skill of Galdone's three-colour illustrations, which follow the colours of the *tricoleur* in order that Mousetown can be truly patriotic.

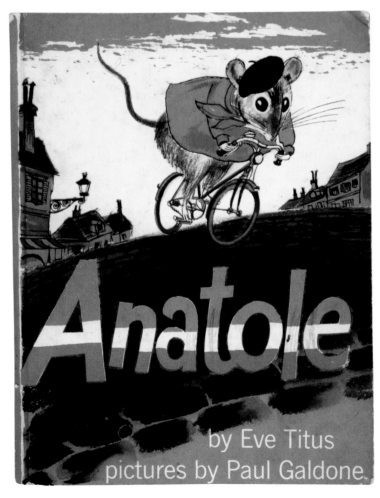

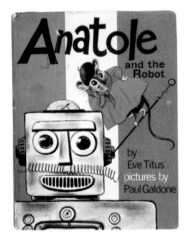

↑ *The Red Balloon* Albert Lamorisse (author), London, George Allen & Unwin, 1957. 312 x 222mm (12¼ x 8¾in)
These stills from a popular short film by Lamorisse were used to produce one of the rare children's books of the period that used photography. The story concerns a small boy's magic balloon and those who scheme to steal it. It was partly, of necessity, printed in colour to show the balloon with a mind of its own, and its charm now consists mostly of the background settings that show an unmodernized Paris.

← *Anatole and the Robot* Eve Titus (author), Paul Galdone (illustrator), London, The Bodley Head, 1961. 255 x 185mm (10 x 7¼in)
In the third *Anatole* book, Anatole and his friend Gaston succeed in sabotaging a robot called Cheezak, who has replaced Anatole as the factory's cheese-taster.

Peaceable kingdoms
Tove Jansson & the Provensens

The first of the Moomin books by Tove Jansson (1914–2001) appeared in her native Finland in 1946. Equally at ease with images and words, she created an intensely realized but never over-defined fantasy world, inhabited by imaginary creatures with many human traits. The strong story lines also convey a depth of feeling about nature, the passage of the seasons, and the need for mutual affection. Bettina Hürlimann wrote, "For all the crazy things they get up to, these merry little fellows have an inner wholesomeness, and they have greatly enriched the world of fantasy." The books appeared in hardback in England in the 1950s, and later became widely popular in Puffin paperbacks. In the USA, they were published by Walck in the 1960s.

Martin Provensen (1916–87), and his wife Alice (b. 1918), both born in Chicago, worked in the Disney studios, but their crisp and slightly primitive style of illustration comes from different sources. They collaborated on a range of books, specializing in non-fiction ideas such as their books based on the Charge of the Light Brigade or Blériot's flight across the English Channel. "We do not indulge in random experimentation," they wrote, "working rather towards the goal of directness and simplicity, the ultimate objective being the authentic statement."

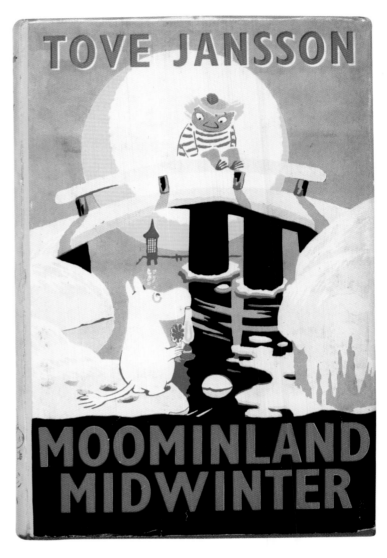

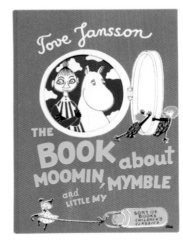

↑ *Moominland Midwinter* Tove Jansson (author and illustrator), London, Ernest Benn, 1958. 205 x 130mm (8 x 5in)
After *Moominsummer Madness* (1955), this next book explored the strange world of winter. The cover evokes the deep north.

← *The Book about Moomin, Mymble and Little My* Tove Jansson (author and illustrator), London, Sort of Books, 2001. 285 x 209mm (11⅕ x 8¼in)
This is a new translation of a book first published by Benn in 1953. It has a cut-away front board, introducing a series of cut-away pages.

← *Finn Family Moomintroll* Tove Jansson (author and illustrator), London, Ernest Benn, 1950. 190 x 125mm (7½ x 5in)
This was the second book in the series, but the first published in English. Its sober jacket is typical of the 1950s.

↓ *The Glorious Flight Across the Channel with Louis Blériot July 25, 1909*
Alice and Martin Provensen (authors and illustrators) New York, The Viking Press, 1983.
The cover gives a snapshot of the moment when Blériot was about to take off on his prizewinning flight. The book won the 1984 Caldecott Medal.

→ *A Visit to William Blake's Inn: Poems for Innocent and Experienced Travellers*
Nancy Willard (author), Alice and Martin Provensen (illustrators), New York, Harcourt Brace Jovanovich, 1981.
260 x 205mm (10¼ x 8in)
The cover for this book of sixteen poems for children incorporates lettering into the design of the imaginary inn.

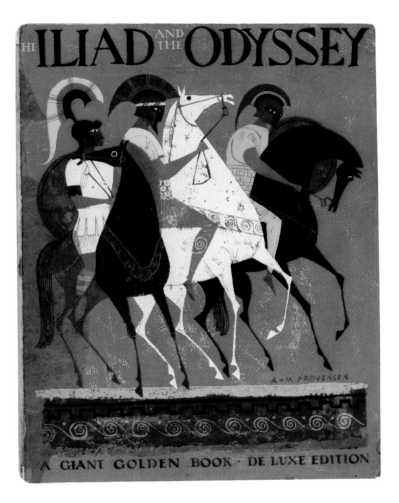

← *The Iliad and the Odyssey* Jane Werner Watson (adaptor), Alice and Martin Provensen (illustrators), New York, Simon & Schuster, 1956. 330 x 255mm (13 x 10in)
Described as "a Giant Golden Book De Luxe Edition" this version, with illustrations derived from the stylized flatness of Greek vase paintings, has much in common with the work of 1950s artists such as Bernard Buffet. The hand lettering contributes to the quality of the design.

↑ *A Peaceable Kingdom: the Shaker Abecedarius* Alice and Martin Provensen (illustrators), Harmondsworth, Penguin Books, 1981. 170 x 257mm (6⅔ x 10in)
The rhyming text of animal names comes from The Shaker Manifesto, 1882. In this title, the Provensens bring animals and humans together in a New England folk-art style. They use an imitation of time-mottled paper, and mottos from Shaker writings provide another layer of commentary.

Wild things
Maurice Sendak

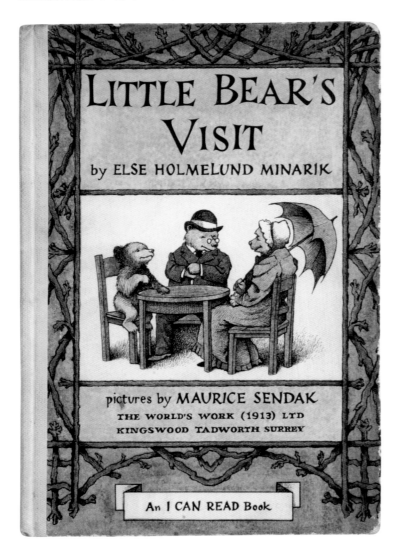

In 1963, Maurice Sendak (b. 1928) transformed the status of picture books with *Where the Wild Things Are*. His skill in drawing in a 19th-century woodcut style with close hatching was first developed in the late 1950s with the *Little Bear* books. The story of Max and the Wild Things challenged Sendak to pare his text down to the bone as the best picture book writers had done before, and this irreducible quality contributed a kind of classicism to the tale of child anger which shocked a number of readers and librarians. Sendak had been illustrating professionally since 1951 and in the words of the critic Brian Alderson, had "the whole history of illustration at his fingertips."

Sendak was not the first author-illustrator to blur the boundary between adult understanding and books intended for children, but his success in doing so marked a new point in the development of children's books in the 1960s. If some child readers (or listeners) and conventionally minded adults find the works disturbing, then many enjoy the way they imply so much that is otherwise excluded from other depictions of the mental and physical world. Sendak discovered he could imaginatively reconstruct the suppressed feelings of early childhood, going beyond issues of "good taste" and connecting the writing of children's books with a world no less wide than that of adult literature. As John Cech writes about *In the Night Kitchen*, "the trip itself – well, that trip is a plunge into everything that is usually repressed in children's books: death, the body, sexuality, the dynamics of the unconscious, and the work of the soul. And so it was for Sendak... an artistic 'coming forth' on behalf of that divine child at a time in our cultural history when we sought a fresh spirit that could move us into the future."

In later books, Sendak has continued to engage in humour, social criticism, and fantasy. His work has attracted considerable criticism, reflecting his own view, when recalling the message he received from the work of William Blake, "that childhood [is] such a damned serious business."

↑ *Little Bear's Visit* Else Holmelund Minarik (author), Maurice Sendak (illustrator), Tadworth, The World's Work, 1962. 220 x 150mm (8⅔ x 6in) These illustrations have a gentleness not always found in Sendak's other work.

→ *Schoolmaster Whackwell's Wonderful Sons* Clemens Brentano (author), "retold by Doris Orgel", Maurice Sendak (illustrator), New York, Random House, 1962. 242 x 157mm (9½ x 6⅛in) Sendak borrows some of the quality of the chapbook tradition for this cover.

→ *Where the Wild Things Are* "Story and pictures by Maurice Sendak", London, The Bodley Head, 1967. 235 x 260mm (9¼ x 10¼in) Sendak was insistent on being present for the printing of his colour books to check the proofs and ensure that the colour quality should not be lost.

↓ **Outside Over There** Maurice Sendak (author and illustrator), London, The Bodley Head, 1981. 235 x 260mm (9¼ x 10¼in) One of Sendak's most adult books, it refers to the way his elder sister Ida had to take care of him as a young child, and to Mozart's *Magic Flute* which he was designing for the stage at the same time.

↓ **We Are All in The Dumps with Jack and Guy** Traditional rhyme, Maurice Sendak (illustrator), New York, Michael di Capua Books, HarperCollins 1993.
210 x 280mm (8¼ x 11in)
This is a commentary on homelessness in New York, seen through an apparently innocent traditional rhyme. The mouth on the cover invites the reader in, and the title details only appear on the back.

↑ **In the Night Kitchen** Maurice Sendak (author and illustrator), New York, Harper & Row, 1970/London, Bodley Head, 1971. 285 x 220mm (11¼ x 8⅔in) Here is the dream tale of Mickey's miraculous night flight over New York, escaping from three Oliver Hardy look-alike bakers in a dough aeroplane before being deliciously immersed in milk. Sendak has interpreted the story as Mickey's problem, "How do I stay up all night and see what the grownups do, and have the fun that is denied to me as a child?"

→**The Bee-man of Orn** Frank R. Stockton (author), Maurice Sendak (illustrator), London, The Bodley Head, 1975.
210 x 194mm (8¼ x 7⅔in)
First published in identical format by Holt, Reinhart & Winston in New York in 1964, this is one of a pair of stories by Stockton (1834–1902). It is illustrated by Sendak with humour appropriate to the circular morality of a foolish man's search for happiness.

4

When we all dressed up: the '60s and '70s

When *Rolling Stone* magazine asked John Lennon what he thought had happened during the 1960s, his reply was "What happened in the sixties was that we all dressed up". Lennon could have been referring to many aspects of the decade, not least to the feeling, encouraged by Lennon and the Beatles, that nobody need really grow up, in the sense that the child's direct, candid view of the world might be preferable to the adult's loss of idealism and submission to convention. Commitment to improve the quality of children's books, through to all levels of production and distribution, was now as widespread a feature in Britain as it had previously been in America. The librarian and critic Marcus Crouch wrote in 1962, "children have never, in their own homes or in the school and public library, had a better chance of finding, wherever their choice falls, books which have style, intelligence, and an original viewpoint. It is no bad thing to be a child in the sixties."

← *Midnight is a Place* Joan Aiken (author), Pat Marriott (illustrator), London, Jonathan Cape, 1974. 205 x 135mm (8 x 5⅓in) Most of Joan Aiken's juvenile fiction was illustrated by Pat Marriott, who always found a way to capture its mixture of the comic and frightening. This jacket, on which the lettering is placed with unself-conscious ease, can be compared to the more conventional jacket of the American edition (illustrated on p. 116).

When we all dressed up: the '60s and '70s

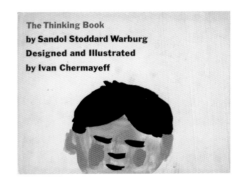

The pastel shades and sharp colour accents of 1920s interiors were echoed in the presentation of books, and subsequent changes in style were tracked in the decades thereafter. The 1960s began with a burst of colour that was equally typical of the transformation from the neat, small-scale patterning of the '50s towards the abundant and unrestrained at the beginning of the '60s, as seen in interior decoration and clothing. New films, too, were now in colour almost as a matter of course. It is difficult to reconstruct an image of quite how drab the world had become, specially in post-war Britain. If we pick out examples of books that were propelled by what Harold Macmillan, the British Prime Minister, famously called "the winds of change", the difference is often one of presentation style as much as content.

Brian Wildsmith's ABC, published in 1962 is one example. In style it was quite different from the delicacy and restraint of most books at the time although the theme could not have been more old-fashioned. Wildsmith's previous book for Oxford University Press, *The Arabian Nights* (1961), had been described by a reviewer as "aimless scribbles... splashed lavishly and untidily with bright smudges of paint." Wildsmith's editor, Mabel George, was encouraged rather than deterred. Judith Graham tells

the story, "As a printer's daughter who had previously worked in the technical side of publishing, she already knew about the four-colour process. She was confident that photo offset litho techniques could preserve Wildsmith's vibrancy, visible brush strokes, and depth. When her Austrian printer Bruder Rosenbaum used thicker-than-usual paper the end results were spectacular." The starburst of colour created by Wildsmith was made possible not only by his own artistic

impulse, but also by an astute and courageous editor, backed by a carefully selected printer. The book may have upset adults but it worked as intended with children, operating on a level of purely visual awareness that typified abstract expressionist painting of the period. As Wildsmith says, "the shapes and colours seep into the child's artistic digestive system, and he is aroused and stimulated by them."

← *The Thinking Book* Sandol Stoddard Warburg (author), Ivan Chermayeff (designer and illustrator), Boston/Toronto, Little, Brown & Company, 1960.
205 x 260mm (8 x 10¼in)
Recognized as "one of the best two picture books of 1960" by the *New York Herald Tribune*, this was the first children's book illustrated by Ivan Chermayeff (b. 1932) – one of the leading American designers of the post-war period. His work is usually spontaneous in feeling, like this informal cover.

← *The Snowy Day* Ezra Jack Keats (author and illustrator), London, The Bodley Head Ltd, 1962.
206 x 233mm (8 x 9in)
With this book, Ezra Jack Keats made a jump from a conventional illustration style to something immediately recognizable as his own. The colour, boldness of outline, and urban subject matter are all indicative of the change in children's books in the 1960s.

← *A Letter to Amy* Ezra Jack Keats (author and illustrator), London, The Bodley Head, 1969.
209 x 231mm (8¼ x 9in)
Without losing the graphic directness found in his earlier book, Keats introduces a watercolour texture for the stormy sky. The fly-away letter begins to tell the story straight away.

→ **Brian Wildsmith's ABC** Brian
Wildsmith (author and illustrator),
London, Oxford University Press, 1962.
190 x 255mm (7½ x 10in)
The depth and strength of colour seen
on the jacket of this famous book of the
early 1960s were seldom seen before,
and would be equally unobtainable with
modern printing. The close-up apple
works as an abstract shape against the
lettering. On the back is an
advertisement for Harold Jones's
Lavender's Blue, an Oxford success of
1954 (see p. 59), but already
representative of another world.

→ **Alexander and the Wind-up Mouse**
Leo Lionni (author and illustrator),
London, Abelard Schuman, 1971.
280 x 223mm (11 x 8¾in)
Like Ivan Chermayeff, Lionni was a
versatile graphic and interior designer
before making his first children's book in
1959. *Alexander and the Wind-Up Mouse*
uses collage to create artwork for
reproduction, continuing the visual
experimentation of Jack Ezra Keats.

→ **Why Mosquitoes Buzz in People's Ears**
Verna Aardema (author), Leo and Diane
Dillon (illustrators), New York, Dial Books
for Young Readers, 1975.
257 x 258mm (10 x 10in)
The masked airbrushed style of the
artwork by Leo and Diane Dillon
captures the spirit of the African
folktales by Verna Aardema (1911–2000)
who specialized in these retellings. This
book won the Caldecott Medal in 1976,
and in their acceptance speech, the
artists spoke of their pleasure in seeing a
shift back to an emphasis on craft in
teaching and producing art.

On the other side of the Atlantic, publishing
in the United States experienced a similar
sense of liberation. American graphic design
was made bolder by the influence of European
Modernism from the 1930s, with its emphasis
on visual rather than verbal communication.
The skill of eliminating superfluous material
without becoming boring was crucial, both for
advertising and for illustration, especially in books aimed at very young children. Increasingly
illustrators worked to achieve this. As Steven Heller writes of the illustrator Paul Rand's work of
the late 1950s, "remove the cigars from the El Producto advertisements and the fanciful paper
cut-outs could easily have been created as children's book illustrations." Rand collaborated with
his wife on four children's books between 1956 and 1970, and Ivan Chermayeff, a younger designer
in a similar vein, as a sideline to his professional work, also produced children's books with a
sensitive marriage of text and simple imagery.

Among dedicated children's books artists, it was Ezra
Jack Keats whose stylistic breakthrough came in the
same year as Wildsmith's *ABC*. Born in 1916 in Brooklyn,
Keats already had experience of mural painting and book
jacket design when, in 1962, he took a new step and used
collage and paint together to create *The Snowy Day*. It
was an unusual book in that the protagonist was a black
city child, whose delight in the unexpected fall of snow
captured a universal theme. As Brian Alderson has

written of Keats, "colour was for him a way of talking".

Leo Lionni also used collage to create a distinctive style that the new colour process cameras
could translate on to the printed page without losing the quality of the original. In a typically

1960s way, he saw himself not as a jobbing illustrator
but as "an artist exploring the possibilities of self-
expression and communication" who happened to
have found in children's books the most effective
medium. As a European by birth and education,
Lionni also expressed a political position in response
to the conventionality of the New World, writing
"most of all, I try to give children doubt... more than
anything else... that will keep us free".

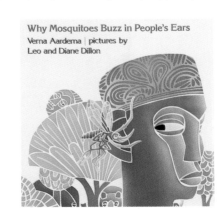

The liveliness of children's book publishing in the '60s and '70s was reflected in a growing awareness of the historical dimension of the subject. Since the beginning of children's book publishing, publishers were pleased when they could reissue older texts free of financial obligation to an author, but these were usually a small range of perennial titles such as *Goody Two Shoes*. Conscious historicism could, however, extend beyond the range of such "classics". *Sir Gibbie*, relaunched by Blackie in 1967 with a jacket in a contemporary realist style by Margery Gill, is actually a text of 1879. It is a story of a "street Arab" who makes his way in the world, and is written by George MacDonald, an author more famous for *At the Back of the North Wind* and other fantasy stories.

This was a period when much of the production of children's books was aimed towards schools and public libraries, for whom the selection criteria were different to those of the open commercial market. Jacket designs did not necessarily need much attention, if the books were going to be sold through the recommendation of reviews and specialized advertising, and indeed there were many cases where the exterior of the book might be quite perfunctory. Nevertheless, many publishers had a sense of pride in their products and commissioned the best illustrators, even for editions whose purpose was primarily educational.

The historical novel had a resurgence in the 1940s, following a lapse since the time of G. A. Henty. The new generation of authors wrote of heroes with existential doubts appropriate to the age of Sartre. C. S. Forester's *Hornblower* books are about a young naval officer in the Napoleonic period who suffers from more inner doubts than any of Henty's heroes. The first of these, *The Happy Return*, was published in 1937, and the series, intended for adults but was eagerly read by children, was resumed with *Mr Midshipman Hornblower* in 1950. Rosemary Sutcliff tended to write about children and adolescents whose families were on the losing side in history, and she also went back in time before the period of imperial conquest which was the favourite setting for the Edwardians. Illustrators such as Charles Keeping (1924–88) used the new loose style of drawing, inspired by abstract expressionism, together with the new liking for strong colour, to develop a graphic style that closed the gap between past and present.

← *Sir Gibbie* George MacDonald (author), Margery Gill (jacket illustrator), London, Blackie & Son Ltd, 1967. 201 x 137mm (8 x 5⅜in)
Here is a Victorian historical text brought back with a fresh cover, although one in which there is perhaps too much detail to be successful. The smaller lines of text get lost awkwardly in the tonal areas of the watercolour.

← *The Mark of the Horse Lord* Rosemary Sutcliff (author), Charles Keeping (illustrator), Oxford, Oxford University Press, 1965.
Charles Keeping began to illustrate Rosemary Sutcliff's books for Oxford University Press in 1957, beginning with *The Lantern Bearers*. The illustrations on the page were in black and white, but the covers allowed Keeping's bold colour sense to develop, with a magnificent sense of motion in the horse shown here.

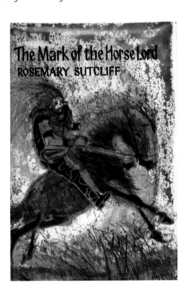

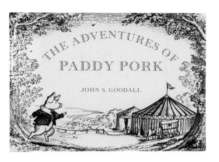

→ *The Adventures of Paddy Pork* John S.
Goodall (author and illustrator), London,
Macmillan, 1968. 132 x 181mm (5¹⁄₅ x 7in)
Goodall had a good sense of graphic
design and his drawing wraps neatly
around the title wording on this cover,
creating an overall sense of period that
matches the style of the whole book.

→ *The Erie Canal* Peter Spier (illustrator),
Kingswood, Surrey, The World's Work Ltd,
1971. 210 x 264mm (8¹⁄₄ x 10²⁄₅in)
The book describes a journey on
America's first important canal, and the
cover is a foretaste of this pictorial
adventure which depends on small
everyday details humorously recreated
in the imagination of the artist.

→ *The Butterfly Ball and the
Grasshopper's Feast* William Plomer
(author), Alan Aldridge (illustrator),
London, Jonathan Cape, 1973.
283 x 218mm (11¹⁄₅ x 8¹⁄₂in)
The polished execution of Alan Aldridge's
illustrations was often criticized in the
world of children's books as an intrusion
of inappropriate adult sensibility. Even
so, his books are redolent of a particular
moment of luxuriant nostalgia.

History could also be used in a more playful way. For very young children, John Goodall devised a picture-book format, where a wordless story develops through a series of spreads. Every other leaf in the book is half-sized, and carries a variant picture through which the narrative develops like a film or comic book. *The Adventures of Paddy Pork* shows Goodall's skill in period pastiche line drawing, which he extended later into full colour as his nostalgic evocations of the Victorian period became increasingly fashionable in the 1970s.

With *The Erie Canal*, Peter Spier drew attention to America's industrial archaeology, taking the text of a traditional ballad about the journey along New York state's first major inland waterway. The drawings are packed with detail and gentle humour, creating an immersive

experience as the well-laden boat travels through cities and landscapes on the way to Buffalo.

If siren voices of the 1960s assured young adults that it was their political duty not to grow up, then they also succeeded in creating confusion between adult and children's books, as the technical and production expertise developed for children's books crossed over into illustrated titles such as

The Butterfly Ball. The illustrator Alan Aldridge (b. 1943) had a meteoric rise in the 1960s with his airbrush style. As George Percy wrote when the book was launched, Aldridge virtually changed the course of British graphic design: "The then-voguish advertisements, with squared-up photographs and chunk sans serif headlines were exchanged for fantasy and airbrush artwork and hand-drawn lettering that managed to look both old-fashioned and wildly trendy at one and the same time." A reworking of a popular but largely forgotten text by William Roscoe of 1806, *The*

Butterfly Ball was created as a vehicle for Aldridge's illustrations by Tom Maschler at the London publishing house Jonathan Cape. He turned the "picture flat" as such books are called in the trade, into a new genre of adult publishing, described by the cartoonist Barry Fantoni as "gasp" books, because, as Brian Alderson puts it, "the reader was called upon to make speechless exclamations when confronted by page upon page of paintings which had not only been executed with great minuteness of effect but were also printed with painstaking exactitude."

The Butterfly Ball (see p. 97) was a hangover from the '60s, a coffee-table book implying that stronger stimulants than coffee should accompany its reading. The impulse to rebellion has been an aspect of most of the best children's books throughout history. They work like a covert political movement against too-literal readings of the world that ignore imagination and intuition. Russell Hoban's *The Mouse and his Child* takes an old theme, the toy that comes to life, and gives it a subtext of personal liberation, in the desire by the toy mice to become "self-winding". Perhaps this is a commentary on Hoban's own transition from the advertising industry to become a full-time writer. The cover, drawn by Lilian Hoban, is surprisingly downbeat in style, although charming in its drawing.

Hoban's book includes a parody of Samuel Beckett, indicative of adult references that can create a more substantial kind of adult-child crossover than *The Butterfly Ball* did. Many authors and illustrators have felt an obligation to entertain parents or other adults who may be reading to a child, by introducing layers of reference only a few of which may be understood by the child, even if the others are dimly grasped. This multiple construction has occurred in literature throughout history, but at the end of the 1960s it acquired a theory and a name, as Post-Modernism, in reaction against the singleness of Modernism. Children's books have carried Post-Modernism by undercover means into public libraries, schools, and homes that might otherwise have resisted the concept. The possibility of deliberate slippage between word and image is one of the many aspects of Post-Modernism's acceptance of the imperfection of the world and the relativism of any of the ways we may try to understand it. *Helen Oxenbury's ABC of Things* selects incongruous groupings of words and then uses the drawings to rationalize them – the cover shown here illustrates how "Hippopotamus" and "Hospital" may be joined. Her husband John Burningham made notable use of this technique of disassociation in three books about a little girl, Shirley, who dreams in pictures against a banal adult commentary. Several of the books by Janet and Allan Ahlberg, from their early *Each Peach Pear Plum* to the trilogy of the *Jolly Postman* books, are virtually entirely constructed out of references to other children's books.

← *The Mouse and his Child* Russell Hoban (author), Lillian Hoban (illustrator), New York, Harper & Row, 1967. 243 x 160mm (9½ x 6⅛in)
This well-known story carries a sober cover in a rather traditional border with an illustration by Lillian Hoban, the author's wife. For the mouse and his son, rescued from a dustbin and sent on their travels, even the security of the doll's house depicted on the cover turns out to be ambiguous.

← *Helen Oxenbury's ABC of Things* Helen Oxenbury (author and illustrator), London, William Heinemann, 1971. 270 x 145mm (10⅔ x 5¾in)
The book has an unusually tall format and the cover drawing, taken from one of the spreads, wraps effectively around to the back of the book, with a bold use of a black background.

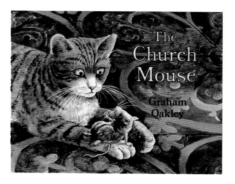

→ **The Church Mouse** Graham Oakley (author and illustrator), London, Macmillan, 1972.
203 x 260mm (8 x 10¼in)
Graham Oakley's illustrations have the high high level of detail found in Kathleen Hale's *Orlando* books (see p. 51). On the original hardback editions, each picture extends around front and back, although the paperback editions tend to repeat the same design back and front, one horizontal and one vertical.

→ **The Church Cat Abroad** Graham Oakley (author and illustrator), London, Macmillan, 1972.
210 x 260mm (8¼ x 10¼in)
The *Church Mice* books involve a series of variations with the same characters in different settings. In this book, the opportunity offered to Sampson to raise money to repair the vestry roof by appearing in a TV cat food commercial goes predictably wrong.

→ **Hildilid's Night** Cheli Durán Ryan (author), Arnold Lobel (illustrator), London, Longmans Young Books, 1973.
182 x 233mm (7 x 9¼in)
The cover is not only a skilled illustration, but a well-considered piece of design, making the best use of the solid black, with lettering placed to make a tight relationship between the moon and the running figure. Arnold Lobel (b. 1933) began working as an illustrator in the late 1950s, but also wrote his own texts.

In its embrace of the past and scepticism about the effectiveness of action for change, Post-Modernism represented the thinking of the 1970s and beyond. It is seen in the difference between Rosemary Sutcliff and Joan Aiken, each a superb writer in their field. While Sutcliff writes about a period with as much historical authenticity as possible, Aiken treats history as a room in which the furniture can be rearranged, often with surreal wit, to provide a setting for stories that transmit important issues about character and values against a picturesque background.

Maurice Sendak showed in the 1950s how older drawing styles could hold their value in the face of experiments inspired by modern art (see pp. 90–1). The 1970s saw a conservative reaction in favour of traditional skills, including drawing, although some of the most renowned results displayed laborious craftsmanship at the expense of keeping a story moving. Graham Oakley's very English series of books about the Church Mice, begun in 1972, reverse the normal relationship in that the cat, Sampson, is submissive while the mice, who take over the church vestry where he once enjoyed solitude, are led by a pair of know-alls whose misplaced optimism provides the basis of a variety of story lines. Oakley's detailed drawings discard traditional good taste by completing every detail in strong colour.

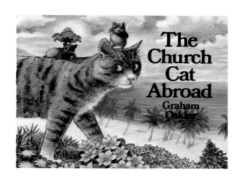

The plethora of colour that printing technology introduced in the 1970s could be overwhelming in its effects, but on rare occasions it was still possible to use black and white for positive and deliberate effect, as in Arnold Lobel's illustrations for *Hildilid's Night*, a story on the perennial childhood theme of fear of the dark. In the work of John Lawrence (see p. 109), the traditional skill of wood engraving was given a new lease of life through a fresh approach to drawing style and imagery. His work was already colourful enough without any colour-washes needing to be applied. The publication of David Macaulay's *Cathedral* in 1973 (see p. 126) marked the continuation of the Puffin Picture Book spirit of imaginative non-fiction with well-researched and accurate information in black-and-white drawings.

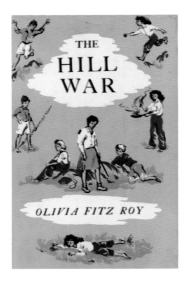

The description given by author-illustrator Shirley Hughes of the production of her first picture book, *Lucy and Tom's Day* in 1960, indicates the relative amateurism in the children's publishing business at the beginning of the period. Compared to the high-speed operation it became twenty years later. Her publishers were Victor Gollancz in London, well-known for their adult list but as yet inexperienced in children's books, lacking even a design department of their own. "The management lashed out recklessly on a set square and ruler for Livia [Gollancz] and we set about designing the book," Shirley Hughes recalls. Despite being printed in a small run by a reputable London firm, at the outset *Lucy and Tom's Day* made little impact. This is astonishing, given the later fame of the book and its successors which give a child's eye view of an ordinary day. However it was understandable in the context of the low ambitions still common in 1960. Soon all that began to change, including the almost invariable printing of books overseas for reasons of economy, and the increasing professionalization of book publicity and marketing.

Like many picture books of the '60s and '70s, Hughes worked in the manner of a cartoon book, with action driving across each spread, so that her covers are scarcely representative of the experience. She was, however, also a popular cover artist, working with Kaye Webb at Puffin Books, at a time when Puffin Picture Books were launching into full colour. Hughes's work has the quality of loose but characterful drawing not often found among younger illustrators, but her best-known subjects operate in a world reminiscent of British middle-class life in the 1970s – with stripped pine kitchen tables, Aga stoves, and loose draperies.

The urban street made relatively few appearances in picture books, even in the socially aware 1960s. Children from ethnic minorities were equally rare, but John Steptoe's *Stevie*, written when the black author-illustrator himself was only seventeen and published in 1969, gave a realistic but hopeful view of a life

← **The Hill War** Olivia Fitz Roy (author), Shirley Hughes (illustrator), London, Collins, 1950. 193 x 130mm (7²/₃ x 5in)
The cover of Shirley Hughes's first illustration commission uses coloured versions of the line drawings in the text, which concerns a quarrel between teenage siblings on holiday in the Highlands that develops into a Arthur Ransome-style story.

← *Stevie* John Steptoe (author and illustrator), New York, Harper & Row, 1969. 236 x 181mm (9¼ x 7⅛in)
The story involves a simple interior monologue in convincing dialect by Bobby, whose only-child existence is invaded by a young visitor. After Stevie has gone, he begins to remember the good times. The cover gives a specimen of the intense close-up illustration style throughout, emphasizing the limited emotional horizons of the character.

← *Corgiville Fair* Tasha Tudor (author and illustrator), New York, Farrer Strauss, 1971. 215 x 255mm (8½ x 10in)
Tasha Tudor, an illustrator of an older generation in the United States, began her career in 1938 and supported her family as an illustrator and author. Living barefoot in Vermont "in the manner of the nineteenth century", Tudor was a precursor of the alternative lifestyles that arose out of the social upheavals of the 1960s. She also anticipated the soft, nostalgic style of illustrating of the later 1970s.

→ **Duffy and the Devil** Harve Zemach (author), Margot Zemach (illustrator), New York, Farrer Strauss, 1973. 261 x 215mm (10¼ x 8½in)
The American educator Harvey Fischtrom (1933–74) used his wife's surname when collaborating with her on children's books. The cover's spirited nostalgia recalls Quentin Blake's work and the title is set in Chisel, a typeface designed by Robert Harling in 1939. The book won the Caldecott Medal in the year before the author's untimely death.

→ **The Four-Storey Mistake** Elizabeth Enright (author), Shirley Hughes (cover), Harmondsworth, Puffin Books, 1967. 180 x 111mm (7 x 4⅜in)
One of a number of covers drawn by Shirley Hughes for Puffin in the 1960s for a book by a well-known American author from 1942. The back cover forms a panorama, although interrupted by a pink spine. The children have the lively expression typical of Hughes's drawing.

→ **Alfie Weather** Shirley Hughes (author and illustrator), London, The Bodley Head, 2001. 226 x 272mm (9 x 10¾in)
Brother and sister Alfie and Annie Rose continue the series of everyday life stories that began with *Lucy and Tom's Day*. This cover comes together effortlessly as a design with the title arched into the rainbow and an intense use of colour.

in New York's Harlem or a similar neighbourhood. Although it is a world removed from Shirley Hughes's owner-occupied and upwardly mobile inner suburbs, the story and its emotions, expressed through a distinctive style of illustration, transcend the social issues and achieve universality.

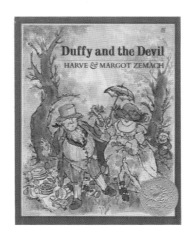

Such specific settings give authenticity to a book, but the pressure on the publishing business in the 1970s meant that publishers increasingly tried to produce their books in international co-editions. In this way, the same set of colour plates, the major cost investment, could serve for editions in several languages, helping to spread the cost. With the growth in children's book publishing in the 1960s came

the danger that more and more "product" would flood the market, much of it imitative and mediocre, and that fewer publishers would be willing to take risks and support original and unusual styles or ideas. The economic structure of the industry also changed from the traditional model in which a hardback would be published first at a higher price, and refund the initial set-up costs for a title before a paperback was considered, to one in which immediate paperback publication shaved the profit margins and required a larger volume of assured sales. Even books which had been radical in design and production when they first appeared, such as *Brian Wildsmith's ABC*, became tamer in effect in reprinted editions as newer, high-speed printing technology proved unable to deliver the intense colour that was possible from older techniques in the hands of master-craftsmen.

The perceptible shift in children's publishing from innovation in the 1960s to safety and nostalgia in the '70s was the result of these factors. Both Britain and America began to pull back in the 1970s from post-war commitment to welfare, publicly funded culture, and the American idea of "The Great Society". This change, meant, among other things, that there was increasingly less money available for schools and libraries to buy books.

"There's nuffin' like a Puffin"

When, in 1961, Eleanor Graham retired as editor of Puffin Books, the children's imprint of Penguin, she was succeeded by Kaye Webb. It was a timely appointment: with the market for children's books expanding, Puffin was well placed to grow. Any resistance to the idea of paperbacks for children had finally vanished for ever. The acquisition of reprint rights became more competitive, however, as other publishers started their own paperback series, but Webb was highly persuasive in this role. She also commissioned new titles, notably *Stig of the Dump* by Clive King (1963), with illustrations by Ardizzone (see p. 77). She paid a lot of attention to the appearance of books, and recalled "We want children to be readers, not merely lookers, but reading has to start with looking, and the cover of a book and its general appearance have an enormous effect on a child. I took a lot of trouble with the covers and I am sure it helped." As Sally Griffin comments, "Indeed it did. By 1965 sales had increased by 300 percent."

Early covers of the Kaye Webb period recall the polite traditions of the 1940s and '50s, but soon new artists were introduced, and more dynamic styles emerged, sometimes more or less reproducing the artwork of the hardback, as for example with *The Weirdstone of Brisingamen*, a Puffin of 1963 (see p. 115). Webb persuaded Collins, Oxford University Press, and Faber & Faber that it was worthwhile selling paperback rights to Puffin to ensure maximum sales for their best titles. One of the keys to this was the allocation of bookshop space to particular imprints, which meant that Puffin could easily predominate in a children's book section of a shop. Webb achieved another major publishing success in 1973 with *Watership Down*, first published the previous year by an obscure hardback house. This was given a sensitive cover by Pauline Baynes, the illustrator of the Narnia books.

Webb also paid attention to what children themselves wanted and founded the Puffin Club in 1967. This was in the tradition of magazine-based clubs of the time, but she spent much time personally answering letters and producing a quarterly magazine. On her retirement in 1979, she expressed the hope that her books were "all the time pushing back the barriers, making life and minds wider and richer and more full of possibilities."

↑ *Sabotage at the Forge* Richard Armstrong (author), L. F. Lupton (illustrator), Harmondsworth, Puffin Books, 1960 180 x 111mm (7 x 4⅓in) Self-evidently a boys' story, first published by Dent in 1946, this book has a forceful two-colour cover in a style that would soon appear rather dated.

← *Heidi* Johanna Spyri (author), Cecil Leslie (adaptor), Eileen Hall (translator), Harmondsworth, Penguin Books 1964. 180 x 111mm (7 x 4⅓in) Illustrations that ran from front to back cover were typical of earlier Puffins, as they were of some hardbacks. Puffins carried their promotional "blurb" on the half-title page inside the cover, and the absence of extra text on the outside was an indication of their confidence.

→ **Black Beauty** Anna Sewell (author),
Charlotte Hough (illustrator),
Harmondsworth, Penguin Books 1964.
180 x 111mm (7 x 4⅓in)
The way the image of the horse fills the
cover is an effective indication of scale.
The coloured band running along the
bottom, spine, and back is part of the
series identity. Anna Sewell died in 1878,
the year her book was published, and
thus her classic could be republished by
Puffin without having to negotiate rights.

↓ **The Phantom Tollbooth** Norton Juster
(author), Jules Feiffer (illustrator),
Harmondsworth, Puffin Books, 1965.
180 x 111mm (7 x 4⅓in)
The tale of Milo's adventures in a land
where language and mathematics
become physically embodied was an
unexpected success on first publication
in 1962, owing in part to the drawings by
Jules Feiffer, a well-known cartoonist.

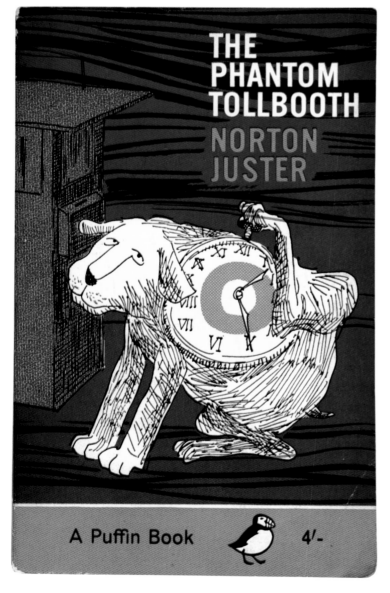

↑ **On The Run** Nina Bawden (author),
Shirley Hughes (cover design),
Harmondsworth, Puffin Books, 1967.
180 x 111mm (7 x 4⅓in)
This was Nina Bawden's third book. The
cover shows the new look for Puffins
introduced in the mid-1960s, with a
cartoon-style bird symbol. Shirley
Hughes's cover uses a fashionable
orange background, a colour often found
in children's bedrooms of the time.

← **Anne of Green Gables** L. M.
Montgomery (author), Crispian
Woodgate (cover photo),
Harmondsworth, Peacock Books, 1974
180 x 111mm (7 x 4⅓in)
First published in 1908, this popular book
has often been filmed. As colour printing
became easier, it was possible to use
film tie-in covers such as this. Peacock
Books was a parallel series to Puffin for
slightly older readers.

A world of facts
Ladybird Books

The British printers Wills & Hepworth of Loughborough began publishing books in 1915, promising "pure and healthy literature". However, the fame of "The Ladybird Series" originated in the Second World War, when small hardback books with fifty-two pages were introduced in 1940 at a price of 2/6d. A page of text faced a full-colour illustration in a realistic style.

Ladybird specialized in non-fiction and were popular for use in schools. History was represented by the deeds of great men and women, "People at Work" showed contemporary life, while in another series, Alison and John accompanied their businessman father to various countries. The "Ladybird Key Words Scheme" was launched in 1964 with virtuous children called Peter and Jane who were depicted in the period charm of a vanished age.

Up to 1964, Ladybirds had loose paper jackets reproducing the same imagery as the paper binding over the thin boards underneath. In 1972, a year after officially adopting the Ladybird name, Wills & Hepworth were bought by the Pearson Group and the image became more contemporary, with a return to fiction titles like *He-Man* and a book on the royal marriage of 1981 produced within five days of the event. In 1999, Penguin, which had previously acquired Frederick Warne, joined the the Pearson empire, meaning that Ladybird had access to the extensive Warne backlist.

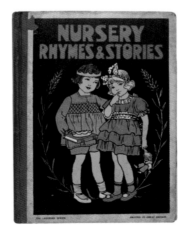

↑ *Tales of the Train* The Ladybird Series, Loughborough, Wills & Hepworth, n.d. 250 x 189mm (9⁴/₅ x 7¹/₂in) A charmingly naive cover on a popular theme in the quarto format of the early Ladybird books.

← *Nursery Rhymes & Stories* The Ladybird Series, Loughborough, Wills & Hepworth, n.d. 250 x 185mm (9⁴/₅ x 7¹/₄in) The "Christopher Robin" smock worn by the boy in this depiction of "Lavender's Blue" dates this to the 1920s, although the book itself carries no date.

← *Fairy Tales* The Ladybird Series, Loughborough, Wills & Hepworth Ltd, n.d. 250 x 186mm (9⁴/₅ x 7¹/₄in) The Art Nouveau style of the draperies and hair really belongs to the 1890s, but shows how long this style survived at a popular level, even after the First World War.

→ **Flight Four: India** David Scott Daniell (author), Jack Matthew (illustrator), Loughborough, Wills & Hepworth, 1960. 176 x 119mm (7 x 4²/₃in)
It would have been too expensive to print a book of colour photographs at this date in the Ladybird price range, but the illustrations are carefully composed to provide accurate information.

↓ **The Story of Captain Cook** L. Du Garde Peach (author), John Kenney (illustrator), Loughborough, Wills & Hepworth, 1958. 176 x 119mm (7 x 4²/₃in)
The Ladybird illustrators had a consistent style. They probably painted the original artwork in gouache in the style widely taught in the "commercial art" courses.

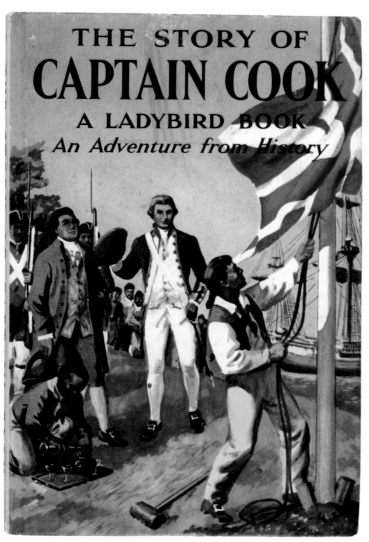

↑ **Fun and Games** W. Murray (author), J. H. Wingfield (illustrator), Loughborough, Wills & Hepworth, 1966. 176 x 119mm (7 x 4²/₃in)
Peter and Jane helped a generation to read. "The full-colour illustrations have been designed to create a desirable attitude towards learning – by making every child *eager* to read each title" claimed the blurb. The small format was equally conducive to reading.

← **"People at Work": The Nurse** Vera Southgate and I. & J. Havenhand (authors), John Berry (illustrator), Loughborough, Ladybird Books, 1963. 176 x 119mm (7 x 4²/₃in)
The focus of the book is on children in hospital, and is intended to allay fears.

Author-illustrators
Raymond Briggs & John Burningham

Raymond Briggs (b. 1934) and John Burningham (b .1936) can be bracketed together as two illustrators whose work appeals strongly to adults as well as to children. Raymond Briggs became a household name through a series of cartoon-like books in the early 1970s, notably *Father Christmas* and *The Snowman*, which led on to more adult themes in the same format such as *When the Wind Blows* (1982), an anti-nuclear tale. The covers usually have one single large-size image, leaving the reader to discover the richness of the multiple images on the pages inside.

John Burningham, whose first book was published in 1963, is famous for the diversity of his materials, employed in an almost abstract expressionist manner to achieve experimental effects. In the 1960s, these were a way of getting over the imperfect printing techniques of the time. He now uses a computer for cover designs, while continuing to use "ink, crayon, gouache, acrylic, photographs, cut paper, anything." His imaginary worlds are equally poised on a fine line between chaos and perfection.

← *The Forbidden Forest and Other Stories* James Reeves (author), Raymond Briggs (illustrator), London, Heinemann 1973. 240 x 160mm (9½ x 6⅓in) The innocent abroad is a recurrent Briggs theme, depicted here with a painterly richness of background that makes an effective cover. James Reeves (1909–78) was a prolific, consistently fine author, many of whose books were illustrated by Edward Ardizzone.

↓ *The Snowman* Raymond Briggs (author and illustrator), London, Hamish Hamilton, 1978. 303 x 213mm (12 x 8⅜in) The soft crayon lines continue through the thirty-two pages of the book, which features the wordless Snowman and his magical night journey with the boy who builds him.

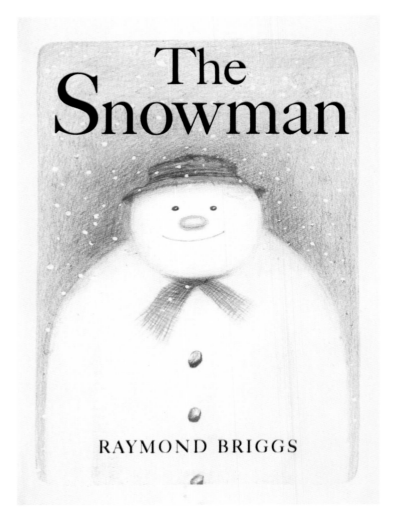

↑ *The White Land* Raymond Briggs (author and illustrator), London, Hamish Hamilton, 1972. 196 x 243mm (7¾ x 9½in) The extraordinary usually happens in a Raymond Briggs book in a totally matter-of-fact way. With its imperturbable giant, this early jacket gives an indication of things to come.

← *Father Christmas* Raymond Briggs (author and illustrator), London, Hamish Hamilton 1973. 254 x 2 17mm (10 x (8¼in) Grumpy Father Christmas breaks out of his frame in a simple drawing that shows Briggs's skill in characterization through attention to detail. The real meat of the book with its cartoon strips is inside, and the cover is bland by comparison.

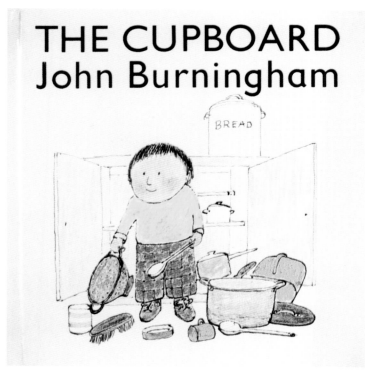

← **Trubloff: The Mouse who Wanted to play the Balalaika** John Burningham (author and illustrator), London, Jonathan Cape, 1967.
273 x 215mm (10¾ x 8½in)
The drawing style is exaggerated compared to later works, but the background group in the sledge shows Burningham's skill in giving a rather awkward and individualistic life to simple shapes.

← **The Cupboard** John Burningham (author and illustrator), London, Jonathan Cape, 1975.
165 x 160mm (6½ x 6½in)
The series of board books, of which this title forms part, makes toddler activities into the serious work that they are. The typesetting in a sans serif typeface suits the simplicity of the concept.

↑ **Come Away From the Water, Shirley** John Burningham (author and illustrator), London, Jonathan Cape, 1977.
197 x 273mm (7¼ x 10¾in)
In the two linked books (see also below), Shirley's mother's familiar words are a world away from the child's imagination. The covers make the point immediately, and should remind adults how boring they can be.

↓ **Time To Get Out Of The Bath, Shirley** John Burnginham (author and illustrator), London, Jonathan Cape 1978.
197 x 273mm (7¼ x 10¾in)
The cover of the second book about Shirley's imagination is even more successful in conveying the idea of fantasy breaking into everyday life. The horse's hooves in the meadow add a sense of depth.

Masters of the zany
James Marshall, Quentin Blake, & John Lawrence

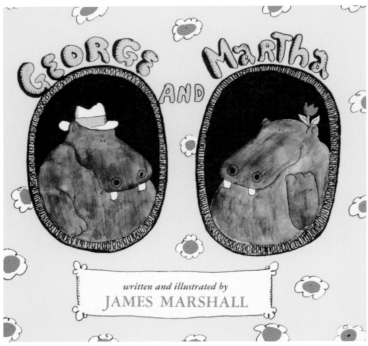

← **George and Martha** James Marshall (author and illustrator) Boston, Houghton Mifflin, 1972. 208 x 220mm (8¹/₅ x 8²/₅in) Marshall uses the limited colour range and flat tints of an earlier era to achieve a striking poster-like quality for one of his early titles about the domestic oddities of a couple of hippos.

→ **How Tom Beat Captain Najork and His Hired Sportsmen** Russell Hoban (author) Quentin Blake (illustrator), London, Jonathan Cape, 1974.
270 x 215mm (10²/₃ x 8¹/₂in)
In the style of a Renaissance title page, the cover introduces the main characters, including Tom's Aunt Fidget Wonkham-Strong in her iron hat.

↓ **Mr Horrox and the Gratch** James Reeves (author), Quentin Blake (illustrator), London and Toronto, Abelard-Schuman, 1969. 241 x 214mm (9¹/₂ x 8¹/₂in)
This cover shows Blake's style, including his characteristic hand lettering, use of line and colour, and sense of spontaneity.

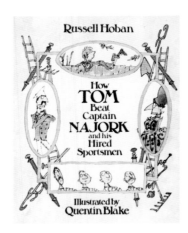

The drawing style of James Marshall (1942–92) perfectly captures the goofy nature of the characters. Another illustrator with a zany style is Quentin Blake (b. 1932). He draws people belonging to the wiry and active type, often with a manic glint in the eye. Blake began to find fame as a children's illustrator in the 1970s and his loose line and wash style is found in several generations of titles, especially those of Roald Dahl, but also in many of his own texts. Blake has taken a public role in promoting drawing, as "Children's Laureate" and as an advocate of the "Campaign for Drawing" which holds an annual festival involving children and grown-ups alike.

John Lawrence (b. 1933) works whenever possible in the traditional medium of wood engraving, often adding colour. He is a prolific illustrator, who has also brought many adult texts to life for publishers such as the Folio Society. Lawrence's illustrations often produce their own parallel text through a network of visual references, or, as shown here with *Nothingmas Day*, he produces a cover design that brings the individual illustrations of the book into a composite picture.

← **The Stupids Die** Harry Allard (author), James Marshall (illustrator), Houghton Mifflin, 1981. 215 x 265mm (8¹/₂ x 10¹/₂in)
"Something really stupid is going to happen today," predicts Stanley Q., head of the house of Stupids in this, the third book in a series begun in 1974, in which children can enjoy the bizarre logic of this irrepressible family. When the lights fuse, the Stupids think they must have died.

JACKANORY STORIES

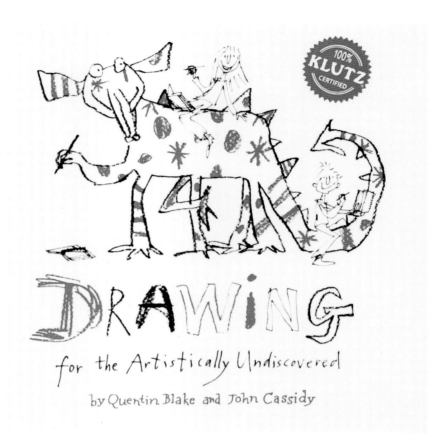

↑ **Jackanory Stories: Tales of Arabel's Raven** Joan Aiken (author), Quentin Blake (illustrator), London, Jonathan Cape, 1974. 235 x 152mm (9¼ x 6in)
Joan Aiken created this series of stories for the BBC programme *Jackanory*, when Blake first illustrated them. Aiken describes the "virtuous and sensible" Arabel as a personfication of the *Ego*, while Mortimer, "her utterly unbridled and unpredictable raven", is the *Id*.

↑ **Rabbit & Pork, Rhyming Talk** John Lawrence (author and illustrator), London, Hamish Hamilton, 1975. 163 x 190mm (6½ x 7½in)
As much an adult as a children's book, this revival of the chapbook form is typical of the sophisticated adoption of childish things by adults in the 1970s. After a long wait, Lawrence was allowed to use wood engraving for a book and the printers Lund Humphries added delicate colour overlays.

↑ **Drawing for the Artistically Undiscovered** Quentin Blake and John Cassidy (authors and illustrators), Palo Alto, Klutz, 1999. 230 x 230mm (9 x 9in)
Blake's belief that everyone can draw is put into practical form in this appealing sketch-workbook which comes with its own drawing tools attached. The book itself is black and white, and the cover, like the pencils provided, is two-colour only.

← **Nothingmas Day** Adrian Mitchell (author), John Lawrence (illustrator), London, Allison and Busby, 1984. 255 x 180mm (10 x 7in)
The publishers created a colour poster of this jacket, and rightly so, as it is a masterpiece of ingenuity. One needs to be able to follow the illustrations to this collection of poems to understand how each stands on its own on the page, yet also forms part of the sequence making a complex interlocking design for the cover, all engraved on a single wood block.

Romanticism revisited
Tomi Ungerer & Errol Le Cain

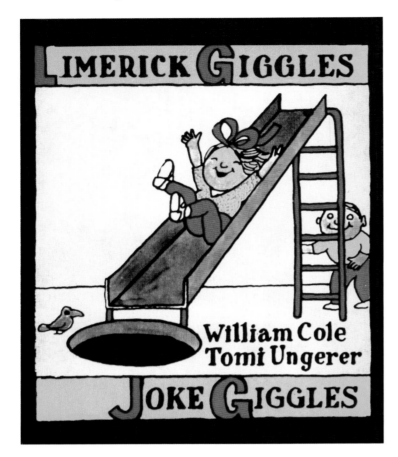

← *Limerick Giggles, Joke Giggles*
Collected by William Cole, Tomi Ungerer
(illustrator), London, The World
Publishing Co., 1969.
170 x 139mm (6²⁄₃ x 5½in)
First published in the USA in 1966, the
cover has a strong graphic quality
enhanced by Ungerer's sense of mischief.
William Cole is known as the author of
Flat Stanley, a book about a child who
becomes two dimensional.

↓ *Zeralda's Ogre* Tomi Ungerer (author
and illustrator), London, The Bodley
Head, 1970. 310 x 237mm (12¹⁄₅ x 9¹⁄₃in)
Zeralda's cooking is so good that the
giant ceases to eat humans. This cover,
with its Gothic aedicule framing the
ogre and black letter title, demonstrates
the strong German roots in Ungerer's
work which gives it an unusual strength.

The author and illustrator Tomi Ungerer was born in 1931 in Strasbourg,
France, where his family were watchmakers. Before moving to the United
States in 1957, he served in the Camel Caravan of the French Desert Police.
His list of publications starts in 1957 and includes not only children's
books but illustrated books for adults, both in the literal and euphemistic
senses. Ungerer's international background has given him a political
attitude, but this does not interfere with his ability to tell a story. Michael
Patrick Hearn suggests that only in a period of material prosperity like
the 1960s could offbeat illustrators such as Maurice Sendak, Edward
Gorey, and Tomi Ungerer have flourished, although each of them employs
very traditional skills of drawing and storytelling. Ungerer uses line and
colour in a style that was much imitated for years after he gave up
illustrating in 1976 on moving to Ireland.

Errol Le Cain was born in Singapore in 1941 and was evacuated to India
during the Second World War. In London he worked on the design of
animations, including the famous title sequence of the Tony Richardson
film *The Charge of the Light Brigade* (1968). Fascinated by the East, Le Cain
developed a detailed manner of illustration, which was very different from
Ungerer's, but also popular and influential. Le Cain's delight in a flat
oriental style is part of a general nostalgia during the 1970s, looking back
to the similar illustrations by Edmund Dulac for the 1907 "gift book" edition
of the *Arabian Nights*.

← *The Sorcerer's Apprentice* Barbara Hazen (author), Tomi Ungerer (illustrator), London, Methuen Children's Books, 1971. 313 x 232mm (12²/₃ x 9in)
A picture book on a popular theme, which combines the comic and scary on its cover.

→ *The Flying Ship* Rosemary Harris (author), Errol Le Cain (illustrator), London, Faber & Faber, 1975. 253 x 190mm (10 x 7¹/₂in)
Decorative borders, which are part of the design vocabulary of many illustrators, create a sense of stability that can become static. On this occasion, the dynamism with which the surface of the sea is depicted could have been allowed a more free rein.

↓ *The Cabbage Princess* Errol Le Cain (author and illustrator), London, Faber & Faber, 1969. 250 x 210mm (9⁴/₅ x 8¹/₄in)
Le Cain's style of enamelled detail adds just the required air of surrealist strangeness to make this a highly effective cover, in which the plain black background prevents visual indigestion.

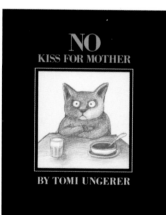

↑ *No Kiss for Mother* Tomi Ungerer (author and illustrator), New York, Harper & Row, 1973.
246 x 197mm (9²/₃ x 7³/₄in)
This black-and-white tale of human behaviour in cat form has a perfect linkage of title words and image. Seeing this, one is already on the way to guessing the subject matter.

↑ *Das Kleine Liederbuch* Collected by Anne Diekmann, Tomi Ungerer (illustrator), Zurich, Diogenes Verlag, 1975. 71 x 58mm (2³/₄ x 2¹/₄in)
A miniature version of *Das Grosse Liederbuch*, in which Ungerer indulged in some nostalgia for the age of the Brothers Grimm. In East Germany this brought him some criticism. Ungerer's drawing here is close in spirit and accomplishment to Sendak's.

The Ahlbergs & Jan Pieńkowski

Janet Ahlberg (1944–94) and her husband Allan (b. 1938) have been described as "a two-headed illustrator". Janet's developing career as an illustrator was the stimulus for Allan to give up teaching and begin to write: "It was as though someone had turned a key in my back," he has said. Their work often has nostalgic qualities which were increasingly appreciated through the 1970s and beyond, but the popularity of their work from *Brick Street Boys* (1975) onwards owes as much to skill, hard work, and an understanding of the medium and the audience, since they have a special ability to catch children's attention with detail and memorable phrasing. Without actually being part of the new fashion for pop-up books, their three *Jolly Postman* books show much ingenuity in cutting and assembly, with letters and documents in envelopes that form pages of the book and carry the story forward.

The covers of Janet Ahelberg's books are well integrated with the rest of the book's style, giving away as much or as little of the story as necessary, and often using her own lettering skills. Allan Ahlberg worked with other authors, notably in the *Happy Families* series for Viking Kestrel, (1988), a series of school "Readers" which blew away the old-fashioned tedium of everyday life situations in favour of socially relevant content. Here children discovered a timeless late-Victorian world in which ridiculous but perfectly logical things happened, within a limited vocabulary.

Jan Pieńkowski was born in Warsaw in 1936, and his Polish background can be seen in his bright folk-art colours and cut-paper silhouettes. Coming to England in 1946, Pieńkowski worked briefly in advertising and then, in 1960, began to design book jackets for Jonathan Cape. Like the Ahlbergs, Pieńkowski has paid great attention to the way that his books are printed, knowing that without constant vigilance the quality can slip, and that without inventiveness new discoveries cannot be made. The *Meg and Mog* books are one example, and his eager participation in pop-up books is another, extending to such adult toys as *Botticelli's Bed and Breakfast*, which was a gift sensation in 1996. The serious side of Pieńkowski's illustration can be seen in *M.O.L.E.* (1993 – see p. 128).

↑ *Each Peach Pear Plum* Allan Ahlberg (author), Janet Ahlberg (illustrator), London, Kestrel Books, 1978.
195 x 250mm (7⅔ x 9⅚in)
This commentary on nursery rhymes satisfies adults and children alike in its simple cross-references and story lines. The cover is an old-fashioned cover design, rather than an excerpt from the book.

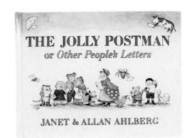

↑ *The Jolly Postman or Other People's Letters* Allan Ahlberg (author), Janet Ahlberg (illustrator), London, William Heinemann, 1986.
154 x 200mm (6 x 7⅘in)
This complex piece of book design and assembly was an instant hit. The series style is set with a simple cover in which the drawing is tight and characterful.

↑ *The Better Brown Stories* Alan Ahlberg (author), Fritz Wegner (illustrator), London, Viking, 1995.
205 x 130mm (8 x 5in)
Many of Wegner's skills are displayed here, including his ability to combine a small scale with a larger sense of design, his superb comic narrative drawing, his sly humour (author portrait), and his excellent lettering.

← *Funnybones: Dinosaur Dreams* Allan Ahlberg (author), André Amstutz (illustrator), London, William Heinemann, 1991. 220 x 179mm (8⅔ x 7in)
André Amstutz was one of Janet Ahlberg's tutors at Leicester Polytechnic in the 1960s. He influenced her work and and remained a friend. The simple flat colour illustrations are carefully detailed without becoming over-elaborate.

→ **Snow White: The Fairy Tale Library** Jan
Pieńkowski (author and illustrator),
London, William Heinemann with
Gallery Five, 1977.
110 x 82mm (4⅓ x 3¼in)
Six different stories were contained in a
boxed set. The cover is in an Edwardian
revival style, although the silhouette
looks like one of the cut-out animations
of the 1920s by Lotte Reiniger.

↓ **Meg and Mog** Helen Nicoll (author),
Jan Pieńkowski (illustrator), Harmondsworth, Picture Puffin, 1975.
202 x 202mm (8 x 8in)
First commissioned by Judith Elliott at
Heinemann in 1972 after going the
rounds of many publishers, the *Meg
and Mog* books were an instant success
and grew into a series over the course of
ten years. The colours are printed pure
rather than as part of a half-tone screen,
reverting in some respects to methods
used before the war, but with more
luminous results.Pieńkowski designed
his images with flat colouring in order
to achieve this effect.

↑ **Haunted House** Jan Pieńkowski
(author and illustrator), Jane Walmsley
(assistant illustrator), Tor Lokvig (paper
engineer), London, William Heinemann,
1979. 300 x 198mm (11⅘ x 7⅘in)
Pieńkowski's delight in theatre and in the
various forms of book production found
a perfect outlet in pop-up books, which
experienced a sudden renaissance at this
time, as a result of the combination of
high-tech printing and cheap but skilled
hand labour in Colombia. The cover joins
in a growing taste in the children's book
market for the deliciously scary or nasty
that had previously been confined to
comic books.

The truth of fantasy
Lucy M. Boston & Alan Garner

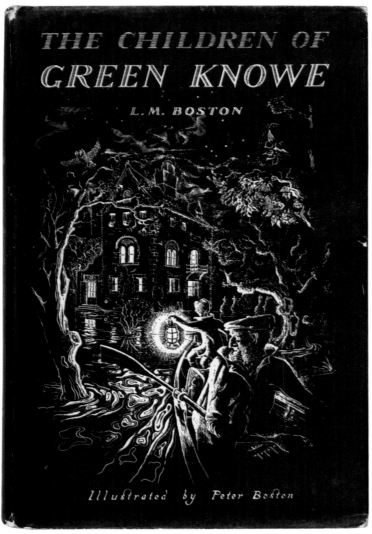

← *The Children of Green Knowe* Lucy M. Boston (author), Peter Boston (illustrator), London, Faber & Faber, 1954.
205 x 135mm (8 x 5⅓in)
The cover of the first title reproduces the frontispiece, showing the arrival of Tolly to stay with his great-grandmother.

↓ *A Stranger at Green Knowe* Lucy M. Boston (author), Peter Boston (illustrator), London, Faber & Faber, 1973.
186 x 124mm (7⅓ x 4⅔in)
First published in 1961, this is the first paperback edition of the most powerful of the *Green Knowe* stories.

↓ *The Stones of Green Knowe* Lucy M. Boston (author), Peter Boston (illustrator), Harmondsworth, Puffin Books, 1979.
180 x 111mm (7 x 4⅓in)
First published in 1976, this was the last of the *Green Knowe* stories and returns to the origin of the house. Peter Boston drew a new set of covers when Puffin took over the paperbacks.

↓ *The Chimneys of Green Knowe* Painting c.1995 by Peter Boston for the Puffin Books edition. Peter Boston's watercolours have since been replaced by more conventional designs.

Lucy M. Boston (1890–1990) was over sixty when she published her first children's book. She was inspired by her home, said to be the earliest inhabited house in England, and set in the flat, flood-prone country north of Cambridge. In the stories, the Norman manor house becomes Green Knowe, a place where children find an understanding of mysteries of the past, which are often frightening, but also serve to reflect on the dark forces of unfeeling conformity at large in the modern world. Lucy Boston's son, Peter, illustrated nearly all her books with tender but unsentimental black-and-white drawings and scraperboards.

Lucy Boston's seriousness about myth and magic, and the relationship to actual places, are aspects also found in the work of Alan Garner (b. 1934). *The Weirdstone of Brisingamen* (1960), takes place in Alderley Edge, Cheshire, an area of rural seclusion not far from industrial centres of population. The supernatural quest story is packed with action. Following its success, Garner's books became increasingly complex and dark, dealing with modern social themes without losing their mythological dimension.

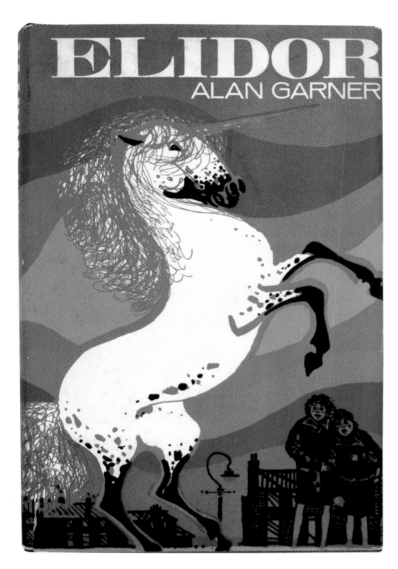

ELIDOR
ALAN GARNER

← *Elidor* Alan Garner (author), Charles Keeping (illustrator), London, Collins 1966. 214 x 142mm (8¼ x 5½in) Set in the decaying suburbs of Manchester, where supernatural horror invades a family, Garner's second novel has a theme that remains relevant today. Working for printing in colour line block, Charles Keeping (1924–88) used a lot of texture to overcome the implicit flatness of the medium. He was one of the great illustrators of the 1960s onwards.

↓ *Red Shift* Alan Garner (author), Arthur Smith (jacket photography), London, Collins, 1973. 215 x 140mm (8¼ x 5½in) "Probably the most difficult book ever to be published on a children's list" was one opinion of *Red Shift*, which combines the stories of three teenagers, depicting the darkness and hopelessness of their worlds. The photographic cover shows Mow Cop Castle, a famous landmark in Garner's part of Cheshire.

→*The Weirdstone of Brisingamen* Alan Garner (author), George Adamson (jacket), London, Collins, 1960. 214 x 142mm (8¼ x 5½in) Garner's first novel is set on Alderley Edge in Cheshire where he grew up, and returned to live as a writer after cutting short his classics degree at Oxford. The cover shows one of the characters from a mythical realm in which contemporary children become involved, although his cheerful expression is unlike the mood of danger that prevails in the story.

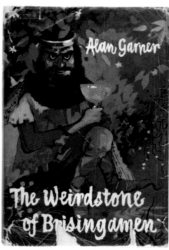

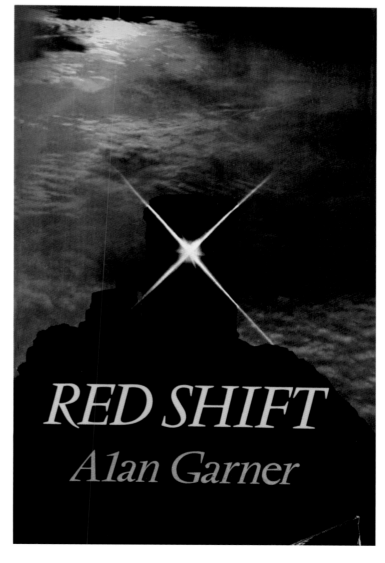

RED SHIFT
Alan Garner

"Unhistorical romance"
Joan Aiken

The daughter of the American poet Conrad Aiken, Joan Aiken wrote books capable of being enjoyed by readers or listeners of various ages. She was born in 1924 and grew up in England, beginning her writing career for children with a book of stories in 1953. It was the publication of the first of a sequence of "unhistorical romances", *The Wolves of Willoughby Chase*, in 1962, which, boosted by a review in *Time* magazine, established her reputation in America. The books, sometimes called the "James III" series are funny, dramatic, and touching at the same time, continued with *Black Hearts in Battersea*, published in 1964. They are loosely linked by characters or settings carried over from one to another, notably the irrepressible cockney waif, Dido Twite. Joan Aiken's most recent title in the series is *Limbo Lodge* (1999), set on an island in the China Seas. It deals with issues of colonialism, ecology, and feminism, allowing these themes to structure the plot rather than obstruct it. There is also an independent set of three novels set in 18th-century Spain that Aiken claims as her personal favourites.

The line illustrations in the earlier titles are by Pat Marriot (b. 1920), who has also done most of the covers and succeeds very well in capturing the quality of exaggerated drama inherent in the texts. The success of Joan Aiken's work, which has been adapted for television on several occasions, has inevitably meant that Marriott's covers have been replaced by more commonplace and literal renderings for the current paperback editions, so that the earlier hardbacks are well worth seeking out. Edward Gorey's covers for the American hardback editions in the 1990s are old-fashioned in flavour and decorative, but lack the brio appropriate for Aiken's rollicking plots. Aiken has also worked with other illustrators in her books for younger readers. The books about Arabel and Mortimer were illustrated by Quentin Blake (see p. 109). In the early 1990s, Blake's drawings were adapted as puppets for dramatized versions of the stories, later published in book form, in which Aiken collaborated with her daughter Lizzie. Finally, several of Aiken's books of short stories are illustrated by Jan Pienkowski (see p. 113).

↑ *Black Hearts in Battersea* Joan Aiken (author), Pat Marriot (illustrator), London, Jonathan Cape, 1964. 205 x 135mm (8 x 5⅓in) The original English hardback cover visualizes a sublime moment from the story in Pat Marriot's theatrical line and wash style. The incorporation of lettering on the banners flying from the balloon is a felicitous touch.

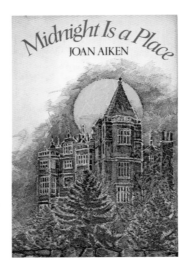

← *Black Hearts in Battersea* Joan Aiken (author), Edward Gorey (illustrator), Boston, Houghton Misslin, 1999. 217 x 145mm (8⅓in x 5⅓in) The rather sober cover from the series designed by Gorey for American reprints of Joan Aiken's titles uses a patterned background, two portraits of the main characters, and twin cartouches.

← *Midnight is a Place* Joan Aiken (author), Murray Tinkelman (jacket design), New York, The Viking Press, 1974. 240 x 160mm (9⅓ x 6⅓in) Compared to Pat Marriot's cover for the English edition, this rendering of a "'Gothic" mansion, from which the book takes its title, lacks a sense of drama.

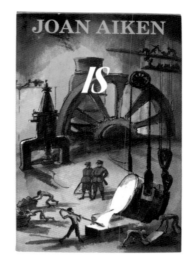

← *Night Birds on Nantucket* Joan Aiken (author), Pat Marriot (illustrator), London, Jonathan Cape, 1966.
205 x 135mm (8 x 5¼in)
With a wonderful crossing over of different story lines, including one based on *Moby Dick*, this continuation of the adventures of Dido Twite has an atmospheric cover that skilfully integrates the title lettering.

← *Is* Joan Aiken (author), Pat Marriot (illustrator), London, Jonathan Cape, 1992. 204 x 134mm (8 x 6¼in)
Aiken's story, named after Dido Twite's sister, reflects in an exaggerated form the British Industrial Revolution and its cruelty. The Piranesian machinery and scurrying figures of Marriot's cover set the tone.

↓ *A Necklace of Raindrops* Joan Aiken (author), Jan Pieńkowski (illustrator), London, Jonathan Cape, 1968.
254 x 172mm (10 x 6¾in)
The early Pieńkowski illustrations indicate this book of short stories is intended for younger readers.

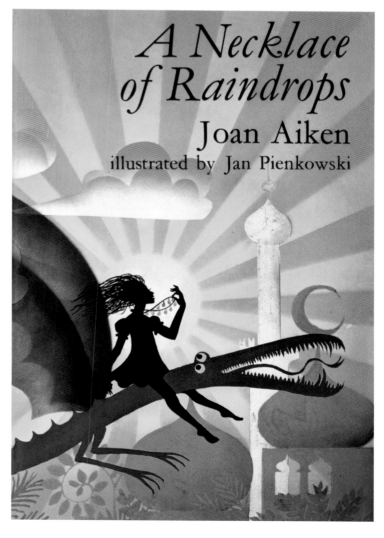

↑ *Go Saddle the Sea* Joan Aiken (author), Pat Marriot (illustrator), London, Jonathan Cape, 1978.
205 x 135mm (8 x 5¼in)
The turn away from hand lettering to typesetting indicates the loss of

confidence in the children's book trade at the end of the 1970s, since no risk could be taken that the title could be secondary to the image. The fine panorama extending to the back cover is a compensation, however.

Out of the chocolate factory
Roald Dahl

Roald Dahl (1916–90) emerged as a children's author late in his career: his first children's book, *James and the Giant Peach*, was published in 1961, nearly twenty years after his initial success as an adult author with *The Gremlins*. As a creator of parallel worlds and their inhabitants, Dahl had much in common with his contemporaries. His stories, described by one reference as "a mixture of the glutinous and the cruel", backed by inventiveness of language, proved immensely successful with children and have remained so.

Dahl's life spanned both sides of the Atlantic. Born in Wales, he served as a wartime pilot before becoming an air attaché in Washington DC during the Second World War. He first wrote mystery stories for adults, and came to write for children by telling stories to his own family of five. "The writer for children must be a jokey sort of fellow," Dahl said. "He must like simple tricks and jokes and riddles and other childish things. He must be unconventional and inventive. He must have a really first-class plot."

Dahl's first three children's books – *James and the Giant Peach*, *Charlie and the Chocolate Factory* (both 1964), and *The Magic Finger* (1966) – were first published in the United States and then in Britain by Allen & Unwin in 1967 and 1968, at a time when recent cultural changes had created a country better prepared for their unconstrained exaggeration. The first two London editions were slightly larger than usual hardbacks, with illustrated covers back and front by Faith Jacques. They were laminated rather than protected by a wrapper and, in this form, they show an interesting combination of old-style drawing with a new physical treatment that was typical of the year of the Beatles' *Sergeant Pepper* album. *The Magic Finger* was published with illustrations by the notable American fantasy author and illustrator, William Pène du Bois.

From the late 1970s onwards, Dahl's books became inextricably associated with the illustrations of Quentin Blake (b. 1932), whose natural instinct is to focus on the comic aspect rather than on the grotesque. Blake's spindly but spirited little girls are particularly suitable to Dahl characters such as *Matilda* (1988).

↑ *Charlie and the Chocolate Factory*
Roald Dahl (author), Joseph Schindelman (illustrator), New York, Alfred A. Knopf, 1964. 240 x 160mm (9¹⁄₂ x 6¹⁄₃in)
This famous book made its first appearance with a rather tentative dust wrapper. Although the title lettering on the chocolate bar is a good example of the 1960s Art Nouveau revival, it fails to communicate clearly, and the amount of white space on the front cover weakens the overall design.

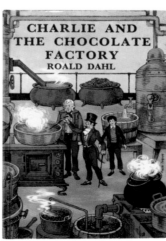

← *Charlie and the Chocolate Factory*
Roald Dahl (author), Faith Jacques (illustrator), London, George Allen & Unwin, 1967. 243 x 170mm (9¹⁄₂ x 6²⁄₃in)
Faith Jacques (b. 1923) has a good eye for Victorian style detail and costume, which is appropriate to the mood of the book, although it also includes modern references to television and chewing gum. The cover shows just what a factory in a story book is supposed to look like.

← *Charlie and the Chocolate Factory*
Roald Dahl (author), Faith Jacques (illustrator), Harmondsworth, Puffin Books, 1973. 198 x 128mm (7⁴⁄₅ x 5in)
As the story became better known, it may have been thought necessary to depict its major characters on the cover of the paperback, as they are seen here.

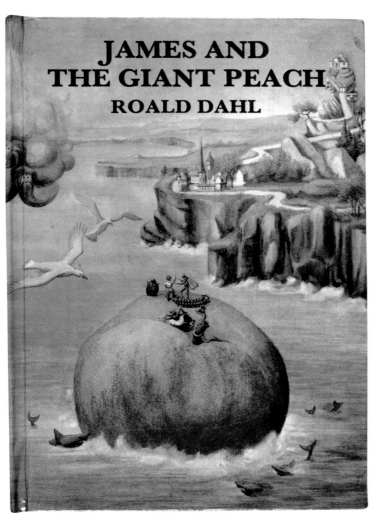

JAMES AND THE GIANT PEACH
ROALD DAHL

FANTASTIC MR. FOX

BY

ROALD DAHL

author of *Charlie and the Chocolate Factory*

ILLUSTRATIONS BY DONALD CHAFFIN

← *James and the Giant Peach* Roald Dahl (author), Michel Simeon (illustrator), London, George Allen & Unwin, 1967. 243 x 170mm (9½ x 6⅔in)
The companion volume in the original Allen & Unwin editions has a softer style of illustration by Michael Simeon, with a touch of Breughel to it.

← *Fantastic Mr. Fox* Roald Dahl (author), Donald Chaffin (illustrator), Donna Lampell (jacket), New York, Alfred A. Knopf, 1970. 235 x 173mm (9¼ x 6⅚in)
This original American edition of a fable about the underdog making good, a role reversal typical of Dahl's world, received a slightly tame-looking cover.

↓ *The Magic Finger* Roald Dahl (author), Quentin Blake (illustrator), London, Viking, 1995. 245 x 160mm (9⅔ x 6⅓in)
The first American edition of this book appeared in 1966. Quentin Blake's cover is skilful in avoiding overcrowding of incident and creating a strong vertical emphasis with a decorative colour scheme.

Roald Dahl
The
MAGIC FINGER
Illustrated by Quentin Blake

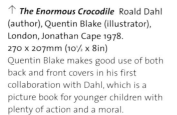

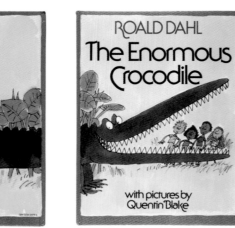

ROALD DAHL
The Enormous Crocodile

with pictures by Quentin Blake

↑ *The Enormous Crocodile* Roald Dahl (author), Quentin Blake (illustrator), London, Jonathan Cape 1978. 270 x 207mm (10½ x 8in)
Quentin Blake makes good use of both back and front covers in his first collaboration with Dahl, which is a picture book for younger children with plenty of action and a moral.

Beware of the Storybook Wolves

Lauren Child

Lauren Child ★ Winner of the KATE GREENAWAY 2001 Award

5

Cold War to Globalization: the '80s and '90s

The appointment of Quentin Blake to the newly-created unofficial position of Britain's "Children's Laureate" in 1999 recognized that children's books were a matter of increasing importance within culture as a whole. More than any other books, it was the *Harry Potter* series that drew adult and child readerships closer together. Every aspect of children's publishing is now a matter of widespread interest and regular press comment. The entrepreneurial success of a publisher such as Sebastian Walker in the 1980s contributed to the change, and some people view the last two decades as a new "golden age" of children's books. On a purely financial level, the fact that the author of the *Harry Potter* books, J. K. Rowling, was ranked higher than the Queen in a 2003 list of British fortunes, indicates the truth of this, and her success has stimulated a renewed interest in children's fiction all over the world.

← *Beware of the Storybook Wolves*
Lauren Child (author and illustrator),
London, Hodder Children's Books, 2000.
300 x 235mm (11⅘ x 9¼in)
Wolf stories may reflect real fears of
people long ago, but they remain a
popular theme of children's books —
especially when retold with a twist.
Lauren Child (b. 1967) often uses collage
in combination with her own drawings.

Cold War to globalization: the '80s and '90s

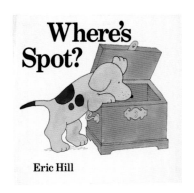

The last two decades of the 20th century have already achieved an identity in cultural terms, even before it is clear what is coming next. The accession to power of Margaret Thatcher as prime minister in Britain in 1979 and Ronald Reagan as president in the USA in 1980 provides a demarcation that separates the 1980s from the '70s. By 1990 the digital revolution had begun to affect media production in many fields, and the remainder of the decade following the fall of communism in Europe accelerated trends towards commercial globalization and economic growth.

Some of these conditions were propitious for children's book publishing. Economic inflation, an enemy of standards in book production during the 1970s, came under control. However, the traumatic remodelling of the printing industry left few firms in Britain or the USA able to compete in price for the printing of colour work, and books began routinely to be printed in Italy, Spain, or the Far East, affecting the previous close relationships between illustrators, publishers, and their printers, since it was usually difficult for illustrators and designers to check work coming off the presses and make adjustments. The advantage, however, was that colour printing became cheaper than ever before and economies such as colour printing on only one side of the sheet, resulting in books with alternate black-and-white and colour spreads, ceased. Traditional printing from metal type was still standard in 1980 but just five years later it had become completely obsolete. Computer setting, available in every home or office, threatened to abolish the traditional design skills of the trade typesetter.

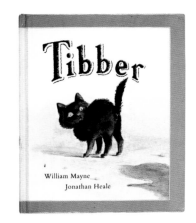

The 1980s saw an expansion in illustration generally, which was in tune with the nostalgic cultural temper of the times and the emergence of a new generation in the late 1970s. This was welcomed by children's book publishers and the strengths of picture books in the 1970s were still further developed. More titles were published catering for the needs of younger children, as child-rearing became increasingly an experience involving shopping and consumption, in line with the growth of consumerism generally.

← *Where's Spot?* Eric Hill (author and illustrator), London, Heinemann Young Books, 1980. 215 x 220mm (8½ x 8⅔in)
Eric Hill's simple formula of lift-up flaps brought the paper-engineering of pop-up books to floor level for very young children. The cover illustrations indicate the simplicity of line and flat colour drawing that lies inside.

← *Tibber* William Mayne (author), Jonathan Heale (illustrator), London, Walker Books, 1986.
232 x 196mm (9 x 7¾in)
Jonathan Heale has been much influenced by William Nicholson and was producing decorative textiles and ceramics at the time this book about a farm kitten was published.

← *Judy the Bad Fairy* Martin Waddell (author), Dom Mansell (illustrator), London, Walker Books,1989.
236 x 177mm (9¼ x 7in)
Martin Waddell was one of the most popular authors for Walker Books, writing *Can't You Sleep, Little Bear?* This cover shows the influence of children's comics on books, with styles of dead-pan narrative and outrageous illustration increasingly used.

→ *Five Minutes' Peace* Jill Murphy
(author and illustrator), London, Walker
Books, 1988. 190 x 229mm (7⅛ x 9in)
This is one of the earliest paperbacks
from Walker, and it followed a hardback
edition in 1986. The back cover is designed
vertically so that the book can be
displayed in two different sizes of stand.

→ *The Rat Race, The Amazing Adventures
of Anton B. Stanton* Colin McNaughton
(author and illustrator), London, Picture
Puffin, 1980. 180 x 227mm (7⅛ x 9in)
First published in 1978, this title was
later taken over by Walker Books. Colin
McNaughton (b. 1951) displays a love of
excess and of action, and gives knowing
references to existing genres of
children's books.

→ *The Mice on the Moon* Rodney Peppé
(author and illustrator), London, Viking
Penguin, 1992. 276 x 195mm (10⅘ x 7⅔in)
Having worked in children's television
and made a number of animated toys,
Rodney Peppé began a series of books
about a family of mice. Each title is based
on a model he has made that plays a
significant part in the story and enables
the mice to outwit their enemy, D. Rat.

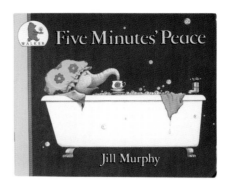

The reliance on co-editions with publishers in other countries to finance every title was an opportunity to keep up producing new titles in a static or contracting market where public spending was being cut. Success came at a price, however, and as the children's book editor Marni Hodgkin said in 1984, "When books are marketed like soap... the result is that a title without mass appeal may easily go out of print within the year of its publication, before the hard-pressed librarians have had a chance to assess it or the children are able to have a go. Publishers are less ready to take risks, and new writers and innovative writing go to the wall."

More significant in its way than the election around 1980 of the two political leaders mentioned, was the decision in the same year by Sebastian Walker to set up his own publishing company specializing in children's books. Born in 1942, Walker had started work in publishing in

1970, in what was an odd role for an Oxford graduate, as a European sales representative for Jonathan Cape. In 1975 he moved on to Marshall Cavendish, a publisher known for part-works and highly illustrated books, again as a European salesman, for which his knowledge of languages, magnetic personality, and salesmanship were suited. He saw at first hand the benefits of much larger print runs (in the region of 60–70,000) than British publishers were used to. He went back to the established mainstream at Chatto & Windus for a while, but as his sister Mirabel Cecil writes, "at thirty-five he wanted to go it alone: he had worked out the figures, mainly on the backs of envelopes, and knew that what he wanted to do was feasible, that the market was there, a global market for selling children's books which were better produced and illustrated than any others, in co-editions of tens of thousands; now he was impatient to get out there and sell them."

Walker Books, as it soon became, was set up in 1978 with Amelia Edwards as the original and long-enduring commissioning editor, and its first titles appeared in 1980. At an early stage Walker experienced the backward nature of British printing, and switched to printing in Italy.

Sebastian Walker asked Helen Oxenbury, already a well-established illustrator, to work for him, and for his second list in 1981 she produced a series of board books for very young children that helped to push the company into sensational profit. His father, Richard Walker, wrote, "Sebastian's original concept of the market for children's books was sound; he supplied a product which was original and excellently designed. He kept costs, particularly overheads, low and so was able to sell his books at prices the customer would pay. His sales policy and methods were imaginative and unencumbered by the tradition and myths of the publishing trade."

While Walker's focus on sales (including a venture with the supermarket Sainsbury's) and international co-editions anticipated later revolutions in bookselling practice, his very personal approach to authors, illustrators, and customers, belonged more to an older period of individualism in publishing. Over time, many of the best artists, illustrators, and authors, including Nicola Bayley and William Mayne, joined the Walker list. When Walker approached the author Jill Murphy she asked to see his catalogue and observed, "It was better laid out and printed than most publishers' actual children's books and... it contained all the people I admired – such as Jan Ormerod, Shirley Hughes, Colin McNaughton, and Helen Craig."

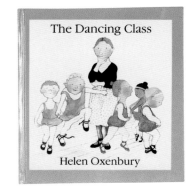

Book covers had been Walker's principal selling tool in his earlier jobs (as they are for most publishers), but when he had his own company he was more inclined to use artwork or proofs from the inside of the books to give prospective buyers a more complete idea of the publication. Walker Books began to produce its own paperbacks in 1988, with royalties for authors and

illustrators that were higher than Penguin's. In 1990, an American branch was set up as Candlewick Books in Cambridge, Massachussetts, but by this time Sebastian was ill with AIDS, which claimed his life in July 1991, though not before he had campaigned to save the historic Opie collection of children's books for the Bodleian Library in Oxford.

← *The Indian in the Cupboard* Lynne Reid Banks (author), Robin Jacques (illustrator), London, Granada Publishing, 1981. 177 x 110mm (7 x 4⅓in)
Robin Jacques (1920–95) was an illustrator with a careful use of line in the manner of old engravings. He illustrated many covers for Dent's *Everyman's Library* when these books were produced in paperback.

← *The Dancing Class* Helen Oxenbury (author and illustrator), London, Walker Books, 1983. 177 x 166mm (7 x 6½in)
Based on her own daughter Emily, these board books by Helen Oxenbury (b. 1938) were one of the early successes of Sebastian Walker's publishing. They are similar in their humorous simplicity to the Cape board books of the 1970s (see p. 107) which are by Oxenbury's husband, John Burningham.

← *Princess Smartypants* Babette Cole (author and illustrator), Harmondsworth, Puffin Books, 1996, (Hamish Hamilton 1986). 229 x 194mm (9 x 7½in)
The official website of Babette Cole (b. 1950) shows a photo of a blonde woman with a toothy grin, amid a record of her achievements as an illustrator and equestrian. Her drawing and lettering brought a new style into children's books from 1976 onwards. This is a typical example of Puffin's picture-book publishing that was challenged by the rise of Walker Books.

The books published by Sebastian Walker had no single type of content and were deliberately diverse, but the years when he was working were marked by a number of successful books, by various publishers, which dealt in imaginative ways with the emotional problems of childhood. Much was written in the 1980s and '90s about adults adopting childish traits of behaviour and clothing, while children seemed, paradoxically, to grow up faster. It is difficult to discern yet whether this was a short-lived

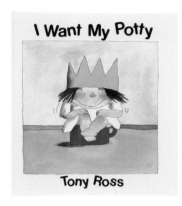

I Want My Potty
Tony Ross

fashion or a profound structural change in society dating from what is known as "the 'Me' decade". While children's writers of many periods have chosen themes involving complex interpersonal relationships, growing pains, and social problems, these became increasingly common as an alternative to pure fantasy, humour, or sentimentality that were dominant in earlier children's literature. The series of books by Lynne Reid Banks about Omri and a magic

cupboard that brings toys to life goes beyond simple magic to deal realistically with emotions about power, attachment, and responsibility, within a compelling and believable story line. A book such as *Princess Smartypants* reflects the feminist movement through humour, by reversing all the stereotypes long-beloved of little girls, while the dramas of everyday infant and child life, such as potty training and going to sleep, are dramatized by Tony Ross and Satoshi Kitamura with a humour that can take pressure off adults and children alike.

Posy Simmonds made her name as a cartoonist for the *Guardian*, depicting contemporary social life, before producing the first of a series of children's books with *Fred* in 1987. Her observant eye for social situations, in which the protagonists fail entirely to understand each other since each is preoccupied with their own thoughts, is found in *The Chocolate Wedding*, drawn in comic book format. Simmonds' newspaper cartoons owe much of their humour to a wicked observation of detail that children are also apt to notice and comment on with embarrassing effect. She has written, "I just go around looking at people. I'm incredibly nosy – so I take a good look at anything that catches my eye – someone's shoes, say, or eyebrows. Then I go home and get it down on paper."

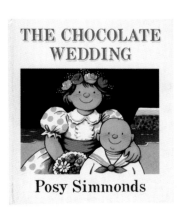

THE CHOCOLATE
WEDDING
Posy Simmonds

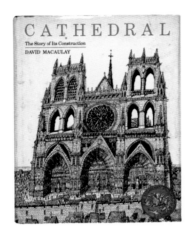

Walker Books began with non-fiction, but the publishing name most closely associated with illustrated factual publishing for children in the 1990s was Dorling Kinderlsey. Peter Kindersley (b. 1941) is the son of a distinguished letter-cutter and type designer, and was brought up with an awareness of the importance of design. He established his company in 1974 with the idea that most publishers failed to understand the way to link pictures and text in information books. In 1987, Kindersley began to publish for children, building on the experience of adult titles such as *Success with Houseplants*. He asked the question "Where are all the exciting books for kids?" and, not finding any, devised an immediately recognizable format for using photographs or drawings isolated against a white background, seen in the *Eyewitness* series. David Macaulay, the American author and illustrator who made his first impact in non-fiction children's books with *Cathedral* (1973) and similar books about the building of historic structures with clear line drawings, produced *The Way Things Work* (1988), which was highly successful in the USA, and led in 1992 to the beginning of a digital publishing partnership between Dorling Kindersley and Microsoft.

Dorling Kindersley were active at an early stage in publishing videos and computer disks. They also found unconventional ways to market books to schools and to parents with a strong sense of mission. The company became a favoured stock on the market after its public launch in 1992, but at the beginning of 2000 it was sold to Pearson following a dramatic fall in profits owing to an over-optimistic investment in *Star Wars* film tie-in books.

The 1990s are associated with J. K. Rowling's *Harry Potter* books, the first of which was published in 1994, but other authors had long been developing plots with a mixture of the fantastic, mythological, and humorous. Diana Wynne Jones (b. 1934), who began to publish in 1973, is outstanding for her ability to give the complexity and depth of real life to her plots and characters while

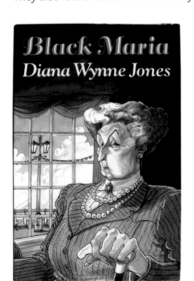

← *Cathedral* David Macaulay (author and illustrator), Boston, Houghton, Mifflin & Co., 1973.
312 x 237mm (12¼ x 9⅓in)
David Macauley was born in England but studied at the Rhode Island School of Design and settled in New England. The cover of *Cathedral* shows a typical drawing, in this case from the last page of the book, after the whole construction process has been graphically charted.

← *Stephen Beisty's Incredible Cross Sections* Richard Platt (author), Stephen Beisty (illustrator), London, Dorling Kindersley, 1992.
273 x 352mm (10¾ x 13⅓in)
The same image is repeated on the boards of the binding. The wrapper feels generous and has oversized flaps, a practical feature for a large quarto title and indicative of the attention to design in Dorling Kindersley books.

← *Black Maria* Diana Wynne Jones (author), Chris Riddell (jacket), London, Methuen, 1991. 205 x 120mm (8 x 4¾in)
Here is a crisp and spirited piece of cover artwork from a well-established illustrator of the 1990s, which does not give too much away about the story of a seaside town which is surreptitiously overtaken by witches.

keeping a story racing along in more than one parallel
world. Her books offer much to reward adult readers,
yet she has not benefited from the mainstream media
attention that has come to Rowling and Philip Pullman in
Britain and Lemony Snicket in the USA, who, to a greater
or lesser extent, have followed in her path.

Anthony Horowitz specializes in parody titles such as
The Falcon's Malteser (2002) and *South by South-East*
(2002), in which elements of famous films provide a basis
for wild narrative improvisation. For child readers, the origin of the plot may only be revealed
years later. Horowitz has also followed an increasing taste for horror stories in the 1990s which

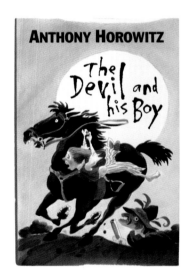

has brought to ever younger readers the thrills previously
reserved for grown-ups as part of the blurring of genre
boundaries between adults' and children's writing.

Part of the confusion comes from the widespread
taste for illustrated books among all ages, and the skills
of many talented artists waiting to be used. Sometimes
the conventions of the children's market are restrictive,
but a cult following can be generated by something
visually appealing and weird enough to catch on. Edward
Gorey (1925–2000) was not the originator of this kind of
cross-over book, but he perfected a visual presentation
for what might superficially appear as a children's book,
often with one line of text for each meticulous black-and-white image. In his study, *The Strange
Case of Edward Gorey* (2001), Alexander Theroux has called them "small and humorously sadistic
parodies of the obsolete Victorian 'triple-decker'", but he also notes the underlying seriousness
of Gorey's revelations of cruelty at work in everyday life, especially between children, as a
pressing contemporary issue.

Poetry for children was once associated with
sentimental or pastoral authors such as Robert Louis
Stevenson and Walter de la Mare, even though the latter
slyly confronted some serious metaphysical issues. Since
the 1970s, all that is past. Michael Rosen's *Mind Your Own
Business* (1974), recaptured the real voices of children and
their love of the nasty and crude. *Walking the Bridge of
Your Nose* is one of a considerable series of his publications.

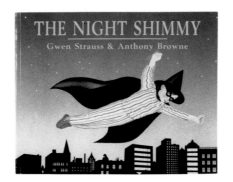

Comparing the 1890s and a hundred years later in a book of 1994, Kimberley Reynolds believed that it would be wrong to think that children's literature at the end of the 20th century was "on the way to becoming a bland and bogus international product. The truth is that the range and diversity of contemporary writing for children has never been greater. In every aspect of the juvenile publishing industry – from picture books through fantasy, history, myth, realist novels, adventure, mystery and so on and so on, innovative, stimulating, and impressive books for readers of all ages and abilities are being produced."

In the same year, however, children's poet Michael Rosen complained in a conference speech that the publishing world was now dominated by, "The inexorable anarchy of capitalism... more titles, more authors, quick, quick, write write, no time to edit, no time to rewrite, get it out, sell it, drop it, pulp it" – the last is a reference to the continuing practice of scrapping of old stock owing to growing costs of keeping copies in the warehouse.

In this world the cover may be crucial to the marketing success of a book. The celebrated commissioning editor David Fickling in London likes his author-illustrators to think of a title first, and then think

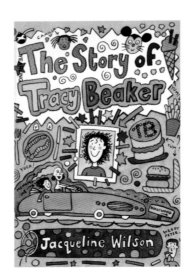

of a book to go with it. As in adult publishing, the cover is proposed by editors and in-house design directors, but often disposed of by the sales force who attempt to predict the reactions of buyers who will probably never read the book.

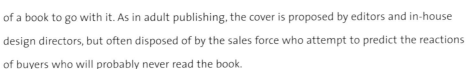

Not all successful children's books of this period have relied on the kind of comfortable nostalgic background that counteracts the fears and insecurities evoked in *Harry Potter*. On the level of a picture book, Anthony Browne (b. 1946) shows aspects of the meticulous craftsmanship of Nicola Bayley and the nostalgia of the Ahlbergs, combined with a preference for getting under the emotional skin of situations, as seen in *The Night Shimmy*, a title that belies the accusations that books of the John Major years in Britain were as bland and

← *The Night Shimmy* Gwen Strauss (author), Anthony Browne (illustrator), "A Red Fox Picture Book" (Random House), 1993. 215 x 260mm (8½ x 10¼in)
Autism among children, and its less severe form of Asperger's Syndrome, became part of common knowledge during the 1990s. This is a tale of a boy who won't speak except through the mask of a secret and imaginary friend. The cover captures some of the delight of a retreat to inward fantasy, although in the end Eric gets a real friend. *The Night Shimmy* was originally published in 1991 by Julia MacRae, whose imprint was linked to Walker Books.

← *The Story of Tracy Beaker* Jacqueline Wilson (author), Nick Sharratt (illustrator), London, Corgi Yearling, 1992. 194 x 130mm (7⅓ x 5in)
First published in 1991, Tracy Beaker has become a bestselling classic with a cleverly delivered message that applies to growing up in any situation.

← *M.O.L.E.* Russell Hoban (author), Jan Pieńkowski (illustrator), London, Walker Books, 1993. 290 x 230mm (11⅖ x 9in)
Although we may be used to Pieńkowski as an optimistic portrayer of brightly coloured fantasy worlds, the mood in this title is very different. *M.O.L.E.* reveals that the progressive stages of the collapse of "civilization" as we know it have a fascination of their own, and prove that everything is subject to change and transformation.

→ **The Iron Woman** Ted Hughes (author),
Andrew Davidson (illustrator), London,
Faber & Faber, 1993.
240 x 161mm (9½ x 6⅜in)
Andrew Davidson has joined the
relatively small number of artists
practising wood engraving at the
highest level at the end of the 20th
century. The ability of this medium to
portray contrasts of light and dark is
specially well used in the cover of Ted
Hughes's sequel to *The Iron Man*,
published by Faber – who are also the
publishers of Hughes's poetry, but
otherwise no longer specialize in
children's books.

→ **Coming to England** Floella Benjamin
(author), Michael Frith (illustrator),
London, Pavilion Books, 1995.
197 x 264mm (7¾ x 10⅜in)
During the 1990s and beyond, there
was a conscious effort to help the Afro-
Caribbean population of Britain tell its
own story about arrival in the 1950s in a
strange and not always friendly land.
This book forms part of a much broader
cultural trend.

→ **Holes** Louis Sachar (author), Nathan
Burton (cover design), London,
Bloomsbury, 2000.
196 x 129mm (7¾ x 5in)
The cover uses two photographs of
desert and sky, with the addition of a
deadly yellow-spotted lizard that plays
its part in the story of a boy unfairly
committed to a correctional camp in
Texas. First published by Frances Foster
Books in New York in 1998, *Holes* has
become a new classic in Britain as well.

risk-averse as the prime minister. Jacqueline Wilson's
Tracey Beaker books have been hugely successful,
although their setting in a children's home, seen through
the experiences of a disturbed but self-aware twelve-
year-old, does not seem to be an easy selling proposition.
The bright candy-coloured cover to what is otherwise a
black-and-white book is in a cartoon style which reflects
an underlying brightness in what might otherwise be a
rather bleak situation.

There is nothing about being a children's book writer
or illustrator that prevents engagement in current issues
of profound importance. In some cases, in fact, a children's story or illustrated book presents a
good opportunity for saying something important that, if said directly, would lose its impact or

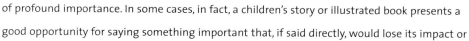

sound sanctimonious or preachy. Although
successful books about serious issues are
relatively rare, the poet Ted Hughes's pair of
linked titles, *The Iron Man* (1968) and *The Iron
Woman*, (1993), created powerful images on the
theme of environmental destruction and its
consequences. *M.O.L.E.* is a book that crosses
the adult-child divide that might have come
from the 1960s had its vision of complete ecological breakdown been envisaged then. Jan
Piećkowski made the drawings, Russell Hoban, who wrote his own post-nuclear disaster book,
Ridley Walker, for adults, added the text, and Sebastian Walker published it as a gesture of
loyalty to a distinguished author and illustrator.

Issues of immigration and race have become
unavoidable in both British and American society since
the 1960s, and educationalists and publishers see the
need to work harder to overcome prejudice and build
self-confidence among minority communities. The
immigration theme is immediately apparent in the cover
of Floella Benjamin's *Coming to England*. Louis Sachar's
Holes is another story that touches on immigration
issues, not in a factual way, but as part of a story that is
part fantasy, part detective novel, and part a symbolic
tale about endurance.

English nostalgia
Ian Beck & Nicola Bayley

The detailed and meticulous talent of Nicola Bayley (b. 1949) was spotted when she showed her illustrations for *One Old Oxford Ox*, a tongue-twisting alliterative counting rhyme, at the graduation show of the Royal College of Art. She has always been able to create the impression of a completely real but separate world on the page of a book, filled with detail. Tom Mashchler of Jonathan Cape immediately saw the potential of the work, which had a dreamy realism similar to Alan Aldridge, although meticulously worked by hand rather than airbrushed, and consequently rewarding a longer and deeper look. Later, Bayley was one of the star illustrators pleased to be wooed by Sebastian Walker, who offered her the opportunity to produce the small format books she felt were more suitable to her gifts but which Cape believed would not represent value for money. In fact, *The Mousehole Cat*, one of her best-known creations, is not particularly small, but was a product of this happy association.

Ian Beck (b. 1947) belongs to the same generation of illustrators who found a ready outlet in the 1980s and '90s for work that is typically nostalgic and English in flavour. He has led a double life, performing with the artist Glynn Boyd Harte in a cabaret duo called *Les Frères Perverts*, which involves mainly French material. Ian Beck is happy to acknowledge the influence of Harold Jones and Edward Ardizzone in his use of line and wash and, since beginning the production of picture books on themes of his own invention, he has developed a strong feeling for creating a narrative like a storyboard for a film. Beck draws with a deliberately shaky ink line, but this is the last element to be added to the drawings which are first built up in colour. His lettering on the cover of *Emily and the Golden Acorn* is skilful in the manner of artists of an earlier generation.

↑ *One Old Oxford Ox* Nicola Bayley (illustrator), London, Jonathan Cape, 1977. 235 x 194mm (9¼ x 7⅔in)
The animals in the traditional rhyme are all gathered together on the cover as if for the finale of some old-fashioned variety show in a winter garden of an Edwardian spa. The format is typical of Jonathan Cape's "picture flats" that were a feature of 1970s publishing.

← *The Mousehole Cat* Antonia Barber (author), Nicola Bayley (illustrator), London, Walker Books, 1990. 230 x 230mm (9 x 9in)
The Mousehole Cat was a handsome buckram-bound hardback on its first appearance (shown here), with a jacket illustrated on the back and front. The inset panel represents Nicola Bayley's yearning to work on a miniature scale.

→ *Oranges and Lemons* Karen King
(compiler), Ian Beck (illustrator), Oxford,
Oxford University Press, 1985.
263 x 205mm (10¹/₃ x 8in)
Ian Beck draws the cover of the book on
the cover, with the implication of an
infinite regression of miniatures contained
in each other. The imagery helps to convey
the idea that this is a book of party
games and songs, a sequel to Beck's
Round and Round the Garden (1983).

↓ *Little Miss Muffet* Ian Beck (author
and illustrator) Oxford, Oxford University
Press, 1988. 261 x 205mm (8¹/₂ x 8in)
Following the success of the rhyme
books, this was Beck's first complete
story, borrowing the idea of a theatre for
its cover, appropriate in its suggestion
that the show inside the book is about
to begin. The typographer has had fun
with italic "swash capitals", a letterform
devised in the 18th century for giving
initial letters a special flourish.

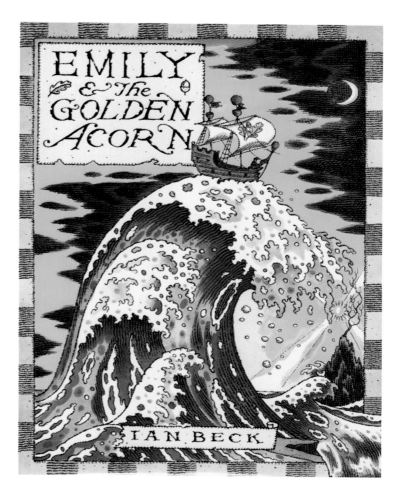

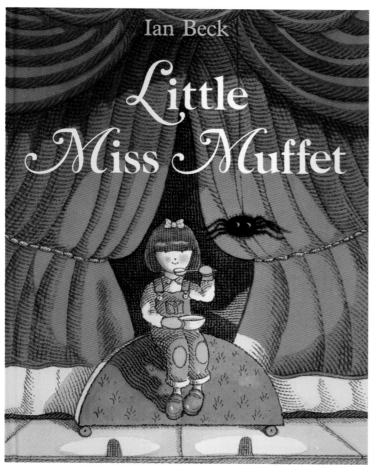

↑ *Emily and the Golden Acorn* Ian Beck
(author and illustrator), London,
Doubleday 1992.
285 x 220mm (11²/₃ x 8²/₃in)
Beck is interested in the layout of the
page, with devices like the framed border
seen here, out of which the picture spills.
The wave in this cover illustration has
been borrowed from the famous
Japanese artist Hokusai (1760–1849).

← *The Oxford Nursery Book* Ian Beck
(author and illustrator), Oxford, Oxford
University Press, 1995.
270 x 208mm (10²/₃ x 8²/₃in)
The influence of Harold Jones's classic
Lavender's Blue (see p. 59) is particularly
apparent in the English summer evening
scene on Beck's cover.

Children's books make news
The Harry Potter phenomenon

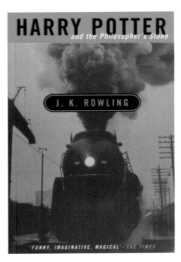

← *Harry Potter and the Philosopher's Stone*
J. K. Rowling (author), Thomas Taylor
(jacket illustration), London, Bloomsbury,
1997. 206 x 135mm (8 x 5⅓in)
The cover of the first Harry Potter book
fixed the appearance of the most
famous boy in fiction.

← *Harry Potter and the Philosopher's Stone*
J. K. Rowling (author), Winston Link
(cover photograph), London, Bloomsbury,
1998. 197 x 128mm (7¾ x 5in)
The black-and-white cover for the adult
edition alludes to the Hogwarts Express.

↓ *Northern Lights* Philip Pullman (author),
London, Scholastic Children's Books,
1995. 222 x 139mm (8¾ x 5⅓in)
The cover to the first in the trilogy is a
conventional fantasy illustration.

First published in Britain by Bloomsbury, the media furore surrounding
J.K. Rowling's *Harry Potter and the Philosopher's Stone* began around the
time the second book, *Harry Potter and the Chamber of Secrets*, was published
in 1997. Parents, teachers, and publishers were all delighted with books
that children absolutely demanded to read, while its edition with an
"adult" cover meant that adults did not have to feel ashamed of being seen
reading it. The American commentator Jack Zipes attributes the success
of these books to "institutional changes of education, shifts in family
relations, the rise of corporate conglomerates controlling the mass media,
and market demands." Other books in the fantasy genre have benefited,
including Philip Pullman's trilogy and Philip Reeve's first novel *Mortal
Engines*. "Lemony Snicket" was almost invented as a media event, since
the real author has cultivated a complex mask of anonymity that has
helped to promote these small hardback texts which have an exaggerated
sense of doom and post-modern reference worthy of Edward Gorey.

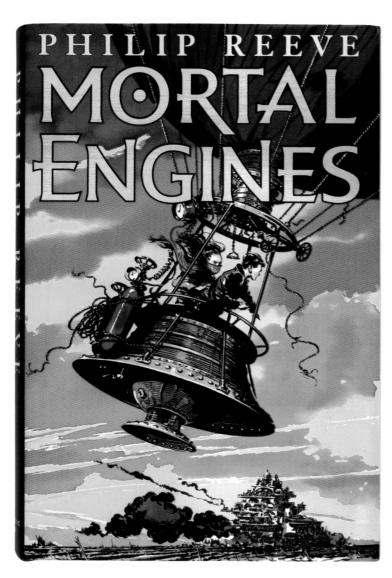

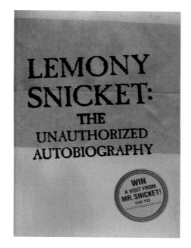

← *Lemony Snicket: The Unauthorized Autobiography* "Lemony Snicket" (author), London, HarperCollins, 2002. 184 x 130mm (7¼ x 5in)
Every publishing success is now followed by the "tie-in" publications, such as this, which fill the gaps between the appearances of the main titles. The reversible jacket is perhaps the best aspect of this cod memoir. The blurb begins: "The book you are holding in your hands is extremely dangerous."

↓ *The Unauthorized Autobiography: The Pony Party* Loney M. Setnick (author), London, HarperCollins, 2002. 184 x 130mm (7¼ x 5in)
When the jacket of Lemony Snicket's autobiography is reversed, it presents a reversal of his own book series, parodying a children's story of fifty years before, complete with an author photo and a letter to the reader.

↑ *Mortal Engines* Philip Reeve (author), David Frankland (jacket), London, Scholastic Children's Books, 2001. 220 x 144mm (8⅔ x 5⅔in)
Philip Reeve is himself an illustrator, but the cover design for his first book is an effective snapshot from an action-packed fantasy of a dystopian future society with echoes of Fritz Lang's *Metropolis*.

→ *A Series of Unfortunate Events: Book the First, The Bad Beginning* "Lemony Snicket" (author), illustrated by Brett Helquist, London, Egmont Books, 2001. 184 x 131mm (7¼ x 5in)
Originated by HarperCollins in 1999, the Lemony Snicket books are successful on both sides of the Atlantic. The formula is akin to other fantasies with a generic Victorian setting, but the packaging is skilful, with a hardback smaller than usual in size and a pleasing page of type. The imitation quarter binding, with patterned endpapers carrying their own bookplate, adds to the effect.

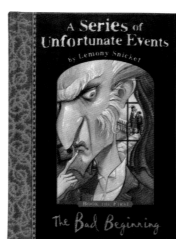

Funny haha and funny peculiar

The children's book as a novelty, rather than just a text, has a history going back to the 18th century, with episodes recurring at intervals. Peter Newell's *The Hole Book* (1908 – see title page), was one instance of a direct link between the book's content and the physical form. In the digital age, one of the advantages of a real book is its tactile quality. Unlike watching a screen, you turn a page of a book by hand, and the book lends itself to various forms of handling and manipulation. There is nothing new in this, but it is satisfying to find that such techniques keep returning and keep giving pleasure. Vladimir Radunsky takes this to an extreme normally only found either in books for very young children or in sophisticated "artists' books" that often resemble them. The idea of learning through the recognition of simple geometrical shapes has an ancestry in the earliest existing theories of education.

In 1988, Joyce Irene Whalley and Tessa Rose Chester ended their *History of Children's Book Illustration* with an anxiety that the result of commercial pressures in illustration might produce "a plethora of mediocre work with slapdash scribbles, or else thin texts supporting paintings that would be better placed in an art gallery." It is hard to think of many books that equal the quality of the best of earlier periods, but it is perhaps too easy to regret the old days with half-closed eyes. This page shows three American books for very young children that refer to traditions of different kinds but present them with a fresh look and are as well produced physically as one could wish. In *This is the House that Jack Built*, Simms Taback even refers to Randolph Caldecott, one of many artists who illustrated this traditional rhyme, and gives him a guest appearance at the end of the book. *I Love Going Through This Book* begins with a cut-away jacket over laminated boards which reinforces the idea of the title.

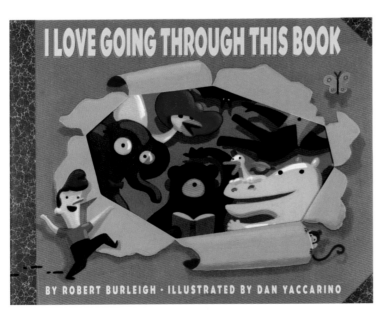

↑ *The House that Jack Built* Simms Taback (illustrator), New York, Putnam, 2002. 286 x 225mm (11¼ x 8⅘in)
The cover, although apparently roughly painted, is carefully balanced in tone and colour. The endpapers continue the idea about the house being for sale, and the back cover has house-building tools.

← *I Love Going Through This Book* Robert Burleigh (author), Dan Yaccarino (illustrator), New York, Joanna Cotler Books, 2001. 210 x 261mm (8¼ x 10¼in)
The idea of actually going into a book has a long life (see *The Hole Book* on the title page). This will lose something in paperback, unless the outer cover can be cut away as the jacket is here.

← *Square Triangle Round Skinny* Vladimir Radunsky (illustrator), Cambridge, Massachusetts, Candlewick Press, 2002. 176 x 160mm (7 x 2⅗in)
Four differently shaped board books are presented in a plastic box. Combining a book and a toy has been part of children's publishing since the time of John Newbery in the mid-18th century.

Conclusion

Children's stories need an ending, but a book about children's books fortunately cannot have one since the books keep appearing and anything may be around the next corner. One interesting development in cover construction, observed during the time the present book was being written, is to make a binding case that is split down the middle of the front board and sealed with a peel-off sticker. This is the style of the UK edition of *Lemony Snicket: The Unauthorized Autobiography* and is evidence of a willingness to try new styles.

The success of *Harry Potter* shows that presentation does not necessarily make a difference to the success of a book. In an earlier generation, the *Harry Potter* books would probably have been illustrated with line drawings at least at the head of each chapter, and the cover would have been an extension of the same style and range of characters, but the readers do not seem to have worried about its absence. The covers may even be nothing special as graphics, although the original artwork for *Harry Potter and the Philosopher's Stone* was sold at auction for £85,000, so this is evidently a matter on which opinions vary.

In two particular ways, the significance of the cover as a symbolic stand-in for the book itself has increased in recent years. Now that books, both old and new, are increasingly bought over the Internet, the closest the prospective purchaser can come to a tangible object is an electronic image of the cover. A buyer handling a copy in a shop can get a more complete feel of a book, both in terms of content and physical presentation, but the cover now has to attempt to carry more subliminal information in a way that could be detrimental to its independence as a

design, or its capacity to interpret the book on more subtle levels. As if in imitation of the Internet, newspapers and magazines now increasingly print a postage-stamp sized reproduction of the book cover to accompany a review. Subtle, complex, or highly detailed cover designs cannot stand up well under these conditions, and it would be distressing to think that they should be relegated to being a thing of the past. However, history shows that everything in children's books goes in waves. What is fashionable one year inspires imitations but, when these have eroded the distinctiveness of the original idea, it is time to try something quite different, so one should not worry that any trend will last for long.

History can also provide inspiration. Looking back over the history of children's book covers, one can regret the passing of older technologies that gave a human touch to the work, whether these were the hand-colouring of the Regency period or the printing of a wood engraving for a chapbook in a hand press. Today, the means for designing illustration and typography to a high level of complexity are widely available. Full colour printing has never been cheaper, but these rich resources are only as good as the vision of the artist or designer controlling them. Fifty years ago, one feels that it was easier to design a cover that would attract attention, since there was so much less competition, not only from books, but from all the other forms of visual stimulation.

The science of marketing and selling children's books may have developed since the time of John Newbery, but fortunately there is still room for diverse approaches, as a visit to any book shop will make clear. Many old covers and binding styles can also be found among the new ones, showing how the inspired guesswork of the past often produced a winning formula. A book cover may seem an unimportant accessory for the proper material of a book, or a collector's fetish that overvalues scarcity without leading to historical understanding. It can, however, be a work of wonder with its own meaning. This makes covers something worth appreciating and thinking about, both in the past and the future.

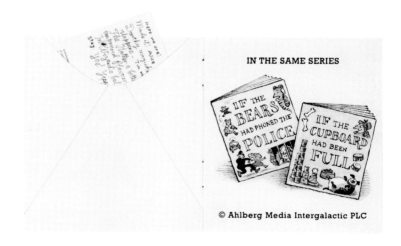

↑ *If The Tyre Had Not Been Flat* Allan Ahlberg (author), Janet Ahlberg (illustrator), London, William Heinemann, 1995. 96 x 96mm (3¾ x 3¾in)
This booklet is the final loose insertion in the Ahlberg's *The Jolly Pocket Postman*. On the small scale of a traditional chapbook, it uses frivolous references to other stories in a manner that has a long history in children's publishing. The final opening has the covers of other imaginary books in "the same series" as a familiar way of ending a book, and suggests other rewritings of traditional tales. The booklet imitates its parent book by having its own envelope pocket, containing a postcard from Lewis Carroll's Alice and Frank Baum's Dorothy.

Bibliography

General

Alderson, Brian, *Sing a Song for Sixpence, The English Picture Book Tradition and Randolph Caldecott*, Cambridge, Cambridge University Press in association with the British Library, 1986

Bland, David, *A History of Book Illustration*, London, Faber & Faber, 1958

British Council, *Magic Pencil, Children's Book Illustration Today*, (selected by Quentin Blake with essay by Joanna Carey), London, The British Council, 2002

Carter, James, *Talking Books: Children's Authors talk about the craft, creativity and process of writing*, London and New York, Routledge, 1999

Connolly, Joseph, Children's *Modern First Editions: their value to collectors*, London, Macdonald Orbis, 1988

Carpenter, Humphrey, *Secret Gardens, A Study of the Golden Age of Children's Literature*, London, Allen & Unwin, 1985

Carpenter, Humphrey; and Mari Prichard, *The Oxford Companion to Children's Literature*, Oxford, Oxford University Press, 1984

Cott, Jonathan, *Pipers at the Gates of Dawn, The Wisdom of Children's Literature*, London, Viking, 1984

Crouch, Marcus, *Treasure Seekers and Borrowers: Children's Books in Britain 1900-1960*, London, The Library Association, 1962

Dalby, Richard, *The Golden Age of Children's Book Illustration*, London, Michael O'Mara Books Ltd., 1991

Darling, Howard, *From Mother Goose to Dr Seuss, Children's Book Covers 1860-1960*, San Francisco, Chronicle Books, 1999

Darton, F. J. Harvey (revised by Brian Alderson), *Children's Books in England: Five Centuries of Social Life*, London, The British Library, 1995 (Revised Third Edition)

Egoff, Sheila; G. T. Stubbs and L. F. Ashley, *Only Connect, Readings on Children's Literature*, Toronto/New York, Oxford University Press, 1980

Eyre, Frank, *20th Century Children's Books*, London, Longmans, Green & Co. for the British Council, 1952; expanded as *British Children's Books in the Twentieth Century*, London, Longman, 1971

Felmingham, Michael, *The Illustrated Gift Book*, Aldershot, Scholar Press, 1988

Hearn, Michael Patrick; Tinckett Clark and H. Nichols B. Clark, *Myth, Magic, and Mystery, One Hundred Years of American Children's Book Illustration*, Boulder, Colorado, Roberts Rinehart Publishers, in association with The Chrysler Museum of Art, Norfolk, Virginia, 1996

Horne, Alan, *The Dictionary of 20th Century British Book Illustrators*, Woodbridge, Antique Collectors' Club, 1994

Hunt, Peter, ed., *Children's Literature, an illustrated history*, Oxford/New Tork, Oxford University Press, 1995

Hürlimann, Bettina, *Three Centuries of Children's Books in Europe* (translated by Brian Alderson), London, Oxford University Press, 1967

Jacques, Robin, *Illustrators at Work*, London, Studio Books, 1963

Kingman, Lee; Joanna Foster and Ruth Giles Lontoft, compilers, *Illustrators of Children's Books, 1957-1966*, Boston, The Horn Book Inc., 1968

Kirkpatrick, David L., ed. *Twentieth Century Children's Writers*, London, Macmillan, 1978 (and subsequent editions)

Lewis, John, *The Twentieth Century Book*, London, Studio Vista, 1967

Mahony, Bertha E.; Louise Payson Latimer and Beulah Folmsbee, *Illustrators of Children's Books 1744–1945*, Boston, The Horn Book Inc, 1947

McLean, Ruari, *Victorian Book Design and Colour Printing*, London, Faber and Faber, 1972

McLean, Ruari, *Victorian Publishers' Book-Bindings in Paper*, London, Gordon Fraser, 1983

Martin, Douglas, *The Telling Line, Essays on Fifteen Contemporary Book Illustrators*, London, Julia MacRae Books, 1989

Horn Book Papers Series, published by The Horn Book Inc., Boston:
No.1 Miller, Bertha Mahony and Elinor Whitley Field, eds., *Newbery Medal Books 1922–1955*, 1955
No.2 Miller, Bertha Mahony and Elinor Whitley Field, eds., *Caldecott Medal Books: 1938–1957*, 1957
Kingman, Lee, ed., *Newbery and Caldecott Medal Books: 1956–1965*, 1965; *Newbery and Caldecott Medal Books: 1966–1975*, 1975; *Newbery and Caldecott Medal Books: 1976–1985*, 1985

Muir, Percy, *English Children's Books*, London, B. T. Batsford Ltd., 1985 (Fourth Impression)

Opie, Iona and Peter, *A Nursery Companion*, Oxford, Oxford University Press, 1980

Opie, Iona; and Robert and Brian Alderson, *The Treasures of Childhood: Books, Toys and Games from the Opie Collection*, London, Pavilion Books Ltd., in association with Michael Joseph, 1989

Reynolds, Kimberley and Tucker, Nicholas, eds., *Children's Book Publishing in Britain since 1945*, Aldershot, Scolar Press, 1998

Rustin, Margaret and Michael, *Narratives of Love and Loss: Studies in Modern Children's Fiction*, London/New York, H. Karnac, 2001 (Revised Edition)

Smith, Lillian H., *The Unreluctant Years*, Chicago, The American Library Association, 1953

Toronto Pubic Library (The Osborne Collection of Early Children's Books), *Plain and Fancy, An Exhibition of Book Covers and Bindings*, (catalogue) 2001

Townsend, John Rowe, *Written for Children*, London, The Bodley Head, 1995 (Sixth Edition)

Viguers, R.H.; Marcia Dalphin and Bertha Mahoney Miller, *Illustrators of Children's Books 1946-1956*, Boston, The Horn Book, 1958

Whalley, Joyce Irene, and Chester, Tessa Rose, *A History of Children's Book Illustration*, London, John Murray with the Victoria and Albert Museum, 1988

Zipes, Jack, *Sticks and Stones: The Troublesome Success of Children's Literature from Slovenly Peter to Harry Potter*, London, Routledge, 2001

Monographs

Alderson, Brian, *Edward Ardizzone, a Bibliographic Commentary*, Pinner, The Private Libraries Association, 2003

Alderson, Brian, *Ezra Jack Keats: Artist and Picture-Book Maker*, Gretna, Louisiana, Pelican Publishing Company, Vol. I, 1994; Vol. II, 2002

Avery-Quash, Susanna, "The Most Beautiful Delightful Wonderful Fairy Tale Books, All Printed with Pictures": *The Contribution of Henry Cole's Home Treasury Series to Children's Books*, Toronto, Toronto Public Library, 1997

Cecil, Mirabel, *Sebastian Walker 1942–91: A Kind of Prospero*, London, Walker Books, 1995

Hale, Kathleen, *A Slender Talent*, London, Frederick Warne,1998

Hammond, Wayne G., *Arthur Ransome, a Bibliography*, Winchester/New Castle Delaware, Oak Knoll Press, 2000

Hughes, Shirley, *A Life Drawing, Recollections of an Illustrator*, London, The Bodley Head, 2002

Lanes, Selma G., *The Art of Maurice Sendak*, New York, Harry N. Abrams Inc., 1980

Smith, Brian, *Rupert: The Rupert Bear Dossier*, London, Hawk Books, 1997

Theroux, Alexander, *The Strange Case of Edward Gorey*, Seattle, Fantagraphics Books, 2000

White, Gabriel, *Edward Ardizzone*, London, The Bodley Head, 1979

Articles

Carrington, Noel, "A Century for Puffin Picture Books", *Penrose Annual* Vol.51, 1957, pp.62–64

Lock, Margaret, "Bindings on Nineteenth Century Children's Books", *Canadian Bookbinders and Book Artists' Guild Newsletter,* Winter 2002, pp.3–15

Thomas, David, "Children's Book illustration in England", *Penrose Annual,* 56, 1962, pp.67–74

Index

Acknowledgments

To my godchildren: Oliver, Richard, Agnes, Imogen, Stephen, and William.

Author's Note and Acknowledgments

An explanation of the selection principles for a book of this kind should be offered to the reader. The possible range is vast, and the first decision made was that the book should combine British and American examples, with a small representation of European ones. Much more from continental Europe could justifiably have been included, but the depth in other areas would have been diminished and Europe itself could constitute another survey of this kind. Although the story carries through from the 1770s to the present, the period before 1914 was somewhat compressed, in relation to the later decades, in order to bring the examples closer to most readers' own experience of children's books.

Within this chronological and geographical field, at least three approaches offered themselves. Selections could be made primarily on grounds of design quality, in order to represent the history of publishing and book production, or in order to show the designs that have been found on the covers of books by the best-known authors regardless of quality. What has resulted is a mixture of each approach, with some bias towards personal favourites and a fondness for the odd and unusual. I am aware of many gaps in all respects, and apologize to readers who find that artists, authors, or individual books they particularly value are missing. We couldn't fit everything in, even if we could have obtained the pictures in the time and within the constraints of a pretty generous budget.

Book jackets and covers are under-explored areas partly because it is hard to find examples. Reference libraries, which one would depend on to provide books for study, do not normally keep loose dust jackets, and, even though many children's books have designs as part of their binding, this is less often the case with examples from the mid-twentieth century. One exception is the Osborne and Lilian H. Smith Collection of Children's Books in the Toronto Public Library, where jackets are valued as they should be. I am grateful to the librarian, Leslie McGrath, and her staff for helping me on a too-brief visit. For the rest, it has been necessary to rely on the kindness of private collectors and dealers. We have been very fortunate in this respect, with a majority of the books coming from a single source, supplemented by other specific requests, answered with great speed and courtesy by those involved.

Dimensions of books have been provided, since the relative scales at which they are reproduced are not consistent. Height is followed by width, and the latter is the overall bulk of the book, which in some cases escapes accurate measurement. These dimensions should therefore be treated as indicative. Publication details are as complete as seemed appropriate for a general survey of this kind, but in some cases there are further levels of complexity that required further elucidation.

I am grateful to Brian Alderson, one of the most eminent authorities in the history and criticism of children's books, for his help and advice on many points. Any deficiencies in selection, errors of fact, or doubtful interpretations are my own, but without him there would have been many more. Finally, I am most grateful to the team at Mitchell Beazley who have worked on this book, specially to Emily Asquith and Emma O'Neill, and to Roger Dixon who took the majority of the photographs.

AP

Picture Acknowledgments

Mitchell Beazley would like to thank those publishers credited alongside each illustrated book cover who have kindly given permission to publish copyright images. In some cases ownership has changed since original publication and we would also like to acknowledge and thank those additional individuals and publishers credited below who have supplied material or granted permission. Where we have been unable to make contact with the copyright holders we would welcome any information concerning the ownership of copyright images not acknowledged. Special thanks to Jo Ann Reisler and her husband, and to Stella and Rose's Books for kindly supplying images from their collections and valuable information. Thanks also to Leonora and Anne Excell at Bookmark Children's Books, Don and Sue Gallagher at the Gallagher Collection, and Sue Bell at Green Meadows Books for kindly supplying images and books from their collections.

Key t top **b** bottom **l** left **c** centre **r** right **OPG** Octopus Publishing Group

James Wall-Wild, Books by Netsifters 100 c HarperCollins Inc; **Ruth Allen of Bufo Books, Hampshire** 44 c The Random House Group Ltd; **Cotsen Children's Library. Department of Rare Books and Special Collections. Princeton University Library** 85 tr © 1951, renewed 1979 by Random House Inc. Used by permission of Golden Books, an imprint of Random House Children's Books, a division of Random House Inc, 89 tr Harcourt Inc, 95 b; **Sue Bell, Green Meadow Books** 44 t Hamlyn Books, 78 tl, 79 tl Hamlyn Books, tr, bl cover image as taken from The Castle of Adventure by Enid Blyton and illustrated by Stuart Tresilian 1946, by permission of Macmillan Children's Books, London & br Sampson Low Ltd. All Enid Blyton covers reproduced by kind permission of Enid Blyton Ltd (A Chorion Company); **Adrian Harrington Rare Books** 81 bl © C S Lewis 1950. Illustrations by Pauline Baynes © C S Lewis Pte Ltd. Illustrations reprinted by permission of C S Lewis & HarperCollins Publishers Ltd; **OPG/Roger Dixon** 5 HarperCollins Inc, 6 b, 7, 10 t, c, 11 t, c, b, 13 t All Arthur Rackham pictures are reproduced with the kind permission of his family/The Bridgeman Art Library, 14 t, bl, br, 15 tl, tc, tr, bl, 16 t, bl, br, 17 tl, tr, bl Sampson Low Ltd, br, 19 t, bl, bc, br, 20 t The Orion Publishing Group, b The Random House Group Ltd, 21 cl The Random House Group Ltd, r Kingfisher Publications Plc, bl Sampson Low Ltd, br, 22 t, bl, br, 23 tl, tr cover of An Alphabet by William Nicholson (William Heinemann 1898) (c) Elizabeth Banks, bl The Random House Group Ltd, br by permission of Sir Henry Brooke, 24 bl The Wind in the Willows by Kenneth Grahame, illustrated by E H Shepard. Jacket colour plate © 1959 E.H. Shepard, reproduced by kind permission of Curtis Brown Ltd, London, br, 25 tl Egmont Books Ltd, tr All Rights Reserved. Reproduced by permission of Scholastic UK Ltd, Wild Wood cover illustration © Andrew Kulman 1993, bl & br Egmont Books Ltd, 26 t (c) Frederick Warne & Co 1908, bl (c) Frederick Warne & Co 1902, br (c) Frederick Warne & Co 1909, 27 tl (c) Frederick Warne & Co 1905, tr (c) Frederick Warne & Co 1908 & br Illustration (c) Frederick Warne & Co 1930. All reproduced by permission of Frederick Warne & Co, 28 t, b, 29 tl, tr, bl, br reproduction permitted courtesy of Bloomsbury Publications Plc. Illustration (c) John Bendall-Brunello, 30 t, bl, bc reproduced by permission of Frederick Warne & Co, br, 31 tl reproduced by permission of Frederick Warne & Co, tr, bl, bc, 32 tl, tr reproduced by permission of Frederick Warne & Co, c, b cover from The Owl and the Pussycat © 1991 Louise Voce. Reproduced by permission of Walker Books Ltd, London, 33 tr, bl cover image as taken from The Hunting of the Snark by Lewis Carroll and illustrated by Henry Holiday 1876, by permission of Macmillan Children's Books, London, br Alice's Adventures in Wonderland illustrated and abridged by Tony Ross, published by Andersen Press Ltd, London, 34 tl & tc The Random House Group Ltd, b, 35 tl, tr, br, 36 tl, tr, b, 37 tl, tr, c, bc, br, 38, 40 b © The Estate of Cicely Mary Barker 1925, reproduced by permission of Frederick Warne & Co, 41 t Bookmark Children's Books. Egmont Books Ltd, c, b, 42 c, b, 43 t Kingfisher Publications Plc, 43 b & 44 b Bookmark Children's Books. Kingfisher Publications Plc, 45 t, b Egmont Books Ltd, 46 t, c The Random House Group Ltd, b, 47 t Kingfisher Publications Plc, c, b Pearson Education, 48 t, b Private Collection, 49 tl cover of The Pirate Twins by William Nicholson (Faber & Faber, 1929) © Elizabeth Banks, bl, br The Culture Archive, by kind permission of The Wanda Gág Estate, 50 t & b Hachette Jeunesse, 51 tl, 51 tr © Kathleen Hale 1949, c © Kathleen Hale 1942, bl Bookmark Children's Books © Kathleen Hale 1939 & br © Kathleen Hale 1952. All reproduced by permission of Frederick Warne & Co, 53 tr Sampson Low Ltd, bl & br Bookmark Children's Books. © Express Newspapers, 54 t, bl, br, 55 tl, tr The Lutterworth Press Ltd, bl, br, 56 t & bl The Random House Group Ltd, br, 57 t, bl & br The Random House Group Ltd, 58 t © 1937 Estate of Harold Jones, Walter de la Mare, illustrated by Harold Jones, Faber & Faber, bl © 1937 Estate of Harold Jones, M E Atkinson, illustrated by Harold Jones, The Bodley Head/The Random House Group Ltd & br © 1958 Estate of Harold Jones, William Blake, illustrated by Harold Jones, permissions granted by the author's Estate,

59 tl, 59 tr © 1947 Estate of Harold Jones, Faber & Faber & bl © 1961 Estate of Harold Jones, Charles Kingsley, illustrated by Harold Jones, Gollancz/The Orion Publishing Group, permissions granted by the author's Estate, 61 tl © 1939 by Virginia Lee Burton, renewed 1967 by Virginia Lee Demetrios. Reprinted by permission of Houghton Mifflin Company. All rights reserved , tr Don & Sue Gallagher, The Gallagher Collection. From Abraham Lincoln (Jacket Cover) by Ingri & Edgar Parin d'Aulaire. Used by permission of Random House Children's Books, a division of Random House Inc, c & cl Bookmark Children's Books, br, 62 © 1964 Estate of Edward Ardizzone, The Bodley Head/The Random House Group Ltd, permission granted by the author's Estate, 64 t, b, 65 t, c, b The Random House Group Ltd, 66 t reproduced by kind permission of SPCK, c, b, 67 t, b, 68 t, c, b, 69 t, c The Culture Archive, b The Culture Archive. Egmont Books Ltd, 70 b Egmont Books Ltd, 71 t, c, 72 t, c, b, 73 tl, tr, bl, br, 74 tl, tc, tr & b The Random House Group Ltd, 75 tl, tr, bl, br, 76 t © 1936 Estate of Edward Ardizzone, Oxford University Press, bl © 1947 Estate of Edward Ardizzone, Noel Langley, illustrated by Edward Ardizzone, & br © 1948 Estate of Edward Ardizzone, Cecil Day Lewis, illustrated by Edward Ardizzone, Putnam & Co, permissions granted by the author's Estate, 77 tl © 1963 Estate of Edward Ardizzone, Clive King, illustrated by Edward Ardizzone, Penguin, tr © 1965 Estate of Edward Ardizzone, Oxford University Press, cr © 1962 Estate of Edward Ardizzone, Brockhampton Press, bl © 1967 Estate of Edward Ardizzone, Christianna Brand, illustrated by Edward Ardizzone, Brockhampton Press & br © 1974 Estate of Edward Ardizzone, Graham Greene, illustrated by Edward Ardizzone, The Bodley Head/The Random House Group Ltd, permissions granted by the author's Estate, 78 tr Bookmark Children's Books, bl & br reproduced by kind permission of Enid Blyton Ltd (a Chorion company), 80 t The Orion Publishing Group, bl Harcourt Inc, br, 81 tl Illustrations by Pauline Baynes © C S Lewis Pte Ltd, tr Bookmark Children's Books. Illustrations by Pauline Baynes © C S Lewis Pte Ltd. The Random House Group Ltd & br Illustrations by Pauline Baynes © C S Lewis Pte Ltd, illustrations reprinted by permission, 82 t © 1941, renewed 1969 by Robert McCloskey. Used by permission of Viking Penguin, a division of Penguin Young Readers Group, a member of the Penguin Group (USA) Inc. All rights reserved, 83 bl & br HarperCollins Inc, 84 t, b Egmont Books Ltd, 87 tr © Albert Lamorisse 1957, reprinted by permission of HarperCollins Publishers Ltd, bl & br The Random House Group Ltd, 88 t, bl, br by kind permission of Sort of Books, 89 bl © 1956 by Random House Inc, renewed 1984 by Random House Inc. Used by permission of Golden Books, an imprint of Random House Children's Books, a division of Random House Inc, br, 90 t Egmont Books Ltd, bl translated by Doris Orgel, copyright by Doris Orgel, by permission of Alfred A Knopf, an imprint of Random House Children's Books, a division of Random House Inc, br The Random House Group Ltd, 91 t Bookmark Children's Books. The Random House Group Ltd, cl & cr The Random House Group Ltd, b HarperCollins Inc, 94 t Ivan Chermayeff, c The Random House Group Ltd, 95 t Bookmark Children's Books, 96 t, b, 97 t, c, b The Random House Group Ltd, 98 t HarperCollins Inc, b Egmont Books Ltd, 99 t & c Bookmark Children's Books. Covers taken from The Church Mouse 1972 & The Church Cat Abroad 1972 by Graham Oakley, by permission of Macmillan Children's Books, London, b, 100 t by kind permission of Shirley Hughes, 101 c by kind permission of Shirley Hughes, 102 t, bl, bc, 103 tl, tr by kind permission of Shirley Hughes, bl, br, 104 l, tr & br © Ladybird Books Ltd, 105 tl © Ladybird Books Ltd 1960, tr © Ladybird Books Ltd 1966, bl © Ladybird Books Ltd 1958 & br © Ladybird Books Ltd 1963. All reproduced by permission of Frederick Warne & Co, 106 t, cl cover from The White Land © Raymond Briggs (Hamish Hamilton 1972), bl cover from Father Christmas © Raymond Briggs (Hamish Hamilton 1973) & br cover from The Snowman © Raymond Briggs (Hamish Hamilton 1978). Reprinted by permission of The Penguin Group (UK), 107 tl, tr, bl & br The Random House Group Ltd, 108 tl © 1972 by James Marshall & bl illustrations © 1981 by James Marshall. Reprinted by permission of Houghton Mifflin Company. All rights reserved, 108 tr The Random House Group Ltd & br/AP Watt Ltd on behalf of Quentin Blake, 109 tl The Random House Group Ltd & tr by permission of Klutz/A P Watt Ltd on behalf of Quentin Blake, 109 bl, br by kind permission of Alison & Busby Ltd, London, 110 t, b The Random House Group Ltd, 111 tl Egmont Books Ltd, tr, bl HarperCollins Inc, bc © 1975 Diogenes Verlag AG Zürich, br, 112 t cover from The Better Brown Stories © Allan Ahlberg (Viking, 1995) & bl cover from Each Peach Pear Plum © Janet & Allan Ahlberg (Kestrel Books, 1978), reprinted by permission of The Penguin Group (UK), bc & br Egmont Books Ltd, 114 tl, tc, tr & br reproduced by kind permission of Diana Boston, 115 tl © Alan Garner 1966, bl © Alan Garner 1960 & br © Alan Garner 1973, reprinted by permission of HarperCollins Publishers Ltd, 116 bl, br Jacket art by Murray Tinkelman, © 1974 by The Viking Press Inc, jacket illustration, from Midnight is a Place by Joan Aiken. Used by permission of Viking Penguin, a division of Penguin Young Readers Group, a member of Penguin Group (USA) Inc. All rights reserved, 117 tr The Random House Group Ltd, bl & bc Bookmark Children's Books. The Random House Group Ltd, br A Necklace of Raindrops © Jan Pieńkowski (Jonathan Cape, 1968) The Random House Group Ltd, 118 t text & illustrations © 1964, renewed 1992 by Roald Dahl Nominee Ltd, by permission of Alfred A Knopf, an imprint of Random House Children's Books, a division of Random House Inc, bl © Roald Dahl 1967, reprinted by permission of HarperCollins Publishers Ltd, br, 119 tl © Roald Dahl 1967. Reprinted by permission of HarperCollins Publishers Ltd, tr Bookmark Children's Books. Text © 1970, renewed 1998 by Roald Dahl Nominee Ltd. Illustrations © 1970 by Donald Chaffin, by permission of Alfred A Knopf, an imprint of Random House Children's Books, a division of Random House Inc, bl & bc Bookmark Children's Books. The Random House Group Ltd, br A P Watt Ltd on behalf of Quentin Blake, 120 Beware of the Storybook Wolves by Lauren Child. Reprinted by permission of Hodder & Stoughton Ltd, 122 t Egmont Books Ltd, b cover illustration © 1989 Dom Mansell from Judy The Bad Fairy written by Martin Waddell & 123 t cover from Five Minutes' Peace © 1988 Jill Murphy, reproduced by permission of Walker Books, London, c © A & C Black Publishers Ltd, b © Rodney Peppé, 124 t © Lynne Reid Banks 1981, reprinted by permission of HarperCollins Publishers Ltd, c cover from The Dancing Class © 1983 Helen Oxenbury. Reproduced by permission of Walker Books Ltd, b cover from Princess Smartypants © Babette Cole (Puffin 1996) reprinted by permission of The Penguin Group (UK), 125 t I Want My Potty by Tony Ross, published by Andersen Press Ltd, London, c When Sheep Cannot Sleep: The Counting Book by Satoshi Kitamura, reproduced by permission of Andersen Press Ltd, London, b The Random House Group Ltd, 126 t © 1973 by David Macaulay. Reprinted by permission of Houghton Mifflin Company. All rights reserved, c cover from Stephen Biesty's Incredible Cross-Sections (Dorling Kindersley 1992), © 1992 Dorling Kindersley Ltd, b cover from Black Maria by Diana Wynne-Jones © Chris Riddell 1991. Egmont Books Ltd, 127 t, c cover illustration © 1998 Tony Ross from The Devil and his Boy written by Anthony Horowitz. Reproduced by permission of Walker Books Ltd & b reproduction courtesy of Bloomsbury Publications Plc, illustration © Edward Gorey, 128 t & c The Random House Group Ltd, b cover illustration from M.O.L.E. © Jan Pieńkowski 1993, written by Russell Hoban (Walker Books), 129 t, c, b reproduction courtesy of Bloomsbury Publications Plc, cover design © Nathan Burton, 130 t The Random House Group Ltd & b cover illustration © 1990 Nicola Bayley taken from The Mousehole Cat written by Antonia Barber. Reproduced by permission of Walker Books Ltd, London, 131 tl, tr The Random House Group Ltd, bl, br, 132 tl Illustration © Thomas Taylor & tr Photograph © Winston Link, reproductions courtesy of Bloomsbury Publications Plc, br All Rights Reserved. Reproduced by permission of Scholastic UK Ltd, 133 tl All Rights Reserved. Reproduced by permission of Scholastic UK Ltd. Mortal Engines. Cover illustration © David Frankland 2001, bl Egmont Books Ltd, tr © Lemony Snicket & br © Loney M Setnick 2002, reprinted by permission of HarperCollins Publishers Ltd, 134 t © 2002 by Simms Taback. Used by permission of G P Putnam's Sons, a division of Penguin Young Readers Group, a member of Penguin Group (USA) Inc, bl, br Square, Triangle, Round, Skinny © 2002 Vladimir Radunsky. Reproduced by permission of Walker Books Ltd, London, 135 t & b Egmont Books Ltd, 144; **OPG/Ken Adlard** 31 br Estate of Rex Whistler 2003. All Rights Reserved, DACS., 34 tr The Random House Group Ltd, 86 tr All Rights Reserved. Reproduced by permission of Scholastic UK Ltd. Madeline. Cover illustration © Ludwig Bemelmans 1938, 87 tl, 113 tr Haunted House © Jan Pieńkowski 1979 (Heinemann); **OPG/Henry Sotheran Ltd** 70 c © Michael Bond 1958. Reprinted by permission of HarperCollins Publishers Ltd; **OPG** 113 b Meg & Mog © Jan Pieńkowski 1975 (Puffin); **Courtesy of the Friends of the Osborne and Lillian H Smith Collections and The Osborne Collection of Early Children's Books, Toronto Public Library** 12 b; **Courtesy of The Osborne Collection of Early Children's Books, Toronto Public Library** 6 t, 8, 10 b/The gift of Elizabeth Budd Bentley to the Osborne Collection of Early Children's Books, Toronto Public Library, 15 br, 18 t, b, 33 tl All Arthur Rackham pictures are reproduced with the kind permission of his family/The Bridgeman Art Library, 42 t Kingfisher Publications Plc, 52 t, bl & br Line illustrations by E H Shepard copyright under the Berne Convention/reproduced by kind permission of Curtis Brown Ltd, London; **The Random House Group Ltd** 92, 94 b, 101 b by kind permission of Shirley Hughes, 116 t, 117 tl images supplied by The Random House Group Ltd and reproduced by permission; **Jo Ann Reisler and her husband** 3 HarperCollins Inc, 12 t, 13 b HarperCollins Inc, 27 bl (c) Frederick Warne & Co. 1906, reproduced by permission of Frederick Warne & Co, 40 t, c, 49 tr, 60 t © 1934 by Ludwig Bemelmans, renewed 1962. Used by permission of Viking Penguin, a division of Penguin Young Readers Group, a member of Penguin Group (USA) Inc, bl © 1936 by Munro Leaf and Robert Lawson, renewed 1964 by Munro Leaf and John W Boyd. Used by permission of Viking Penguin, a division of Penguin Young Readers Group, a member of Penguin Group (USA) Inc, br, 82 bl HarperCollins Inc, 83 tr HarperCollins Inc, 85 tl copyright TM & © by Dr Seuss Enterprises, LP 1940, renewed 1968, by permission of Random House Children's Books, a division of Random House Inc, bl © 1957 by Dr Seuss. Copyright renewed 1985 by Theodor S Geisel & Audrey S Geisel, by permission of Random House Inc, 86 bl, br ©1951, 1953 by Ludwig Bemelmans, renewed © 1979, 1981 by Madeleine Bemelmans and Barbara Marciano. Used by permission of Viking Penguin, a division of Penguin Young Readers Group, a member of Penguin Group (USA) Inc, 89 tl, 100 b, 101 t; **Royal Library, National Library of Sweden** 70 t; **Sotheby's** 13 c, 24 t Egmont Books Ltd, 32 cl; **Stella and Rose's Books of Tintern, Monmouthshire and Hay-On-Wye, Herefordshire** 52 c cover illustration © E H Shepard, reproduced by kind permission of Curtis Brown Ltd, London, 53 tl © Express Newspapers, 71 b © Hergé/Moulinsart 2003, 82 br The Random House Group Ltd, 83 tl © Margaret Wise Brown 1992, reprinted by permission of HarperCollins Publishers Ltd, 85 br © 1962, renewed 1990 by Random House Inc. Used by permission of Golden Books, an imprint of Random House Children's Books, a division of Random House Inc, 95 c, 113 c Snow White: The Jan Pieńkowski Fairy Tale Library © Jan Pieńkowski 1977 (William Heinemann with Gallery Five) 122 c cover illustration © 1986 Jonathan Heale from Tibber written by William Mayne. Reproduced by permission of Walker Books Ltd, London.

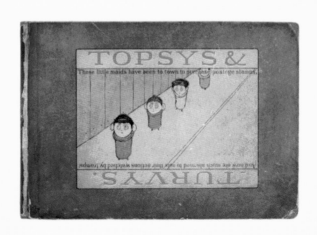